Public Theology and Violent Rhetoric Examined in a Queer Womanist Critical Ethnography

T&T CLARK STUDIES IN SOCIAL ETHICS, ETHNOGRAPHY, AND THEOLOGY

Over the last half century, there have been numerous calls for Christian theology and ethics to take human experience seriously—to delve into particular economic, socio-political, racial-ethnic, and cultural contexts from which theological and moral imagination arises. Yet actual theologies that draw upon descriptive-rich, qualitative methods—methods that place such particularity at the center of inquiry and performance—are few and scattered. **T&T Clark Studies in Social Ethics, Ethnography, and Theology** is a series that addresses this gap in the literature by providing a publishing home for timely ethnographically-driven theological and ethical investigations of an expansive array of pressing social issues, ranging from armed conflict to racism to healthcare inequities to sexuality/gender and discrimination to the marginalization of persons with disabilities. The scope of the series projects, taken together, is at once global and intensely local, with the central organizing conviction that ethnography provides not only information to plug into a theology, but a valid and vibrant way of *doing* theology.

Public Theology and Violent Rhetoric Examined in a Queer Womanist Critical Ethnography

Teresa L. Smallwood

t&tclark

LONDON • NEW YORK • OXFORD • NEW DELHI • SYDNEY

T&T CLARK
Bloomsbury Publishing Plc
50 Bedford Square, London, WC1B 3DP, UK
1385 Broadway, New York, NY 10018, USA
29 Earlsfort Terrace, Dublin 2, Ireland

BLOOMSBURY, T&T CLARK and the T&T Clark logo are
trademarks of Bloomsbury Publishing Plc

First published in Great Britain 2025

Copyright © Teresa L. Smallwood, 2025

Teresa L. Smallwood has asserted her right under the Copyright,
Designs and Patents Act, 1988, to be identified as Author of this work.

Cover design: Gita Kowlessur
Cover image: Tulips and Windmill, photograph by JacobH © IStock

All rights reserved. No part of this publication may be reproduced or transmitted
in any form or by any means, electronic or mechanical, including photocopying,
recording, or any information storage or retrieval system, without prior
permission in writing from the publishers.

Bloomsbury Publishing Plc does not have any control over, or responsibility for,
any third-party websites referred to or in this book. All internet addresses given in
this book were correct at the time of going to press. The author and publisher regret
any inconvenience caused if addresses have changed or sites have ceased to exist,
but can accept no responsibility for any such changes.

A catalogue record for this book is available from the British Library.

Library of Congress Cataloging-in-Publication Data
Names: Smallwood, Teresa L., 1959- author.
Title: Public theology and violent rhetoric examined in a queer womanist
critical ethnography / Teresa L. Smallwood.
Description: London ; New York : T&T Clark, 2025. | Series: T&T Clark
studies in social ethics, ethnography, and theology | Includes
bibliographical references and index. | Summary: "This book shares the
insight of LGBTQIA+ persons surveyed and interviewed to describe how
they have experienced the violent rhetoric of black church public
theology as a means toward developing a philosophical paradigmatic shift
that generates spiritual renewal for all, particularly those in the LGBTQIA+ community
and those who provide them pastoral and teaching leadership"– Provided by publisher.
Identifiers: LCCN 2024022397 (print) | LCCN 2024022398 (ebook) |
ISBN 9780567711236 (pb) | ISBN 9780567711243 (hb) |
ISBN 9780567711250 (epub) | ISBN 9780567711267 (pdf)
Subjects: LCSH: Black theology. | Queer theology. | Womanism.
Classification: LCC BT82.7 .S58 2025 (print) | LCC BT82.7 (ebook) |
DDC 230.086/6–dc23/eng/20240904
LC record available at https://lccn.loc.gov/2024022397
LC ebook record available at https://lccn.loc.gov/2024022398

ISBN:	HB:	978-0-5677-1124-3
	PB:	978-0-5677-1123-6
	ePDF:	978-0-5677-1126-7
	eBook:	978-0-5677-1125-0

Typeset by Integra Software Services Pvt. Ltd.
Printed and bound in Great Britain

To find out more about our authors and books visit www.bloomsbury.com
and sign up for our newsletters.

CONTENTS

Preface vi

Introduction 1

1 The Least of These 17

2 The Bully Pulpit: Untying the Ties That Bind 31

3 Whiteface and the "Face of the Other" 73

4 "Wounded Healers" Wound People 99

Epilogue 131

Appendix A: Death Documents for Lillie Ruth Mitchell 138
Appendix B: Survey Questions 141
Appendix C: Transcription of the Sermon by Pastor Anderson 142

Index 146

PREFACE

What Are Our Publics?

Pondering the meaning of public theology and its implications for LGBTQIA folks led me to this work. The unadulterated truth is that faith-based meeting places are public spaces, whether they are churches, temples, synagogues, mosques, or tents. What is said in them, how it is said, and by whom it is said, leave indelible impressions on those who hear the message. Public theology, as a discipline, is relatively new. Yet religious leaders have generated public theology for millennia. In many respects, the shaping of a message, particularly about faith, requires meditative thought, contemplative approaches, and spiritual guidance. Without these, public theological discourse can and often does hurt people. In fact, some public theological discourse amounts to violent rhetoric, which exacts a price on its hearers as it orders them to live up to and into certain provisos, which are employed to control. As I reflect on the serious scholarship on public theology, I realize there are no black female lesbian voices in the discourse proper. Moreover, I note that Womanist methodology is needed to explicate the myriad ways that violent rhetoric impacts LGBTQIA folks involved in faith-based institutions. Womanism is devoted to the "survival and wholeness of entire people."[1] It offers a framework for truth-telling that employs narrative contextually as lived theology. That is important when subjectivity crashes into belief.[2] The collision will cost you something. This book evaluates the violent rhetoric of some public theology and points readers toward healing practices. Because the pulpit is a very pubic platform for theological impartation, the experiences of LGBTQIA persons presents evidentiary relevance to the harm caused by violent rhetoric as pronounced by bully pulpit preachers.

E. Harold Breitenberg Jr. asks the question "Will the Real Public Theology Please Stand Up?" in his 2003 article, which appeared in the *Journal of Christian Ethics*.[3] This question signals that public theology has taken on many forms and has been given many meanings. It also queries whether there is any one correct way to approach public theology. Christian practitioners ought to locate their understanding of public theology within the simplicity of the gospel message to "love your neighbor as yourself." After all, Jesus's ministry was a public ministry, and much of our theology is bound up with Jesus's ministry. That message isn't limited to the Christian tradition: a common thread running through many faith systems encourages devotees to love their neighbor.

Fundamentally, public theology beckons us to live our faith out loud. The words "public" and "theology" connote an open, outward expression of one's inner convictions. In the eleventh century, St. Anselm posited that theology is "faith seeking understanding," *fides quaerens intellectum*.[4] If we connect that basic thought to the mission of public ministry, public theology is taking that quest—that desire to seek understanding—to the public square.

What are our publics? They are literally everywhere. Public theology beckons us to find meaning in everyday life, to find ways for all people to be made whole—that is, healthy, loved, accepted, cherished as God's good creation. This requires our practice of public theology to seek justice in the face of injustice in the world. The justice of God should be of paramount importance to people of faith. You cannot study the sacred texts and conclude differently. The work of the prophets summons "prophetic activism"—a term offered by Helene Slessarev-Jamir in her manuscript *Prophetic Activism: Progressive Religious Justice Movements in Contemporary America*.[5] Prophetic activism, as employed in public theology, speaks to an unadulterated commitment to social change, resistance to empire, the advancement of community solidarity, and engagement and alignment with diversity, equity, and inclusion. LGBTQIA folks have been tortured in the public sphere in the name of God. This book offers a corrective. Interestingly, a short survey of works on public theology over its roughly fifty-year history reveals a gaping hole where LGBTQIA folks are concerned and a measure of invisibility where black folks are concerned.

Harvey Cox, a professor at Harvard Divinity School, wrote a treatise in 1967 that moved public theology toward an evaluation of the clash between the sacred and the secular. His book, *Religion in the Secular City: Towards a Postmodern Theology*, clearly delineated secularization as "an authentic consequence of biblical faith," in hopes that it would spawn a revolution of religionists shaping the world around them in keeping with God's prophetic mandates. He stated, "We are trying to live in a period of revolution without a theology of revolution. The development of such a theology should be the first item on the theological agenda today."[6] Cox favored a postmodern theology that addressed the dispossessed people of the world—namely, women, minorities, and the poor. However, his myopic public theology, which follows fundamentalist categories that identify "insiders" and "outsiders," falls short of portraying an all-inclusive God and offers little to LGBTQIA folks.

Martin Marty, a church historian at the University of Chicago, wrote an article regarding Reinhold Niebuhr in response to Robert Bellah's seminal 1967 essay on civil religion.[7] He denounced Bellah's suggestion that America has a "civil religion" based on religious practices one might observe in American culture: reciting the pledge of allegiance, singing the national anthem, emblazoning "in God we Trust" on our currency, asking that God bless America, praying at the inauguration of a new president, and so forth.[8] Marty's book *The Public Church: Mainline, Evangelical, Catholic* is the first manuscript defining public theology as a discipline in the field of religious studies. By confining public theology to "the church," this description fails to offer convincing insights for ecumenism and religious pluralism in the practice of public theology.[9]

The concept of public theology has morphed into a serious inquiry for Christian social and theological ethics. Marty focused on "the three constituencies," as he referred to them: mainline, evangelical, and Catholic churches.[10] His *The One and the Many: America's Struggle for the Common Good* more specifically delineates the difficulty in identifying one national storyline for Americans, which gravely impacts our sense of community. As a "Balm in Gilead," Marty offers an analysis of the "common good" and finally suggests that "citizens" tell their origin stories to this end. He states: "Common Life happens most often when one engages in acts of 'plural belonging.'"[11] However, some stories are simply unwanted in the American context. Because what is "common" is generally fraught in the American ethos, many are simply left out or not contemplated at all. My book advances the notion that LGBTQIA folks are important to God, and they deserve a place at the welcome table and the public sphere.

David Tracy, a Catholic theologian, wrote *The Analogical Imagination*.[12] Tracy concerned himself with historical consciousness and the problematic of identifying a foundational Christian principle in the face of religious pluralism. Tracy later identified five basic models for "doing" theology in a revisionist frame: contemporary, orthodox, liberal, neo-orthodox, and radical. Tracy reflects philosophically on the meanings present in common human experience and language, and on the meanings present in the "Christian fact."[13] Yet, there is no conscious regard for those who are "othered" in society.

Richard John Neuhaus, a Lutheran pastor, critiqued the notion of the public square in his 1984 book *The Naked Public Square: Religion and Democracy in America* by examining the intersection of various sociopolitical phenomena with secular and sacred meaning.[14] His argument is that the public square is naked or "bare" without religious speech.[15] More particularly, Neuhaus argues that democracy would be threatened without the moral suasion of faith-based citizens. His popular maxim makes this clear: "Politics is chiefly a function of culture, at the heart of culture is morality, and at the heart of morality is religion."[16] As a pastor at a Lutheran Church–Missouri Synod congregation in Brooklyn, New York, Neuhaus was a "major Protestant figure in the civil rights movement as well as a "salient opponent of the war in Vietnam."[17] At the time, he sought to defend the weak from the powerful and to uphold the rights of the poor and the racially oppressed. However, his commitments switched in the aftermath of the 1973 Supreme Court decision in *Roe v. Wade*, falling down the rabbit hole of partisan politics and later joining the Catholic Church, where he was ordained as a priest in 1990.[18] One could argue that we are seeing his predictions about democracy unfold in real time. Though we cannot claim that the public square is completely naked, the emperor, at the very least, has no clothes.[19] The reality is that the Neuhausian approach is devoid of insight for LGBTQIA folks.

Nonetheless, the role of the public theologian in society is to clothe the naked. This is not a call for pious words. As Allan Boesak correctly opines, "The time for pious words is over."[20] We are compelled to bring order and purpose to God's justice in the public sphere. Max Stackhouse, to that point, identifies four publics to which public theology is called: religious, political, academic, and economic. Issues of injustice emanate from each as they unfold globally.

Linell E. Cady overhauls the notion of public theology in her classic work *Religion, Theology, and American Public Life*. Cady espouses the view that the "common good," as an ethical frame, fails to address public life in America because it is tethered to a deeply privatized exercise of freedoms known only to those with extreme wealth. Consequently, the notion of the "common*wealth*," popular parlance for political groupings like cities or states, functions as coded language signifying those able to participate in the nebulous "common good." Cady offers the alternative concept of a "common public life," which I contend is pivotal to a public theology seeking racial and social justice. Cady states, "The common life of the polis where equals freely participate in debating the meaning of excellence for the body politic has given way to a procedural, watchdog state whose mandate is to secure the private interests of its members."[21] Those members who are LGBTQIA must have a voice and it must be heard; the focus on a common public life makes this possible.

Sebastian Kim's *Theology in the Public Sphere: Public Theology as a Catalyst for Open Debate* offers a global perspective for public theology that considers global Christianity, eco-theology, and struggles against injustice in various parts of the world. He introduces a frame for interactive pluralism in a multicultural society. His focus is in giving public theology a practical application.

From these foundational thinkers we have two basic models for doing public theology: foundational models and action models. The foundational models can be further identified as those which look to the (1) theological (model of disclosure), (2) existential—philosophical (universal model), or (3) sociological (factual model). The action models focus on (1) audience (society, academy, church), (2) apologetics (vs. dogmatics or confessional), and (3) context (Chicago School, Yale School).[22] Sebastian Kim's *Theology in the Public Sphere: Theology as a Catalyst for Open Debate* comes closest to a public theology of plurality by opening the discourse to global contexts; however, it adroitly sidesteps the issues related to LGBTQIA folks.

Public theology is a force within globalization, understanding its place among global religions and seeking to be inclusive, but stopping short of full inclusivity. The Global Network of Public Theology (GNPT), of which United Lutheran Seminary is a founding member, thanks to the scholarly work of Katie Day, meets biennially. The GNPT states, "As a network with member institutions from all continents, we foster scholarly exchange about the contribution of Christianity to public discourse in such diverse fields as social ethics, environmental ethics, and political ethics."[23] The role of the public theologian in society is fundamentally to show up in the public square and to live one's faith out loud.

More recently we have seen an uptick in police brutality, mass shootings, massacres of children, children taken hostage by empire, empire serving families tainted water, attacks on the right to vote, attacks on the right to exercise agency over one's body, a lack of civility toward our neighbors, bloodletting, war, and rumors of war. The cry for the justice of God can be heard by those who have an ear. Our role is not to sit idly by as all hell breaks loose in our streets but to jump into action to bring the balance nonviolently. We have the responsibility to walk as Jesus walked, to concern ourselves with the needs of the poor, and to shape a public theology receptive to collaborating with a wide range of beliefs with the understanding that the entire world may not believe as we do but is still our neighbor. In sum, we are to love our neighbors as we love ourselves. Our role is to model agapé love—unconditional love. A love conditioned on dogma and polity will sometimes justify leaving bodies on the street, but unconditional love sees that as injustice. Our role as public theologians is to keep the doors of the church open to the stranger, to the widow, to the orphan.

Why Queer Womanist?

Pamela R. Lightsey produced the first manuscript of queer Womanist theology titled *Our Lives Matter: A Queer Womanist Theology*. Following from that insightful book is a need to bring specificity to the lived experiences of LGBTQIA persons as they engage with their faith communities. This volume offers the insights of their experiences from a Womanist lens, exploring how violent rhetoric, whether from preachers, teachers, congregants, or observers, promulgates an atmosphere of dissonance related to LGBTQIA persons. The Womanist lens looks to the tenets defined by Stacey Floyd-Thomas—radical subjectivity, traditional communalism, redemptive self-love, and critical engagement—to elucidate the *canon* of inclusivity, the deep need for unconditional love, the nature of nurture, the importance of communal engagement, and the imperative for perspectival correctives.

This volume will take the reader on a journey through the lived experiences of LGBTQIA persons while simultaneously evaluating the violent rhetoric they have endured because of ignorance, insolence, neglect, greed, avarice, and oppression. It offers a path to begin the healing and an understanding of the phenomena that perpetuate violent rhetoric.

Notes

1 Alice Walker, *In Search of Our Mother's Gardens: Womanist Prose* (San Diego, CA: Harcourt Brace Jovanovich, 1983).

2 Kathy Rudy, "Subjectivity and Belief," *Literature and Theology* 15, no. 3 (2001): 224–40.

3 E. Harold Breitenberg Jr., "To Tell the Truth: Will the Real Public Theology Please Stand Up?," *Journal of the Society of Christian Ethics* 23, no. 2 (Fall/Winter 2003): 55–96.

4 Anselm of Canterbury (c. 1033–1109), "Fides quaerens intellectum," cited in Wikipedia, https://en.wikipedia.org/wiki/Fides_quaerens_intellectum (last edited August 21, 2023).

5 Helene Slessavev-Jamir, *Prophetic Activism: Progressive Religious Justice Movements in Contemporary America* (New York: New York University Press, 2011).

6 Harvey Cox, *Religion in the Secular City: Toward a Postmodern Theology* (New York: Simon and Schuster, 1984).

7 Martin Marty's article was written in 1974 about Neibuhr in response to Robert Bellah's article on civil religion.

8 Robert Bellah, "American Civil Religion," *Daedalus* 96, no. 1 (Winter 1967): 1–21, http://www.robertbellah.com/articles_5.htm (accessed July 5, 2024).

9 Martin Marty, *The Public Church: Mainline, Evangelical, Catholic* (Eugene, OR: Wipf and Stock, 2012).

10 Ibid.

11 Martin Marty, *The One and the Many: America's Struggle for the Common Good* (Cambridge, MA: Harvard University Press, 1997), 162.

12 David Tracy, *The Analogical Imagination: Christian Theology and the Culture of Pluralism* (St. Louis, MO: Herder and Herder, 1998).

13 Ibid.

14 See Richard John Neuhaus, *The Naked Public Square: Religion and Democracy in America* (Grand Rapids, MI: Eerdmans, 1984).

15 Ibid.

16 Matthew Rose, "The Liberalism of Richard John Neuhaus,"*National Affairs*, Summer 2016, Accessed (July 5, 2024). https://nationalaffairs.com/publications/detail/the-liberalism-of-richard-john-neuhaus.

17 Richard John Neuhaus, *The Naked Public Square: Religion and Democracy in America*, (Grand Rapids, MI: Eerdmans, 1984)

18 Ibid.

19 Ibid.

20 Allan Aubrey Boesak, *Kairos, Crisis, and Global Apartheid: The Challenge to Prophetic Resistance* (New York: Palgrave Macmillan, 2015).

21 Linell E. Cady, *Religion, Theology, and American Public Life* (New York: State University of New York Press, 1993), 8.

22 Linell E. Cady, "A Model for a Public Theology," *Harvard Theological Review* 80, no. 2 (1987): 193–212.

23 Global Network for Public Theology, https://gnpublictheology.net (accessed July 5, 2024).

Introduction

This Is My Story, This Is My Song

I was nearing my fourth birthday when the march on Washington took place. Despite my youthful innocence, I knew Martin Luther King Jr. His picture hung in our living room beside a European rendition of Jesus. My mother and the women she knew regarded King as the leader of the civil rights movement. Because he was a preacher and could draw large crowds, people from my rural, agrarian community looked to King for direction in their everyday lives. As a child, I could discern that the civil rights movement was the heartbeat of the church. As I matured, the association deepened. Naturally, I loved the movement, what it stood for, and the message it promoted. Preachers held high sway in most black communities, and Dr. King was a standard bearer.

The message of the movement was embodied in the songs sung in those large gatherings, songs that shaped the theological underpinnings of the black church. In particular, the music of Mahalia Jackson, that iconic figure of matronly grandeur, looms large in the collective memory of black people in the mid-twentieth century. Her music serves as a locus of meaning in the formation of an eschatological vision for black people in general and for the black church in particular. Mahalia sang of a future when all could "look back and wonder" how they overcame the difficulties of life. The songs focused on a victory that would be experienced in the "afterlife." The theological import was grounded in delayed gratification.

Mahalia was a favorite of my mother's because it was said that my mother "resembled" her. My mother, Mattie Matilda Cherry Smallwood, was a beautiful black woman. Her skin color was deep dark. She had a towering presence and was well-known in the community because she operated a beauty shop. Getting your hair done was one of the many social outlets for black women in the 1960s. It still is, but back then it was different. All of the news about town and the world, as far as we could connect, was told and retold in the beauty shop. There the body politic of the black community, for women, convened its sessions. There women debated the vote, examined the business of life, and celebrated the commonality of life. New methods for child-rearing, corrective action for the unruly, and how to make ends meet were the standard agenda items. Talk of children, especially their accomplishments, was the highlight of the day. Children held a special place of pride and fulfillment for black women. Every child knew the love of the community. You did not belong only to your parents; you were a child of the community. Neighbors could correct you, just like your parents could. There was a mutual trust in the neighborhood because there was a commonality of purpose; all wanted the same things for their children. It was nothing for a neighbor to give you fifty cents or a dollar for bringing home a great report card.

Influence of the Bible in Community

The women who came to my mother's beauty shop knew how to be in community with each other. Or so it seemed. It appeared that they had each other's backs. If someone in the shop needed something that my mother had, it was given without question. It was as though I could see the person of Jesus in each of those women. Certainly, in my childlike reasoning, their way of being with each other gave the impression that all were valued. Communal sharing serves as a barometer for how the community understands morality. The effervescence that spirituality produces determines the maturity of a faith community. It reminds me of the passage in Galatians where Paul speaks of Christ in the context of a communal spirit:

> It is good to be made much of for a good purpose at all times, and not only when I am present with you. My little children, for whom I am again in the pain of childbirth until Christ is formed in you, I wish I were present with you now and could change my tone, for I am perplexed about you.[1]

My first inclination toward a Christology of inclusion was based on this idea of Christ being formed in someone. The Greek term "formed," *morphóō*, means "to form" or "to fashion," e.g., artists their materials, and in the passive "to take on form" (especially in the womb). This passage is the only New Testament instance, Gal. 4:19, where the growth of Christ in believers is compared to development in the womb. This growth is an ongoing process, both open and secret and both a gift and a task, with maturity as a goal.[2]

My experience with such a Christology became distorted in later years. The good news is that my Christology formed while I was a child. Let me describe how it developed and its meaning for me.[3]

Childhood Connections

Around age six I remember being very curious about my body. My childhood friend and I were playing with our tea set one afternoon, and she put a teacup in her pants. I thought that was riotously funny! We giggled and kept on playing. Later that week her mother confronted my mother about what her daughter had reported. The mother made a point of saying that her child admitted she put the teacup in her pants but that I must have done something to make her do such an unladylike thing. For what seemed like an eternity, my friend and I could not play together. As I celebrated more birthdays, I was described as "tomboyish" and "mannish," which in retrospect must have been a colloquialism or local adaptation of "womanish," as defined by Alice Walker.[4]

When I was fifteen a young woman in our neighborhood who was a known "bulldagger"[5] stopped in the street as she passed my house. Her name was Lillie Ruth Mitchell Carter. I was sitting on the front porch in my favorite swinging chair. I remember the chair was painted green from the summer before (my mother and I painted it to "spruce it up"). When Lillie Ruth stopped, she looked at me intently and said, "You better watch your back! They are trying to make you out to be something you don't even understand." She was roughly twenty-four years old at the time. Lillie Ruth always spoke as she passed by; it was a common neighborly gesture in my community. But this time she addressed me. It is funny because I always wanted her to talk to me. But I knew that if she did, people would confuse our friendliness with something that was clearly not acceptable. In essence, it was unacceptable for me, a church girl, to be friendly with someone so "worldly." Never mind that my mother was friendly with Lillie Ruth's mother, and they all seemed to show each other kindness.

At age thirty-three, Lillie Ruth's body washed up on the shore of the Cashie River; the cause of her death was determined to be suicide. The investigation consists of one page.[6] She had an argument with her girlfriend. Lillie Ruth took her girlfriend's car keys. The girlfriend, through the aid of the police, retrieved her keys. According to the police report, later that night Lillie Ruth asked her mother to take care of her nine-year-old son and indicated that if she did not return home by a certain hour, they would never see her again. Her mother concluded that she killed herself. In the face of Lillie Ruth's death, I lived with the fear of that same fate.

Grievability

The beauty shop talk surrounding Lillie Ruth's death signaled to me that her life was not highly valued. It was assumed that because her lifestyle was so "immoral," the devil tormented her until she surrendered to *his* plan for her life. She simply "did not know the love of Jesus," according to the community. When will we denounce such practices in our churches that deem some lives *ungrievable*? Judith Butler, a Jewish, feminist, lesbian philosopher, writing about frames of war, avers:

> To say that a life is injurable, for instance, or that it can be lost, destroyed, or systematically neglected to the point of death, is to underscore not only the finitude of a life (that death is certain) but also its precariousness (that life requires various social and economic conditions to be met in order to be sustained as a life). Precariousness implies living socially, that is, the fact that one's life is always in some sense in the hands of the other. It implies exposure both to those we know and to those we do not know; a dependency on people we know, or barely know, or know not at all.[7]

The larger faith community deemed the death of Lillie Ruth—and that of others like her—*ungrievable* because she did not fit a very particularized frame of acceptability. She was queer. Because she was queer, it was unimaginable that she could ever have known Jesus. In some sense, Lillie Ruth, as a queer woman, was, in the minds of others, nonhuman. She was an alien to the very folks around whom she lived and breathed. Her death, then, was a phenomenon given to multiple interpretations. Either Lillie Ruth fit no ontological category recognizable by people of faith or her existential reality was incomprehensible to people of faith because of their total indoctrination to a narrative foreign to her ontology. What is remarkable is the sheer insolence at the loss of her life.

Knowledge of Lillie Ruth's death brought to my mind her earlier admonition to me. What did I know about the life of a lesbian in a small northeastern North Carolina town? Who did she *know* and who *knew* her? The beauty shop attendees presumed that Lillie Ruth did not know Jesus. But did she know them? Did they know her? These questions frame important queries for this book. The ways of knowing shaped, in part, by preaching rhetoric present the LGBTQIA[8] person with little ability to be seriously known. When an LGBTQIA life is "ungrievable," it means that ideological wars about who is and who is not part of God's family produce certain casualties. Judith Butler posits that "grievability is a presupposition for the life that matters … Without grievability, there is no life, or, rather, there is something living that is other than life."[9] In large measure, Lillie Ruth's life is an archetype reflected in the postmodern faith context where ideologies battle over whose lives matter: "We might think of war as dividing populations into those who are grievable and those who are not. An ungrievable life is one that cannot be mourned because it has never lived, that is, it has never counted as a life at all."[10] Because Lillie Ruth was "othered" in life and in death, she exemplifies how an LGBTQIA life is ungrievable based on hate-talk disguised as God-talk. If, in the end, this rhetoric lands on the ears of those deemed ungrievable, the very message from the pulpit might catalyze an uptick in alienation or, even worse, suicide.

Sexuality and the Sacred

Ironically, Lillie Ruth's death made me all the more curious about my sexuality. I was scared and intrigued at the same time. I was scared to express my sexuality or what I was beginning to think about it because I did not think I could withstand the kind of scrutiny Lillie Ruth faced. It seemed to me she never knew acceptance because she was "so different." I wanted to avoid that feeling at all costs. Armed with a Nzinghan inner fight, I was not willing to pretend that I was not captivated by what was being made of my developing sexuality; moreover, my own personality dictated a certain positive ownership of my self-definition.

As I lived into my own sexual identity, my spiritual formation anchored me against the tide of indifference I experienced throughout young adulthood. I recall being asked to serve as "mistress of ceremonies" at an anniversary banquet for a local minister. A guest minister from Elizabeth City, North Carolina, came to town to give the keynote address at the banquet. He was flanked by a large number of young girls who appeared to be my age. Displaying a big grin on his face, he called them his "armor bearers." They carried his briefcase, took his hat and coat, and performed a number of menial tasks that I found disgusting. Nevertheless, I executed my duties with respect and humility, and I gave the minister a proper introduction. When he rose to the podium, his first words after his icebreaking banter were "God don't need no lesbian to do nothing for him," spoken as he looked directly at me.

On another occasion, a young man who was one of my childhood friends told me that "people" were calling me a lesbian because I "was not giving it up." He said, "I'm just trying to help you. If you want me to turn you out, I will." In those moments of formation, the bricks of my being were carefully crafted in the kiln of ambiguity.[11] I dated boys, I went to the prom, I did all of the things that "normal" girls did. I genuinely liked the attention I received from my male friends. Yet, I remained curious about the forbidden in my developing sexual orientation. I would not act on that curiosity until I was in law school. I was in my second year of law school when I received the news of Lillie Ruth's death. By that time, I had also "accepted the call to ministry." The call to ministry and the call to self-fulfillment worked a tension in me that felt like an ideological tug-of-war. I often pondered what could have driven Lillie Ruth to such a place of despair and what could have been done to help her overcome it.

Law school completed, I worked a few years in Charlotte, North Carolina, before returning home to work in the district attorney's office. Once I was home, the pastor of my church sought to license me to preach and appointed me to a position as associate minister. I enjoyed public speaking and preaching. Two brothers, William and Glen Peele, who were on the deacon board at Mount Olive Missionary Baptist Church, openly opposed women ministers. But my appointment gave them particular angst because I was "one of those abominations." On Communion Sunday the brothers refused to receive the communion elements when I passed them the plate and cup, claiming I was "unclean."

In one showdown, William Peele told me I was "nothing" to God. Navigating the treacherous waters of open rejection and verbal abuse from within the church caused me to question my relationship with God. These were the same people with whom I had learned Bible verses as a young child. They taught me the foundational dogma of the Baptist faith. Some of their wives were my mother's beauty shop customers. Concomitantly, however, the memory of those innocent times on Saturday morning, as a young child, when I would entertain the children of my mother's customers with my Barbie, my puzzles, my bike, and my Easy-Bake oven gave me a glimpse into the inner workings of the brand of "Christian" sisterhood practiced by those who came to my mother's beauty shop. My soul looks back, but I do not have to wonder how I got over. The experiences I had in the church throughout my development present me with an orientation to the existential anxiety that ultimately framed my personal theology.

I, like womanist theologian Renee Hill, have questioned "Who Are We for Each Other?"[12] I have often wondered how things changed so drastically for me, from being loved by everyone as Mrs. Mattie's little girl to being outcast because of my sexuality. The ambiguous nature of my acceptance and later rejection correlates with womanist theologian Kelly Brown Douglas's assessment of sexuality within the black church.[13] The polar opposites—my acceptance and my rejection—revolve around an axis of difference. It is out of sameness that difference is reified. As long as one is perceived to be just like everyone else, the scrutiny is kept at bay. However, any slight deviation from the cookie-cutter profile of gendered and sexual expression brings on the dagger eyes. In my experience, the critique started with the sense of self-pride, knowledge, and confidence that exuded from me in my high school years.

Womanism and the LGBTQIA Body

I never heard them voice it per se, but I am sure many thought I acted "womanish" within the meaning that Alice Walker describes: "outrageous, audacious, courageous ... wanting to know more and in greater depth than is considered 'good' for one."[14] For as far back as I can remember, and well before I confronted my own sexuality, people in my context whispered about my being "homosexual." It happened to any young girl who did not fit the mode of "Suzy homemaker." Yet, I was a sought-after youth day speaker, I graduated as valedictorian of my high school class, and I graduated from one of the most revered state institutions of higher education in North Carolina—the University of North Carolina at Chapel Hill. The dual nature of my experience can perhaps be understood more specifically through the lens of Kelly Brown Douglas's discussion of homophobia and of a sexual discourse of resistance that deals with the psychological nature of church folk in relationships. It is helpful to explore her development of this concept. Brown Douglas seeks language tools to transform the rhetoric of the black church and the black preaching tradition as a "first step toward helping Black men and women to understand that homophobia threatens Black well-being instead of protecting it." Significantly, she points out that the "discourse of resistance will show that homophobia plays into the hands of White culture and racism." She points to the many forces working against the unity of the community and stresses the importance of resisting the "real enemy."[15] The real enemy, I contend, is the hegemonic rhetoric that scatters lesbian, gay, bisexual, transgender, and queer (LGBTQIA) people away from their families and faith communities in the name of religion.

Estrangement

All too often there is the hierarchically-inscribed perspective that LGBTQIA persons are like bad apples that destroy the entire bunch. This psychological perspective alienates LGBTQIA persons, identifying them as unworthy of the love of God. Though the rhetoric emphasizes that God loves the sinner but hates the sin, it is never really settled just how that might take shape. As a consequence, of all the "sinners" that the black preacher names, this one has a bifurcated "deliverance" that leaves their "salvation" incomplete. This is owing to the nature of "sin," which the black preacher characterizes as being attached to the body, whereby no amount of "cleansing" can really take away the stain because the person remains always in an LGBTQIA body. It is a sin of existence. When one's very existence in an LGBTQIA body is deemed sinful, even the blood of Jesus is presumably ineffective in propitiating it. Brown Douglas suggests that the black preaching tradition promotes this effect when "using the authority of scripture" as a tool of power:

> They take up these tools when they construct sexual discourse against gay and lesbian persons and shelter it under a biblical sacred canopy, suggesting that such sexuality is an abomination to God and that it engenders Black existence. This discourse serves to denigrate and destroy a significant segment of black humanity, in much the same way that White sexual discourse seeks to destroy Black people.[16]

Brown Douglas surmises that the black church has fallen prey to an empty approach to religion driven by the commitment to help the white culture destroy black people. In effect, black church public theology, through the black preaching tradition, judges "the world" while being unwilling to judge itself by those same standards, thereby positioning itself as an idol to be worshipped. Because the church asserts a right to be the judge of "the world," it consequently removes itself from the cultural landscape as an actor. Since there is no escaping culture and therefore no way for the church to remove itself from the cultural landscape, black feminist lesbian poet Audre Lorde's pronouncement that "the master's tools will never dismantle the master's house" brings new revelation.[17]

The black preaching tradition is subject to the same level of scrutiny as that it metes out to "the world." Religion, as well as every act of life, has cultural implications. When the rhetoric of the black preacher serves as a cognitive cacophony for people seeking the "face" of God, it fails the meaning and mission of the Great Commission. It causes an ontological estrangement in LGBTQIA people who hear the message. I am especially concerned with what this estrangement might mean to a young woman struggling with her own sexual identity. How, if at all, does one overcome this estrangement?

The initial inquiry is about having an awareness of one's own humanity. Being aware of my humanity, my own self-worth, and my personal connection to God through the Holy Spirit anchored me in the moments of my spiritual formation when the rhetoric of black church theology deemed me "ungrievable." Culture helps us hold that awareness without breaking under the pressure of the existential reality that we are all finite beings.[18] Art, poetry, and aesthetic creations all bring me the indisputable revelation that God accepts me and loves me. My own sexual discourse of resistance offered me a platform for understanding the dilemma I faced as a young adult. It is instructive to note that my own understanding of sexual preference was initially suppressed under my very real existential anxiety created by a fear of rejection. The women who gathered at the beauty shop were some of the same women I saw on Sunday as my Sunday school teachers, deaconesses, missionaries, and ushers in the church. The rejection I felt happened in direct correlation to the fears of those in my concentric circle. They feared being associated with one who operated in "sin." Sin, for them, constituted death. Members of the LGBTQIA community are literally dead to the community of believers because they have been identified as an abomination to God.

Sin is characterized in my black church experience as that which separates me from God. But thankfully, as a child I had come to realize that there is "*nothing* that can separate me from the love of God,"[19] despite the rhetoric of the church. The fear of association that many projected onto me stemmed from the existential anxiety that threatens all being—the fear of nonbeing. The fear of nonbeing is most prevalent when one is expelled from the community based on "Christian" rhetoric that amounts to nothing more than a complete distortion of the Christian message and a camouflage for intolerance.[20] It is as though you are dead to the world. This is illustrated in Deacon William Peele's assertion that I was "nothing" to God. For a time, I felt estranged from God. I was indeed estranged from my community of faith. But I got over it.

Qualitative Method Informing Public Theology

Ethnography offers many distinct examples of how qualitative researchers explore the spatial relationship between "the said" (*le dit*), "the saying" (*le dire*), and the behavior that follows.[21] What is said and who says it contextualizes the formation of faith in ways that go far beyond the speech act itself. This project investigates what is said from the bully pulpit that directly and often negatively impacts the faith formation of LGBTQIA persons. The description "bully pulpit" is used to describe any places where LGBTQIA persons might hear violent rhetoric such as churches, temples, mosques, and lecture halls. The qualitative approach shaping this work relies on the work of D. Soyini Madison's *Critical Ethnography: Methods, Ethics, and Performance*.[22] Madison infuses the conceptualization of ethnography with attention to performance. Madison's attention to multidisciplinary methodology informs the way that theorists such as Audre Lorde, a black lesbian author and poet, Luce Irigaray, a French feminist philosopher, and Emmanuel Levinas, a Lithuanian Jew and theo-philosophical ethicist, collectively help me conceptualize a paradigm shift such that preaching as a performance art steeped in the art of domination can transform into agapé love.

In dialogue with Madison, I combine what I have learned from qualitative interviews and a focus group with performance theory to expose harmful rhetorical speech. Performance, in this sense, of everyday life, particularly as it relates to worship life, signals the aspects of speech acts performed by bully pulpit preachers that form the gravamen of this manuscript. Specifically, I will show the reader examples of violent rhetoric performed in places of worship. The theory of performativity that Madison espouses is particularly informative as I navigate the reflections of ten LGBTQIA persons when they have encountered this type of violent rhetoric. Madison's approach gives rise to my treatment of performativity as a way to capture the historical moments when participants in my study encountered violent rhetoric. I learned from their particularities as LGBTQIA persons as they remembered their feelings and experiences.

In particular, Madison's analysis of social movements, activism, and performance[23] support the analysis in this work by offering a framework for evaluating the commonality of experiences, the collective conceptualization of resistance, and the hope that lies in resilience in the face of adversity. In short, bully pulpit preachers use their platform to perform the role of "overseer" in service to their allegiance to whiteness. This is shown through an analysis of whiteface mimesis. The pastoral performances of bully pulpit preachers sully biblical ethical mandates and foster dominion over church folks and other people faithful to their own traditions to saddle them with what Na'im Akbar calls "mind slavery."

Through my analysis of the qualitative data comprised of listening to the stories of numerous LGBTQIA persons with experience in the black church tradition, I learned that specific, vibrant understandings/interpretations of notions such as advocacy, ethics of care, and ideologies of freedom emerge from the narratives of LGBTQIA persons who resist/reject the oppression of these high-profile ministers. By countering the insidious patriarchal hegemony from heterosexist and homophobic preachers, this qualitatively-informed public theology seeks to develop public theological affirmations that free LGBTQIA persons to embrace the *imago dei* and to walk in a liberty that calls into question anyone's ability to treat them as less than human or to denigrate their ontological value. Moreover, through critique of sermonic speech-acts, this study exposes the violent rhetoric in many faith institutions, unmasking hate-talk disguised as God-talk. Sharing central aspects of my own story along with those interviewed, reveals the extent of the rhetorical violence experienced by LGBTQIA persons in churches.

I investigated the particular socio-theological ramifications of black church public theology and the effects of rhetorical violence on human subjects who self-identify as LGBTQIA. To do so, I employed three types of analysis: theo-philosophical—a way of establishing philosophical knowledge through theological concepts, theo-ethical—a way of extricating ethical approaches from theological claims, and theo-poetic—a way of acknowledging the creativity ensconced in liberative theological analysis. Ethnographic material is woven into a content analysis of sermons and teachings to introduce a queer womanist public theology. After analyzing the data from the interviews, three important themes emerged from my ethnographic participants:

(1) The homophobic black bully pulpit is a source of oppression for LGBTQIA persons.

(2) LGBTQIA persons are singled out for direct ostracism designed to control their behavior.

(3) Many LGBTQIA persons who are subjected to open critique from the black bully pulpit either internalize the oppression or flee from the site of rhetorical terror to find refuge in different spaces.

I conducted a survey pretest with seventy-eight black subjects who self-identify as LGBTQIA through a protocol that asked ten simple questions.[24] Each participant was asked to state their sexual self-identity as a way to focus on the specialized experiences of a narrowly drawn set of human subjects—black LGBTQIA persons who have experience in the black church tradition. These subjects came from forty cities and forty states throughout the continental United States and Barbados. About a third are Baptist, though of different affiliations; about 20 percent are Church of God in Christ; about 20 percent are currently of nonspecified Pentecostal churches; and about 28 percent selected "other" for their current faith traditions, signifying that they are either presently nonaffiliated or participate in indigenous faith traditions, including Yoruba. In addition, two people are currently Muslim, one is Christian Methodist Episcopal, and one person practices Judaism. The family histories of more than one-third of the respondents included African Methodist Episcopal, African Methodist Episcopal Zion, Presbyterian, Episcopalian, Catholic, United Holy Church, United Church of Christ, and Methodist denominations. Over 90 percent of the respondents identify as either gay or lesbian. Three respondents identify as bisexual, and one identifies as transgender. Over 90 percent reported hearing vitriolic rhetoric from the pulpit or in the teaching of their faith tradition.

After fielding the pretest responses, I scheduled an interview with twelve subjects. I selected them based on availability for interviews, proximity to the scheduled site for interviews, and whether their pretest responses indicated information germane to further inquiry. Each interviewee was given the option of full anonymity. A few desired to remain anonymous, and that desire is honored here by assigning pseudonyms. The majority desired to be identified by their given names. I asked permission to video record the interviews and all agreed. I engaged each person in a face-to-face conversation about their experiences of black preaching on sexual orientation. A transcript was created from the video recording of each conversation. Questions were open-ended, following the thoughts of the interviewee. Next, I invited all twelve interviewees to a focus group session where I played the Sunday morning sermon of Pastor Terry K. Anderson of the Lilly Grove Missionary Baptist Church in Houston, Texas.[25] The sermon was used as an exemplar of the bully pulpit. Eight persons participated. With their permission, I recorded the responses of the group while the video played. I also recorded the group discussion that ensued thereafter.

The purpose of this investigation is to examine the effects of black church theology in its treatment of LGBTQIA persons, focusing on sermons, Bible teachings, group discussion, and individual talks where the issue of sexuality has been a topic. The following list of words and phrases represent a lexicon that signals when in the preaching and teaching moment rhetorical attacks against LGBTQIA persons often emerge: "sinful," "homosexual," "LGBTQIA," "same-sex marriage," "same gender loving," "gay marriage," "gay," "openly gay," "the gays," "queers," "sissy," "sissies," "common," "funny," "faggots," "fags," "dykes," "fairies," "them," "some of them," "that way," "profane," "reprobates," "reprobate mind," "immoral," "that life," "that lifestyle," "nasty," "ungodly," "abomination," "damned to hell," "God hates them," "not Adam and Steve," "punks," "sick," "sickness," "unnatural," "gave up the natural affection," "studs," "two men together," "two women together," "base," "fornicators," "unclean." My data analysis consisted of reviewing videos of the interviews that I conducted, review of the field notes taken simultaneously with the interviews, and review of the observations that I documented during my interaction with the participants. I coded the data according to descriptive markers of things people said that confirmed key themes. In completing a content analysis of sermons and narratives to determine when and whether the sermon or teaching raised issues of sexual orientation/identity, these terms were frequent markers. Although not exhaustive, these terms were used to refer to persons who self-identify as "queer," a term used to positively identify sexually diverse people who, in this research, are linked to the African diaspora by blood, marriage, or ethnicity.

"Otherness" is specifically defined here as those black LGBTQIA persons who populate or once populated the congregations of black churches or majority-black churches and who were subjected to hate-talk disguised as God-talk because of their sexual orientation. My operational definition of black church public theology encompasses the theology of any place, regardless of religious affiliation, where black-identified LGBTQIA persons have received instruction through black teaching and preaching targeting them or condemning them to hell.

In sum, this book identifies some of the historical, theological, philosophical, and psychological dynamics of black church public theology as it operates through teaching and preaching. I interrogate the correlation between the rhetoric and stereotypes generated by white dominant culture, on one hand, and the rhetoric in the Black bully pulpit regarding the treatment of LGBTQIA persons within black church theology, on the other. I analyze and illustrate how black church theology promotes an atmosphere of derision, isolation, fear, and abandonment of LGBTQIA persons. To the extent that black church public theology grounds itself in biblical images and narratives, I explore biblical references that offer a counternarrative to the images cast on LGBTQIA persons within the black community of faith. Through critical ethnography, I critique black church public theology by using the narratives of a nationwide sampling of black LGBTQIA persons. By doing so, I hope to expose the harmful theological practices that cause many to leave "the church." My claim is that the black preaching tradition, fraught with colonized thinking that oppresses the LGBTQIA community, permeates much of the landscape in black faith and life. Scarcely is there "good news" for black LGBTQIA people in black church public theology. Instead, what is espoused is hate-talk disguised as God-talk.

Overview of the Chapters

In Chapter 1, I establish the fundamental disconnect between insider and outsider language used to disgrace LGBTQIA persons and to signal intolerance in society. The first departure from an inclusive society starts with language. When language evokes stereotypical tropes that then emerge in cultural values, it creates a disconnect that licenses rhetorical violence. I evaluate the treatment of LGBTQIA persons within black practical theology considering the theo-poetics of Audre Lorde and the Womanist ethics of

Emilie M. Townes. I explore common themes from history of religions scholar Charles H. Long describing how stereotypes were used to characterize and debilitate enslaved Africans such that they would not survive the dominant culture's social order. I then build on Sarah Ahmed's analysis of *whiteness as an orientation* to frame the work of black bully pulpit preachers oriented toward whiteness in the preaching and teaching moment.

In Chapter 2, I posit that some black preachers are puppets who merely spew rhetorical violence upon their congregants in service to their slavish alignment with postmodern rhetorical violence. They are following the lead of the puppet masters—*those white preachers who are descendants of slave masters and who perpetuate a plantation mentality*. This makes the black bullies in the pulpit and in other public discourse the architects of speech acts that carry the message and narrative of enslavers. These bullies are the progenitors of hurtful words spoken to break down people's self-worth and value.

Moreover, because preachers carry significant influence in the community, congregants and others adopt their violent rhetoric in the mistaken belief that they are in alignment with God. I explore the theological and biblical frameworks that support the black bully pulpit. I trace the rhetoric in the mouths of black bully pulpit preachers to their roots in fundamentalist evangelicalism, drawing out the similarities between black bully pulpit preachers and their white counterparts. As a first ethic of public theology, I advance the notion that violent rhetoric is ungodly and maladjusted for purposes of control. I explore the theological moorings and biblical foundations of hate-talk disguised as God-talk and offer correctives building my public theological framework from a wealth of Womanist and feminist theology and ethics.

In Chapter 3, my focus is on surviving rhetorical violence. I consult the historical antecedents that reflect black people's capacity to survive despite many structural evils in their paths. Gleaning from the survival repertoire of black women in particular, I argue that even though rhetorical violence is prevalent in society generally, it is particularly harmful when it emanates from the mouth of trusted speakers. I contend that the violent rhetoric in the mouth of preachers creates harm that is not easily overcome. I use a sermon preached by a well-known television evangelist/preacher, Rev. Terry K. Anderson, to illustrate the diabolical nature of his rhetorical violence and to expose the rudimentary ways this and other speech-acts like his harken back to a slave mentality. I investigate, through Rev. Anderson's preaching exemplar, the (un)ethical framework by which black public theology guides the mission and ministries of some black churches. I consider the multiaxial dimensions of Christian social ethics associated with the treatment of black LGBTQIA people within black traditional congregations and compare that treatment with the experience gleaned from those participating in this qualitative research.

Consulting womanist and feminist theorists, I identify movements in black church politics that give rise to a disinvestment in the lives of

LGBTQIA people. Specifically, I explore how Levinas situates "Eros," "sexual difference," and "the feminine" considering Audre Lorde's liberative ethos for the purpose of advancing a more wholistic public theology.[26] Thus, I offer a public theological corrective to counter rhetorical violence in all its myriad ways by telling the stories of LGBTQIA persons who have been berated by this rhetoric and who have gained insight, foresight, and hindsight from their encounters and from the spiritual values they have retained, cultivated, and nurtured despite this harmful rhetoric.

In Chapter 4, I evaluate the treatment of LGBTQIA persons within black public theology where rhetorical violence is present. By examining the rhetoric of Rev. Terry K. Anderson's sermon as an exemplar that condemns black LGBTQIA people, I argue that his black preaching and teaching tradition renders him as a black bully pulpit preacher and as a minstrel in whiteface. Moreover, I argue that those who follow Anderson's patterns and practices in public discourse engage in minstrelsy as well. This is evidenced by the responses of my ethnographic focus group as they collectively listened to and commented on Anderson's sermon. I contend Audre Lorde is an exemplar of a lived theology that both liberates and stays connected to an Africentric ethos where spiritual expression, human dignity, and liberty "walk together as little children." My offering to the corpus of public theology argues that violent rhetoric can and should be countered with affirmations of worth and acceptance that meet the biblical mandate of loving one's neighbor.

I further evaluate otherness associated with LGBTQIA persons considering multiple identities, including Muslim, Baptist, and other Black faith identities as well as identities that do not claim a faith tradition. The ideology of genocide and the cultural production of evil serve as the foreground for a discussion of the psychological impact of violent rhetoric from a local and a global perspective. Ethnographic participants share their experiences with violent rhetoric and establish a baseline for coping, conquering, and surviving the longstanding impact of such rhetoric. The focus is on developing one's inner sanctum over all manner of oppositional rhetoric. Joined with my own analysis, the reflections of Franshon, Helen, Mara, Mileece, Patricia, Sadiqua, Zachard, Benjamin, Quincy, and Tadhi will provide guidance, confirmation, affirmation, and strength for the journey toward overcoming the bully pulpit.

Notes

1 Galatians 4:18–20 (NRSV).
2 Gerhard Kittle and Gerhard Friedrich, eds., *Theological Dictionary of the New Testament*, trans. Geoffrey W. Bromiley (Grand Rapids, MI: Eerdmans, 2000), 609.

3   Paul Tillich, *Systematic Theology*, vol. III (Chicago, IL: University of Chicago Press, 1963), 333.

4   Walker, *In Search of Our Mothers' Gardens*, xi.

5   This term is defined as a masculine-identifying lesbian, usually African American. See Urban Dictionary's entry for "bull daggers," http://www.urbandictionary.com/define.php?term=bulldagger; and "Rickey Smiley 'Lesbians ~vs~ Bulldaggers,'" posted by dtm313, YouTube, February 29, 2012, https://www.youtube.com/watch?v=LjJUxyTvQpk</> (both accessed July 5, 2024).

6   See Appendix A.

7   Judith Butler, *Frames of War: When Is Life Grievable?* (New York: Verso, 2016), 13–14.

8   Cody J. Sanders, *Queer Lessons for Churches on the Straight and Narrow* (Macon, GA: Faithlab, 2013), preface. "Queer is a word of unification of those targeted by prejudice and injustice." I will refer primarily to "LGBTQIA," as this term is most commonly used when referring to this community within the black preaching tradition.

9   Butler, *Frames of War*, 14–15.

10 Ibid., 38.

11 Paul Tillich, *Systematic Theology*, vol. I (Chicago, IL: University of Chicago Press, 1951), 81–83.

12 Renee Hill, "Who Are We for Each Other?: Sexism, Sexuality and Womanist Theology," in *Black Theology: A Documentary History*, vol. 2, ed. Gayraud S. Wilmore and James H. Cone (Maryknoll, NY: Orbis, 1993), 345–51.

13 Kelly Brown Douglas, *Sexuality and the Black Church: A Womanist Perspective* (Maryknoll, NY: Orbis, 1999).

14 Walker, *In Search of Our Mother's Gardens*, xi.

15 Brown Douglas, *Sexuality and the Black Church*, 107.

16 Ibid., 107.

17 Ibid.; Audre Lorde, *Sister Outsider: Essays and Speeches by Audre Lorde* (Berkeley, CA: Crossing, 1984), 110. See also Paul Tillich, *Theology of Culture* (New York: Oxford University Press, 1959), 41.

18 Dwight N. Hopkins, *Being Human: Race, Culture, and Religion* (Minneapolis: Fortress, 2005), 116.

19 Romans 8:39 (NRSV).

20 Hopkins, *Being Human*, 29.

21 My use of the French forms of these words signals a direct reference to the work of Emmanuel Levinas. In the final chapter I explore more deeply the significance of these words for Levinasian thought. For our purposes here, they signify the way meaning travels through the spoken word and how that word moves from an utterance to a "truth" statement that then becomes "gospel." This simulates the argument made by Hebrew Bible scholar Nyasha Junior in her essay "Tyler Perry Reads Scripture," in which she evaluates how "the said" is treated as biblical content when it may not even be in the Bible

or when it is conflated with a semblance of biblical truth mixed with people's misguided understanding of the actual Bible that then becomes a "saying" given biblical credence. Nyasha Junior, "Tyler Perry Reads Scripture," in *Womanist and Black Feminist Responses to Tyler Perry's Productions*, ed. LeRhonda S. Manigault-Bryant, Tamura A. Lomax, and Carol B. Duncan (New York: Palgrave McMillan, 2014).

22 D. Soyini Madison, *Critical Ethnography: Methods, Ethics, and Performance* (Thousand Oaks, CA: Sage, 2012).

23 Ibid.

24 See Appendix B for these ten questions.

25 The video is available on YouTube: "What Must The Church Do About Same Sex Marriage? (Matthew 13:24–30)—Rev. Terry K. Anderson," posted by Lilly Grove Missionary Baptist Church, YouTube, April 15, 2012, https://youtu.be/SfpVPydcNrQ?si=vNSGwGUSjG7re_ja (accessed July 5, 2024).

26 Emmanuel Levinas, *Totality and Infinity* (Boston, MA: Kluwer Academic, 1991), 257, 259.

1

The Least of These

I am concerned with preaching that does no more than confuse and hurt people. As a Christian, I preach that Jesus emphasizes ministry toward "the least of these."¹ Separating bad actors from good ones and mooring a commitment to God's justice to the beachheads of radical hospitality are the foci of Jesus's earthly ministry in my estimation. Jesus invoked *ad litem* representation of those who are deemed by society as less than. As such, I contend the disciples of Christ are called to see and feed the hungry, give drink to the thirsty, clothe the naked, receive the stranger, visit the sick and imprisoned. There is no lack of clarity about the intent of the gospel to promote radical hospitality. However, there is evidence that this mandate is abridged in houses of worship when it comes to LGBTQIA persons. LGBTQIA persons are considered less than by ministry leaders who, in many instances, take the liberty to exploit the differences they perceive between heterosexuals and LGBTQIA persons. They create the ethos of insider and outsider among congregants based on sexual orientation. In so doing, ministry leaders often lead LGBTQIA persons to believe they do not belong in the household of faith, no matter which faith communion they engage. LGBTQIA persons are often without recourse when it comes to how they might live out a faith tradition or how they might overcome the faith leaders' rhetoric that feels violent as it lands in their ears.

As Audre Lorde describes in her biographical writings, she discovered indomitable strength that comes with a clear understanding of one's difference. She characterized her own spiritual ascension into a place of purposeful resistance to oppressive structures that compress creativity with this resolution: "Difference is that raw and powerful connection from which our personal power is forged."² Emerging from a place of abasement, degradation, and dejection to a place of "dogged" strength and inimitable courage against the forces of evil facing LGBTQIA persons presupposes a value system and an intentionality capable of transcending the dialectical tension between faith born of struggle and marginalization within the faith community. Possessing the agency to confront that which threatens one's self-identity requires a tenacious grasp of how difference informs one's personal power. This recognition is the entry point into a deeper examination of the (un)ethical practices of the black preaching tradition in its treatment of LGBTQIA persons.

Perpetuating Evil

In her seminal work *Womanist Ethics and the Cultural Production of Evil*, Emilie Townes explores how stereotypes are used to funnel certain images and how those images, particularly within the realm of religious values, tend to distort one's view of humanity.[3] Certain religiously held values have operated within black church theology to create an atmosphere of rejection that leads to banishment for LGBTQIA persons. The historical blackface stereotype and the inverted idea of whiteface mimesis serve as metaphors for how the black preacher promotes the message of white, right-wing fundamentalist evangelicalism in preaching and teaching, which then trickles down to congregants who mimic the same behavior. I cautiously, if decidedly, engaged this stereotypical rendering of the black bully pulpit preacher as a counternarrative critique in hopes that its examination will inspire circumspection and allocution by such preachers and teachers. I do not favor the use of stereotypes for purposes that distort. I hope to inspire all preachers and teachers to develop a healthy critique of stereotypes, to renounce their use, and to identify when rhetorical violence becomes stereotypical. For that reason, I must turn attention to how negative stereotypes can be disemboweled through our *countermemory*.

Countermemory and Whiteface Stereotypes

Relying on an essay written by Manthia Diawara, a cultural theorist and scholar of Malian descent, titled "The Blackface Stereotype,"[4] Townes suggests that the stereotype promotes a distorted view of history that must be redressed with "countermemory," a term coined from an analysis of Antonio Gramsci's understanding of hegemony and Michel Foucault's understanding of imagination. To this end, Townes introduces the "fantastic hegemonic imagination," which "traffics in peoples' lives that are caricatured or pillaged so that the imagination that creates the fantastic can control the world in its own image."[5] In accord with Townes, black practical, public theology is often laced with the white, fantastic hegemonic imagination about LGBTQIA persons, which is ensconced in selective memory. Blacks were seen as animals and in many cases believed by whites to have "tails."[6] This fantastic hegemonic imagination promulgated by whites has now been transformed by black bully pulpit preachers, who preach the same misperception of their own people. The narrative in their mouths is not the voice of God.

Diawara offers yet another layer to my embrace of the whiteface stereotype. He argues that some artists who have embraced the old blackface stereotype, such as Chris Rock appearing in blackface on the front cover of *Vanity Fair*, have done so to incorporate "the criterion of transtextuality," which is Diawara's term for a reappropriation of the old stereotype. Not only has the old stereotype been reappropriated within black practical, public theology, as it relates to LGBTQIA people, it has been transubstantiated from blackface minstrelsy to whiteface mimesis such that its presentation is actually representation. This brings into clearer focus Diawara's contention that "if the old stereotype is the projection of white supremacist thinking onto black people, the new stereotype compounds matters by desiring that image, and deforming its content for a different appropriation."[7] Diawara sees some positives in such (re)appropriation; however, in this study, I do not. On LGBTQIA issues, much of black practical, public theology not only upholds the right-wing fundamentalist evangelical "worldview" but also appropriates that worldview as its own.

Townes argues against the use of stereotypes to describe black reality and introduces a new paradigm, arguing that "we must name ourselves with precise anger and ornery love while churning justice and truth into a new analysis of our ethical dilemma. The dilemma of what it means to shape and name and create an identity forged by the hope found in those who are still here ... regardless."[8] My ethnographic subjects offer wise counsel on this and many issues that stem from whiteface mimesis treated in this book. Franshon, a queer preacher from Chicago, models the idea of naming oneself perfectly by establishing her sense of who God is and how God is situated in her worldview.

Franshon: So, I went through a period in my life, I told you, for two or three years I did not go to nobody's church, and I was not ever going to either. I'm like Jesus's gonna have to step down off the throne and come tell me to go to church. Because I felt like I was being ostracized. I felt two things: I felt called to ministry. I was called. I felt like I was anointed to do ministry and I felt like I wasn't able to do what God was calling me to do because of who I was. But then, I was thinking, "Well, God knew what I was when God called me. It's not a surprise to God, right?" These are all of the thoughts that I'm having in my young mind with myself and not able to articulate that even to my friends because they come from the same background as me and they think that homosexuality is wrong. So, I didn't have anybody to talk to about what I was experiencing. It wasn't just the homosexuality or the homophobic spews; "God said it's wrong, and it's an abomination, and it ain't going to be none of that up in here," and this crazy mess that came out of her mouth that was the issue for me.

Aside from that, I would say in my late teens early twenties I really felt like there was really more to God than what I was getting in church. I always felt like God was bigger.

Arriving at this conclusion was no easy task for Franshon. She moved from a place of complete denunciation of the church to a place of personal acceptance that she was a child of God who was called to ministry and whose gifts were important to God's work. This came from reframing her image of God. Once Franshon allowed herself to embrace her vision of a God who was bigger than what she had encountered in the churches she had been hurt by, she could hold fast to her belief and move forward.

LGBTQIA Persons Navigating Outsider Status in the Church

Despite the hurt caused by black church public theology, there are black LGBTQIA persons who remain inside the gate of the black church and those who feel unwelcome and therefore retire outside the gate. My ethnographic analysis seeks to discern how *countermemory* might inform the way forward for black church public theology in general and LGBTQIA persons specifically. Religionists tend to exude a piety that fosters a belief that some are unworthy. The practical implications of "religious values" dispatched as artillery against LGBTQIA persons are threefold. First, there is a diminution of the self-worth of those targeted by theological venom. Consider Helen, for instance:

> *Helen:* The only reason I go to church now, if I'm at home, is because my granny will ask me to go with her. But, typically if I'm home, I am usually only there for about three or four days anyway, and I usually leave on Sundays, so I don't have to go 'cause I just feel like it's an oppressive place. I always felt like I was pariah in my spiritual setting 'cause it was just stuff that I just didn't understand and that definitely impacted me.

Helen's feelings that she was "pariah" in her "spiritual settings" points to the ways that obnoxious piety creates a wall of confusion and doubt in the LGBTQIA person so overwhelming that her sense of belonging can only exist outside the church. The inside experience is too oppressive to endure on a sustained basis. The harm that comes from that oppression causes her to flee the church. Womanist theologian Frances E. Wood names this oppression a "yoke." Woods notes, "Black women who risk telling their story in this context are shamed, denounced, and treated as pariahs rather than prophets. The yoke of silencing, degrading, ignoring, or dismissing women weighs down the Black Christian community in a conspiracy against its own total liberation."[9]

Second, there is a belief promulgated from the pulpit that LGBTQIA persons are beyond the capacity of God's love. Mara's discomfort and sense of not belonging demonstrate this:

Mara: Because everything that I was taught told me that I was going to hell. I'm in church and you hear a sermon "God created Adam and Eve and not Adam and Steve." You know the famous line. And so, I'm like okay, do I have a place here? It became very uncomfortable for me to be at a place where somebody is preaching that; and it's like "but my sexuality doesn't have anything to do with me loving God or serving Him or worshipping Him."

Mara's loss is a loss of place. She once knew her place in the church, but her status as a lesbian displaced her to a point where she cannot find her footing in church. Cole Arthur Riley opines,

For those whose sense of place speaks more of trauma than of belonging, it is understandable to think that the sole and sacred solution would be to belong nowhere at all. But this is alienation masquerading as freedom … Alienation and trauma of place are best met not with dislocation but with belonging, with a defiant rootedness, even if those roots stretch out to new and safer places.[10]

In those instances one would do well to remember Jesus's pronouncement that "I go to prepare a place for you."[11]

Third, there is a separation from one's traditional congregational life to avoid being shamed or "othered." Sometimes the rhetoric is so damning that remaining in the congregation makes one feel like an alien, as Mileece describes:

Mileece: Disciples of Christ … a little storefront church … it was—very homophobic. The pastor preached hell and damnation for gay and lesbian and trans people. Anyone who was not straight, heterosexual was going to go to hell, and you were in sin, and you do not deserve to be a Christian. I felt demoralized, I felt disrespected, I felt hurt; because we're in this congregation with you, but we are not the same, we're not like you. We have the devil in us, and your job is to get it out of us. That's what your job is because we're different. We're African American, we're women, but we're different. We're possessed, so to speak.

Homophobic rants such as what Mileece experienced point to the power dynamics in black church public theology that seek to relegate LGBTQIA persons to a place of damnation. The feelings this practice engenders give LGBTQIA persons the idea that there is something wrong with them that needs exorcising. Their reaction to this treatment is often anger or woundedness. Either emotion can lead to separation from the church, the community, and sometimes the family.

To the degree that black preaching creates these effects, it is operating within an (un)ethical framework convinced of its (self) "righteousness" and its (adulterated) "truth." In effect, as Townes structures the argument, the culture of black church public theology, which treats LGBTQIA "identity as property," promoting the stereotype of people as "chattel," creates an "evil" perception of LGBTQIA persons within the culture of black religiosity.[12] When such brutal rhetoric falls on the ears of LGBTQIA people, it is traumatic. Consequently, the multiaxial dimensions of Christian social ethics—when bound by the graveclothes of biblical literalism, legalism, and punishment—must be systematically dismantled, deconstructed, and denounced in order to reverse this trend. One must fully understand the historical markers and the roots of such thinking in order to deconstruct it. For that analysis I turn to historian of religions Charles H. Long. Long situates the approach I identify as the *mind slavery* of black bully pulpit preachers at the intersection between European primitivism and Protestant reform.

Cultural Hegemony

The perception of some people as "primitive" emerged to separate them from other people who are "civilized." Long opines that "cultural primitivism" reveals itself as retaining "simpler" forms of existence and denouncing anything that threatens civilization's fundamental approach. As a consequence, cultural primitivism serves as the link between the image of the leper, which "disappeared" at the end of the Middle Ages, and the mythology of the "wild man," which appeared in "folkloric, literary, theatrical, and artistic levels of medieval society."[13] Long connects Richard Berheimer's history of the "wild man" to "Michel Foucault's history of madness, identifying how difference was treated across time and space from the Greco-Roman cultures to the 'New World.'" According to Long, "the wild man is a child of nature ... Nothing about the wild man prepares him for participation in civil society."[14] There was no place in a civilized order for those who were imagined to fit this description:

> Wild men are separated from human society. The natural place for these ambiguous creatures is the forest, removed from habitation. Wild men are tempted to leave the wilds out of an inordinate and destructive desire for human flesh, expressed carnally or cannibalistically. Their biological structure is ambiguous, partaking of the human and the beast, uncontrolled by human reason; their great natural and bestial strength poses a threat to human society.[15]

Advancing Long's argument further, mimicking one's oppressor, through the use of the same descriptions such as "wild man," in order to categorize and isolate one's own kindred as lesser, signifies the deep psychological trauma, fear, and self-loathing emanating from years of chattel slavery and systematic brutality. This constitutes a transference that literally activates mimesis so that what was once the exclusive critique of oppressive "masters" becomes a personal critique and, more importantly, a critique of one's own kindred. As a result of this trauma, transmuted over time and space, a process of internalization gives rise to hierarchical practices of othering and belonging. LGBTQIA persons are othered, and those who adopt the language, content, and meaning of belonging from the mimetic process operate as though they belong by striking verbal blows at those they perceive to be undesirable based upon a skewed, ritualized view of whiteness as a property to be owned.[16] This property, acquired by convergence, takes shape in a "taken for granted," "this is normal," "everybody knows this" kind of dialogue. Because the designation "chattel" conferred no benefit to Africans in America that American jurisprudence recognized or acknowledged, there was no formal or legal nexus between Africans in America and the concept of freedom until after the Civil War.[17] Those who desired to garner a modicum of civilized treatment from whites converged their behavior to that of whiteness. They adopted and adapted whiteness as a social construct for purposes of acceptance and survival.

LGBTQIA persons have been characterized in the same way as enslaved Africans were. Descriptions of enslaved Africans characterized them as animal-like.[18] Because of European influences, from the Middle Ages to the present moment racial hierarchies permeate Western culture. The tragedy of black pastors characterizing their own people using the same terms that Europeans used to describe enslaved Africans positions them as modern-day amanuenses, copying and writing what another dictates. It is particularly troubling when the descriptions of LGBTQIA persons by black public theologians do not deviate from Europeans' totalizing view of black people as sexual predators and as beast-like, grotesque beings occupying a marginal place outside of civil society.[19] "Within the epistemological valence of civilization," Charles Long explains, this is a "false consciousness."[20] *Plessy v. Ferguson* amplified this falsity in the context of American jurisprudence.[21] From the basic contention that there is nothing that whiteness owes to blackness, that legal precedent established a mythology that continues to animate intersubjective exchanges that constantly press people into molds as either in or out of the so-called dominant culture.

Right-Wing Fundamentalism

The flow of rhetorical violence committed against LGBTQIA persons from the black bully pulpit is reminiscent of the way Christianity spread throughout the world. Christianity employed the tactics of military conquest to capture and kill every cultural difference identified as inconsistent with its imperialistic claim to morality, which willingly sacrificed human beings in the name of its supposed superiority and celebrated the same as ordained by God. Traci West describes this phenomenon:

> When inviting discussion of universal Christian moral concerns, I hasten to reiterate my awareness that there is an extensive historical legacy of Christians violently imposing their beliefs on Jews, Muslims, and various indigenous populations who were practicing their own religious traditions before encountering Christians. This widespread legacy of coercion has included an assertion of universality of Christianity for everyone, everywhere, interpreted to mean Christian superiority over other religions. This sense of superiority has justified Christian subjugation and even extermination of peoples.[22]

The universality of this moral framework for right-wing fundamentalist evangelical Christians is exposed in the memoir of a gay, white man, Mel White. In *Stranger at the Gate: To Be Gay and Christian in America*, White tells of his personal battle to overcome the Christian stereotypes at work in right-wing fundamentalism. White details his intimate dealings with leaders of the Moral Majority as he encountered "The Ghost of Silence," "The Ghost of Fear," "The Ghost of Loneliness," and "The Ghost of False Hope," all titles of essays in the book. Eventually, White "gave up the ghost" and found his own voice.[23] White served as ghostwriter for several prominent, right-wing fundamentalist evangelical leaders. Referencing his ghostwriting for Jerry Falwell's autobiography, *Strength for the Journey*, White responded to a scathing fundraising letter sent by Falwell to his constituency:

> I received a copy of the October 1991 fund-raising letter describing me and millions of men and women like me as "perverts" who "unashamedly flaunt their perversion." The letter declares "homosexuality a sin." It warns that "our nation has become a modern day Sodom and Gomorra" and that you have decided to speak out against this "perversion" for the purpose of "moral decency and traditional family values."[24]

Here White clearly identifies the Moral Majority's agenda. The intent to clothe hate-talk in the disguise of God-talk could not be more pronounced. Because the message has a moral overtone and was sent by a preacher, it is easily treated by the recipient as a biblical mandate. The fundraising letter not only demeans the LGBTQIA community but also makes the very being of LGBTQIA persons "sinful." The hegemonic right-wing fundamentalist evangelical dossier, expressed in the fundraising letter, secured these ruthless, negative stereotypes of LGBTQIA persons in the minds of church people, permanently etching those images onto the cultural imagination of those who read the letter. Addressing the net effect of such a correspondence, White directs Falwell to the ethical implications of such teaching:

Jerry, I am hoping that staff or agency ghostwriters wrote that letter and that you didn't have time to read it before it was signed and mailed on your behalf. Did they realize the immediate and long-term impact of its cloud of misinformation, half-truth, and hyperbole? Did they understand the confusion and the suffering that it helps cause in the lives of American families who have gay or lesbian members? Did they know that the letter's misleading statements fuel bigotry, hatred, and violence?[25]

Living the "Good" Life

If living the "good life,"[26] as proffered by Christian ethicist Robin Lovin, is the goal of every human being, it is best approached within an intersubjective relationality. As faithful beings, we must care about "the wellbeing of others indiscriminately, without regard for their worthiness."[27] This signals an important component of the kind of Christian social ethics necessary to embrace the questions White poses to Falwell. In this way, one resists the temptation to conflate "morality" with ethics. There is a distinction between the two that must be considered.

Ethics involves the discernment needed to reach correct decisions whereas morality is the set of guidelines one adopts and follows to enact them. Nuancing the two renders the distinction as between "choices" and "rules."[28] This distinction, though subtle, is helpful in establishing the parameters of a Christian social ethics because it requires one to first distinguish "the moral goods such as justice, honesty, or compassion" from the "natural or nonmoral goods, such as health, wealth, comfort, and security."[29] Distinguishing the two enables Christians to separate "the good life and the Christian life."[30] The two are not always mutually exclusive, but morality is often (mis)placed as superior to Christ, in the context of Christian social ethics, displacing those perceived to threaten the "natural or nonmoral goods."[31] The choice to follow Christ is therefore an ethical one: "the choice between love of God and love of self is so absolute that you really cannot love God and at the same time care about your own good life."[32] The paramount questions that we must answer in evaluating Christian social ethics generally are these: What does God require of those who give pastoral care to LGBTQIA persons? What is the message of hope for the LGBTQIA person? Is there any aspect of the Christian message that calls for denigrating rhetoric and hate-filled sermons? What harm does one cause when one engages in hate-talk disguised as God-talk? Until these questions are sincerely pondered, the tensions created by the alterity of LGBTQIA persons within the context of some Christian settings will continue to produce evil effects. White continues his inquiry to prompt an assessment of the damage such violent rhetoric causes:

Closer home, did anyone consider the tragic consequences of that letter in the lives of the people who see you as their spiritual guide? Certainly you know that in the Thomas Road Baptist Church, in Liberty University, and in the audience of the "Old Time Gospel Hour," there are thousands of Christians struggling with this issue. Did anyone think about the confusion, the anguish, and the despair that the letter's simplistic, judgmental, and erroneous position creates for them and for their families?

I know personally what it means to be a victim of this uniformed and noncompassionate "Christian" position on homosexuality. I went through twenty-five years of Christian counseling and "ex-gay therapy" including electric shock to try to overcome my sexual and affectional orientation. Finally feeling abandoned by God, by the church, and by society, I longed to end my life.[33]

Violent rhetoric increases exponentially when the subject is a black LGBTQIA person. Often the ridicule exemplified by black pastoral leaders, such as Pastor Terry K. Anderson, who is discussed in Chapter 3, is designed to publicly shame the LGBTQIA person, not to liberate them. A line is drawn in the sand that any "holy" person would not dare to cross.

The public shaming is reminiscent of a "spectacle" lynching where it was not enough to kill the person; rather, the body had to be put on display, hanging in the midst of the crowd and ultimately dismembered.[34] Mileece recounts the denigration she felt when she was made a spectacle in the church service:

> *Mileece*: I had no idea that this was going to happen, because we had gone several times before and we heard the preaching, okay, and we knew how they felt, felt about gay people. But, on this day the pastor decided this was the day that we needed to come up and be delivered and have hands thrown on us and pushed us around and hands on your head and you know, violently pushing you. It was violent.

Consequently, the LGBTQIA person "retreats to the wall"[35] by denying their own authenticity or their right to be. White offers that the only way out of this death trap for him was to mount up with courage. Mileece found her courage as well.

> *Mileece*: That, okay, that's not God. I am not going to a place where God is ... first of all God is not limited to a storefront church, especially with hatred involved. That is not God. I don't care what you call it. You can put a gold twenty-foot cross in front of it, lit up. That's not God. And so, I am not going to a place where I've been abused.

Sometimes the courage one finds is internal, and at other times it is external, as White explains:

Now, looking back, I can see God was there, all the time, in the midst of my suffering, leading me to a remnant of faithful, well-informed Christians who had the courage to speak truth whatever it cost them. My most helpful counselor was fired from Fuller Seminary (where I was a professor for fourteen years) because she dared to tell the truth about homosexuality and the false claims that the "ex-gay" movement makes. And though telling the truth cost her her academic position, she saved a lot of lives and ministries in the process.[36]

Mileece's embrace of courage as a self-identified lesbian presents a sound theo-ethical position for the LGBTQIA person. It foregrounds the position that Audre Lorde espouses—difference is power. The courage to embrace one's difference empowers one to be authentic. Katie Cannon would term this "unshouted courage."[37] Mileece expressed her own connection to God born of her own discernment. LGBTQIA persons can and do cultivate the ears to hear what the Spirit is truly saying.

Whiteness as Orientation

Sarah Ahmed, former professor of race and cultural studies at Goldsmiths College, University of London, relying on Frantz Fanon's *Black Skin, White Masks*, argues "whiteness as an orientation."[38] Making a phenomenological claim, Ahmed explains that the peregrination of nonwhite bodies in a white world is "lived as a background to experience."[39] For Ahmed, orientation refers to a "starting point," and whiteness holds the default position. It is the place from which "being," as Husserl suggested, "is directed towards some objects and not others."[40] Position, status, and privilege are objects of the whiteness orientation. To the extent that being is oriented as whiteness, what follows is the probability that "styles, capacities, aspirations, techniques, habits" flow from that orientation. "The analogy works powerfully to produce a particular version of race *and* a particular version of family, predicated on 'likeness,' where likeness becomes a matter of 'shared attributes.'"[41] The particularities find expression "beneath the surface of the body." Consequently, no matter the skin color, the orientation is presented as a "likeness" to the objectified orientation—whiteness. This phenomenon renders the black body, "shaped by histories of colonialism," as invisible but renders whiteness visible within the same black body.[42]

In the preaching moment in black churches, what *being* presents the message? Looking beyond the surface, the moment often operationalizes whiteness as an orientation. Black preachers in the bully pulpit distort the gospel message, pushing the agenda of the religious right, a codification of control mechanisms deployed to divide and conquer. This calls into question the ethical relationship between preacher and congregation. Ahmed's conception of "whiteness as property" speaks to the way some pastors enter ministry and evolve as ministerial presences. When oriented through whiteness, the preached message derives its authority from what is perceived by the minister to be what white folks want them to say considering what white folks are saying. The orientation looks to whiteness for its legitimacy, its standards, it value. By taking on a white orientation, the black body of the preacher attains the status it desires but perceives as otherwise unreachable. The preaching style, method, aims, and intent are designed to reduce the hearer to that which is oriented toward whiteness. Whiteness as "likeness" achieves the goals of signification.

Charles H. Long suggested that religious foci followed a similar trajectory in the Atlantic World. "Religion as orientation in time and space, externally and internally, forms a locus," which created, for Africans kidnapped and forced into it, an "instability." The religious center, now destabilized, forced a new "curiosity."[43] Instability, I argue, is the root cause of the religious fracture giving rise to the vitriolic rhetoric of some black preachers. In the next chapter I further illustrate how this phenomenon unfolds in the life of congregational ministry. Black preachers who bully LGBTQIA persons from the pulpit follow the pattern and practice of the white preachers that Mel White described and that I describe in the following chapter. This mimetic function for black pastors can be understood as a means of embodying whiteness in response to years of social conditioning that names whiteness an unmitigable truth of Christian worth in which the religious validation and belief system bows to whiteness as a moral standard. It is their point of entry into the familial place in whiteness.[44] It is whiteness as likeness.[45]

Notes

1 Matthew 25:40 (NIV).
2 Lorde, *Sister Outsider*, 112.
3 Emilie M. Townes, *Womanist Ethics and the Cultural Production of Evil* (New York: Palgrave McMillan, 2006), 6.
4 Manthia Diawara, "Blackface Stereotype," *Black Cultural Studies*, 1998, https://www.scribd.com/document/209231430/Blackface-Stereotype (accessed July 5, 2024).
5 Townes, *Womanist Ethics*, 18, 21, 43.
6 Nell Irvin Painter, *The History of White People* (New York: W. W. Norton, 2010); Charles H. Long, *Significations: Signs, Symbols, and Images in the Interpretation of Religion* (Aurora, CO: Davies Group, 1999); James H. Sweet, "The Iberian Roots of American Racist Thought," *William and Mary Quarterly* 54, no. 1 (1997): 143–66; R. A. Hogarth, "The Myth of Innate Racial Differences between White and Black People's Bodies: Lessons From the 1793 Yellow Fever Epidemic in Philadelphia, Pennsylvania," *American Journal of Public Health* 109, no. 10 (October 2019): 1339–41.

7 Diawara, "Blackface Stereotype."
8 Townes, *Womanist Ethics*, 55.
9 Frances E. Wood, *"Take My Yoke upon You": The Role of the Church in the Oppression of African-American Women*, ed. Emilie M. Townes (Maryknoll, NY: Orbis, 1993) 39. See also Emilie B. Townes, *A Troubling in My Soul: Womanist Perspectives on Evil and Suffering* (Maryknoll, NY: Orbis Books, 1993), 37–47.
10 Cole Arthur Riley, *This Here Flesh: Spirituality, Liberation, and the Stories That Make Us* (New York: Convergent, 2022), 19.
11 John 14:2b (NKJV).
12 Townes, *Womanist Ethics*, 40–47.
13 Long, *Significations*, 89–91.
14 Ibid., 91.
15 Ibid., 92.
16 Cheryl I. Harris, "Whiteness as Property," *Harvard Law Review* 106, no. 8 (1993): 1716–18.
17 *Plessy v. Ferguson*, 163 U.S. 537 (1896).
18 Painter, *History of White People*, 59–71.
19 For an example of this portrayal of black people, see W. D. Griffith's film *Birth of a Nation* (1915).
20 Long, *Significations*, 95.
21 *Plessy v. Ferguson*, 163 U.S. 537 (1896).
22 Traci C. West, *Disrupting Christian Ethics: When Racism and Women's Lives Matter* (Louisville, KY: Westminster John Knox, 2006), 37.
23 Mel White, *Stranger at the Gate: To Be Gay and Christian in America* (New York: Penguin, 1994), 11–84, 192–221.
24 Ibid., 292.
25 Ibid.
26 Robin W. Lovin, *Christian Ethics: An Essential Guide* (Nashville, TN: Abingdon Press, 2000), 16–17.
27 Ibid., 16–17.
28 Ibid.
29 Ibid.
30 Ibid.
31 Ibid.
32 Ibid., 17.
33 White, *Stranger*, 293.
34 James Allen et al., *Without Sanctuary: Lynching Photography in America* (Santa Fe, NM: Twin Palms, 1999).
35 This phraseology is common among legal scholars in reference to the widely held view that persons who are attacked have a duty to retreat, if such can

be done safely, before using deadly force against their attacker. See Eugene Volokh, "Duty to Retreat 'To the Wall,'" *Washington Post*, December 5, 2014, https://www.washingtonpost.com/news/volokh-conspiracy/wp/2014/12/05/duty-to-retreat-to-the-wall (accessed July 5, 2024).

36 White, *Stranger*, 293.
37 Katie Geneva Cannon, *Black Womanist Ethics* (Atlanta, GA: Scholars Press, 1988).
38 Sarah Ahmed, "A Phenomenology of Whiteness," *Feminist Theory* 8, no. 2 (2007): 149–168.
39 Ibid., 150.
40 Ibid., 151.
41 Ibid., 151, 154.
42 Ibid., 153.
43 Charles H. Long, "Passage and Prayer: The Origin of Religion in the Atlantic World," in *The Courage to Hope: From Black Suffering to Human Redemption*, ed. Quinton Hosford Dixie and Cornel West (Boston, MA: Beacon, 1999), 11–21.
44 Ibid., 19.
45 Ahmed, "Phenomenology," 150–55.

2

The Bully Pulpit: Untying the Ties That Bind

In the previous chapter we explored the parameters of LGBTQIA selfhood in the face of many so-called Christian demarcations of belonging. We established the longstanding stereotypes that characterize the treatment of LGBTQIA persons within white Christian pulpits and signaled this as a precursor to how black preachers operating in the likeness of their white counterparts mimic that rhetoric. What follows is an exemplar of this kind of rhetoric and the ties that it binds to black bully pulpit preaching. On any given Sunday, the connection between faith claims and political issues aimed at extending human dignity toward LGBTQIA persons presents opportunities for these preachers to couch their hatred in terms of God's mandates. Their language expresses their personal angst regarding LGBTQIA persons. They speak their own vitriolic feelings and hide behind God as a shield.

In a 2012 YouTube video, Pastor Charles Worley, a white, evangelical fundamentalist from North Carolina, preached the following message on a Sunday morning:

> … of our president getting' up and sayin' that it was alright for two women to marry or two men to marry. I tell ya right now, I was disappointed bad. Uh, but a, I tell ya right there it's as sorry as you can get. The Bible's agin it, God's agin it, I'm agin it, and if you've got any sense you're agin it. I had a way, I figured a way out; a way to git rid of all the lesbians and queers, but I couldn't get it pass the Congress. Build a great big large fence, hunderd fifty or a hunderd mile long, put all the lesbians in there; fly over and drop some food. Do the same thing with the queers and the homosexuals, and have that fence electrified so they can't get out, feed 'em … And you know what, in a few years, they'll die out … Do you know why? They can't reproduce. If a man ever has a young'un, praise God, it'll be the first one … You just well to say amen cause I'm a preach the hell out of all of 'em.[1]

He continued, in the same sermon, to belittle lesbians and gays by making fun of the idea that someone could love someone of the same gender. As he brought his message to a crescendo, he theorized that in the 2012 presidential election, he would not vote for a "baby killer" or a "homosexual lover."[2] Pastor Worley goes on to say, "God have mercy, it makes me puking sick to think about; I don't even know whether you oughta say this in the pulpit or not, could you imagine kissing some man?" Pastor Worley's sermon is hate-talk disguised as God-talk. His disdain for lesbians and gays extends far beyond some biblical reference, which he does not even offer. This goes deep into his persona as a hatemongering bully. Undoubtedly, his message about voting was aimed at countering then president Barack Obama's changed stance on marriage equality.

On May 9, 2012, during his first term in office, President Obama candidly confessed in an exclusive interview with ABC News that he had wrestled with the constitutional implications of marriage equality and had, over time, reversed his longstanding view that the conveyance of equal rights under the law could and should be made through civil unions as opposed to conventional marriage. However, his change of heart came after much deliberation whereby he concluded that same-gender-loving people are entitled to the same rights under the law as everyone else.[3] President Obama's moral responsibility in setting forth his changed position presumably evoked the death wishes of Pastor Worley upon LGBTQIA persons. This narrative must change. Black pastors must be challenged to rethink their role as pastoral caregivers and to disentangle themselves from the message of the religious right, as it only serves to inscribe the condemnation of LGBTQIA people over and against all the human rights and freedoms that black people fought and died for in this country. Human rights are civil rights, and civil rights are human rights. It will take a concerted effort to deconstruct the black bully pulpit.

Deconstructing the Black Bully Pulpit

Many pulpits tend to be used, in part, to advance the political aspirations and agendas of the leaders who adorn them. Justice represents the inimitable charge to "be prophetic" and to "speak truth to power." Justice is the thesis that undergirds religious studies scholar Marvin McMickle's lament in *Where Have All the Prophets Gone?*[4] McMickle seeks to compel preachers to "restore prophetic preaching to a place of urgency in the life of the American church," principally the black American church.[5] *Where Have All the Prophets Gone* sets forth four challenges that impinge on the possibility of prophetic preaching:

> a narrow definition of justice that does not extend beyond abortion and same-sex marriage, the emergence of an oxymoron called patriot pastors,

the focus on praise and worship that does not result in any duty and discipleship, and finally, the vile messages of prosperity theology that seem to have overtaken the pulpits and the airwaves used by televangelists across this country.[6]

McMickle suggests that authentic prophetic preaching should attend to a much broader corpus than same-sex marriage. Despite implying that marriage equality or same-gender love is a proper topic for prophetic preaching, McMickle does not suggest what position preachers should take on the topic. Rather, he advances a progressive view about the role of a prophetic preacher.[7] More specifically, McMickle admonishes preachers to bring messages of healing and justice. McMickle cautions against messages that bully people and urges the prophetic preacher to be sensitive to the message of Christ through the Spirit of God, which speaks both on themes important to biblical prophets and on new themes that have emerged as humanity has traveled through time.

To deconstruct the central theme held by black bully pulpit preachers that seek to "other" LGBTQIA persons, McMickle's charge serves as a responsible start. Black preachers must seriously consider how their rhetoric harms. The Christian commitment to justice is lost in translation when severe personal attacks are hurled at people from the preachers in the pulpit. This requires a reassessment of the pastoral care practices. Pastors are charged to develop pastoral care for all persons within their congregations. Yet, what we continue to see in black faith traditions are messages that resemble Pastor Worley's. This level of bullying is deeply rooted in an American ethos emanating from a pre-Civil War era where blacks were the object of great ridicule and mockery. However, the connection to damnation preaching in the black church tradition survived slavery's abolition, the renunciation of Jim and Jane Crow laws, and Reconstruction. The close ties to this manner of preaching substantiate the argument that whiteface mimesis is at work. Moreover, the ideological commitments to whiteness function as a mechanism for the black preacher of this ilk to achieve a position of acceptance.[8] In turn, the black bully pulpit preacher takes up the mantle of overseer, whipping his congregation into submission to the will of racist, white "Christianity." Those preachers succumb to a racist ontology, which I will name next.

The Ties that Bind

Many of America's pulpits are platforms for "bullying." While bullying from the pulpit is not a new phenomenon, bullying same-gender-loving persons and denigrating marriage equality has escalated. According to Anderson Cooper, a primetime CNN anchor, Pastor Worley, a white evangelical Christian, has been bullying for over forty years, and his rants echo his preacher-father before him. "I'm against the sin," Worley said, "but I'm not against them. I want them to be saved, but I will not accept that way of life here, nor hereafter."[9] This rhetoric has been an integral part of Pastor Worley's preaching since at least 1978 and presumably several decades before that over the span of his father's preaching career.[10]

In 1978, Pastor Worley reportedly preached this to his congregation: "You know we are living in a day when you know what, it saddens my heart to think that homosexuals can go around, blessed God, and get the applause of a lot of people. Lesbians and all the rest of them, blessed God, forty years ago, they'd of hung them from a white oak tree. Wouldn't they? Amen."[11] In 1938, the time frame Pastor Worley references, young Worley would have been entering the ministry. And he is likely correct, black gay and lesbian people—or at least those accused of being homosexual, whether they were in fact practicing as such or not—would have been hung or at least lived with the threat of such white mob violence.[12] Worley would have been a little lad, perhaps perched on his father's neck or standing beside him as they watched the spectacle lynching of bodies—black bodies accused of sexual expression. He could preach that message with such conviction because he could have witnessed a hanging and the removal of that person's sexual organs for souvenirs.[13] Firmly embedded in his psyche, perhaps since childhood, this ideology seems valid to Pastor Worley. As the congregation absorbs this diabolical rhetoric, a deep suspicion befalls the members, creating a division between insiders and outsiders. LGBTQIA persons become keenly aware of it. The people in the congregation begin to separate some people from others, as Benjamin experienced in his congregation under the leadership of a black pastor:

Benjamin: I paid attention to the people in my congregation, Joseph Gibbs, who was a stellar singer you know with processed hair, but, you know the people said he was a "sissy." And, but, I liked him, you know, I loved the way he could ... he was charismatic and um, you know, just all the people, Gaines Everett Williams, who played the piano and led the choir; and you know, he was married, but he was gay, in my mind at least. And I was always drawn to them, you know. And even my godmother, Juanita Stewart, she and Wilhelmina Marshall were lesbians. They lived like two doors down from us and somehow, she became my godmother, but my parents kept me from her, you know. They made sure that I wasn't able to just go down to their house. So, they were always protecting me from it. And then, in our neighborhood growing up in Colorado Springs, I remember Rudy who was Hispanic, and "Turtle," we called him Turtle, African American, you know they were considered the "fags" in the community. You know, Rudy would wear his shirt sort of tied and he even had sort of a sashay when he walked, and I was intrigued by them you know. And, my family would run to the picture window of the house when they walked by and sort of mocked them. And, I always thought that that was the wrong thing to do. Um so, very much aware of it, very much aware of it.

Benjamin was socialized in church and at home to see members of his community as either social insiders or outsiders. As he took notice of the differences between people, he developed an awareness that helped him identify the evil nature of this divisiveness. Benjamin names this "wrong" despite what some of the adults in his concentric circle modeled. Benjamin's sense of self and his openness to humanity helped him accord dignity to every human being. Benjamin embraced the kind of liberation described by Cole Arthur Riley:

> Our liberation begins with the irrevocable belief that we are worthy to be liberated, that we are worthy of a life that does not degrade us but honors our whole selves. When you believe in your dignity, or at least someone else does, it becomes more difficult to remain content with the bondage with which you have become so acquainted. You begin to wonder what you were meant for.[14]

Audre Lorde's compilation of essays titled *Sister Outsider* speaks to the conundrum forged by such rhetoric. Lorde demonstrates with her title the notion that she is both a "sister," which suggests an insider status with familial connection both biological and platonic, and an "outsider," because of her difference sexually and perhaps socially and politically.[15]

The Invisible Ontology

Ingrained in the rhetoric of bully pulpit preachers are the marks of the invisible ontology of *racecraft*. Sociologist Karen Fields notes:

> In my work on racecraft, I have been struck over and over again by such intellectual commonalities with witchcraft as circular reasoning, prevalence of confirming rituals, barriers to disconfirming factual evidence, self-fulfilling prophecies, multiple and inconsistent causal ideas, and colorfully inventive folk genetics. And to these must be added varieties of more or less legitimized collective action such as gossip, exclusion, scapegoating, and so on, up to and including various forms of coercion (which is to say that the logical and methodological byways of racecraft, like those of witchcraft, are rife with dangers to body as well as to mind).[16]

The circular reasoning pertaining to procreation raised by Pastor Worley is echoed in too many black pulpits. Rev. Keith Butler, a black pastor of the more than 22,000-member Word of Faith International Christian Center, wrote in a 2003 *Detroit Free Press* editorial that "the gay lifestyle is based on a behavior choice that endangers family, children, and the core of society."[17] Bishop Wellington Boone, the black founder of Wellington Boone Ministries, said, to thunderous applause at a "Values Voter Summit" hosted by the Family Research Council, "that when it comes to the matter of this gay stuff, I know that a family is not a man and a man or a woman and a woman. It's a man and a woman. That's the creative order, and I'm not backing down. I'm standing flat-footed on that right there."[18] Commenting on the potential for California to legalize same-sex marriage, Rev. Jesse Patterson, a black pastor in Los Angeles, California, said that "it will destroy the family, especially the black family."[19] In philosophical logic models, circular reasoning is deemed a fallacy.[20] The pronouncement that society is doomed because of the existence of LGBTQIA persons—and specifically that LGBTQIA persons reciting marriage vows is an insurmountable threat—is a familiar trope the logic of which strains the cultural imagination. The idea that LGBTQIA persons are responsible for the breakdown of the family is prevalent, though sociological studies indicate that commitment to family and fidelity is much stronger among LGBTQIA persons than among heterosexuals.[21] Exclusion and scapegoating are the principal tools by which LGBTQIA persons are cast out of the community of believers by the black preaching tradition. And gossip surrounding who is and who is not homosexual is pervasive among black preachers. Whether one is convinced that "witches" exist or not, there is a distinctive relationship between current claims about LGBTQIA people and the way the logic of witchcraft, particularly as historically alleged, has been used to harm people, particularly women.

Ideology is the vehicle through which a certain message travels in time. As Fields asserts, it "must be constantly created and verified in social life; if it is not, it dies, even though it may seem to be safely embodied in a form that can be handed down."[22] It masterfully keeps its principal content intact even though the "terrain" through which it travels and the landscape against which it treads may change. Fields posits:

> Many Christians still think of kneeling with folded hands as the appropriate posture for prayer, but few know why; and the few who do know cannot, even if they choose, mean the same thing by it as was meant by those to whom the posture was part of an ideology still real in everyday social life. The social relations that once gave explicit meaning to that ritual gesture of the vassal's subordination to his lord are now as dead as a mackerel, and so, therefore, is the ideological vocabulary—including the posture of prayer—in which those social relations once lived.[23]

The example of kneeling for prayer serves as a metaphor for how an invisible ontology manifests in the context of black Christian preachers mimicking their white, racist counterparts. The mimicked practices foster patterns that ultimately form structures, which shape the worship modalities into conveyor belts disseminating harmful rhetoric. The original motivation for this rhetoric fades in the shadows while the message itself strengthens through repetition until it becomes a part of the quotidian dynamic of white, racist evangelical "Christian" messaging. In the next section I will review an exemplar of this type of message.

The Racist Ontology of Black Bully Pulpit Preachers

Racecraft connotes "one among a complex system of beliefs, with combined moral and cognitive content, that presuppose invisible, spiritual qualities underlying, and continually acting upon, the material realm of beings and events."[24] Racecraft works a particular magic to conjure certain attitudes about different modes of being, ultimately forming beliefs embedded in moral and cognitive rationalities that take on spiritual qualities.

In the case of black church public theology, the Bible is used to overlay beliefs that buttress a preacher's authority such that through racecraft, hate-filled rhetoric is literally promoted as sanctioned by God. For example, Bishop Rader Johnson of Greater Bethel Temple in Louisville, Kentucky, preached a sermon on March 20, 2010, in which he stated:

> There's a whole lot of folk that are out there selling a bunch of wolf tickets, ah, talking a good game, ah. They don't know who God is, ah. Amen, the homosexual, and homosexual preachers that are out there, Amen. I got homosexuals on my job, Amen, lesbians and uh, gay men or what have you. Amen, and some of them, uh, out here in the world claim to be saved, Amen, ha, but I want you to understand, Amen, they say that because they really don't know God. Let the church shout hallelujah, because if they really knew God, ah, they would understand that He burnt up Sodom and Gomorrah, Amen, [and] two other cities because of their wicked practices, ah, Amen. God is not with you uh, Amen, being a homosexual, God is not with you, ah, being a lesbian. And I know some folk, uh, will get a little bad press on the internet, but that's alright, uh, Amen, because that's what we need to hear, I'm trying to make you mad, ha. Let the church shout hallelujah. You been making God mad for a long time, ha. He said in His word that He's angry with the wicked every day. Amen. So, you get mad about me telling you the truth, you just gone have to be mad, with your gay self. Come on somebody and shout hallelujah. Being a homosexual and a lesbian is a ticket to hell, as well as any other sin. The Bible says the wages of sin is death but the gift of God is eternal life, ha. Amen, you gotta repent of all your sins, ha, whether you are sleeping with a man, whether it's a man/man [or] woman/woman [or]

a she-man woman or a he-man man or whatever, Amen. If you know God you won't lay up like you're laying up ...[25]

Bishop Johnson's claim that God is not "with" the gay or lesbian is clearly refutable in the biblical context.[26] Pastor Johnson's rhetoric is an example of hate-talk disguised as God-talk. He is advancing his own prejudice fostered by whiteface mimesis. Franshon's experience with her black preacher claiming to be giving a similar prophetic word is also indicative of this:

> *Franshon:* I was very much in touch with the fact I was a lesbian, I was attracted to women, I like women. And, I don't believe I ever articulated that out loud at church; but every week the pastor got up and said she had a dream, a vision about penises and uh, vaginas. Just crazy stuff ... she used to say and I'm sitting there and saying like "what is she talking about, you know?" I mean she was trying to say that she knows that somebody in her church was gay. And I, I felt like this: if you want to know the answer to a question, you should ask the question. Getting up talking about stuff over the pulpit is, to me, a form of manipulation and control. It is not confronting the issue. I would have been more than happy to share with her, you know, uh, but, she didn't ask.

While Franshon's fortitude enabled her to transcend the rhetoric and declare that it was utter nonsense, many have been swayed by the false nature of the pronouncements. In actuality, it is merely the invisible ontology of racism holding its value as white supremacist ideology. As a result, the white vestiges of southern religious agenda remains in place, after slavery and its aftermath, held there by black bully pulpit preachers. Black bully pulpit preachers advance the narrative of their white counterparts through mimesis, which causes them to emit racist ideology. The question whether black bully pulpit preachers can be racist is answered, in part, by analyzing the interconnection between racism and racecraft, which I do in the next section.

The Interconnection between Racism and Racecraft

In the example given above, racecraft worked to keep those images of hanging homosexuals in Pastor Worley's mind for decades. Racism justified his feelings about how to resolve the problem as he perceived it. Racecraft generated the narrative of Bishop Rader Johnson's sermon. Racism created the systemic oppression that made that message of paramount importance in Bishop Johnson's toxic theology. Racism operates to give the black bully pulpit preacher the tools to build upon the foundation of the "master's house."[27]

Pastor Worley's sermonic reference to what would have happened to homosexuals, such as them hanging from a tree, seems to have morphed into an indefatigable component of his "Christian" conviction, which he continues to stoke as a fire with his hate-filled rhetoric to younger generations. Stacey Pritchard, the young woman who is a member of Pastor Worley's congregation, was also interviewed by Anderson Cooper.[28] This young woman articulated her pastor's conviction and affirmed its "truth," even though Pastor Worley clearly preached that concentration camps and death chambers should be constructed for all lesbians and gays so that they would be exterminated. Pastor Worley's hatred has metastasized over several decades, creating a perpetual, septic congregational hatred for LGBTQIA persons. In the recording of his sermon, one can hear the congregation responding to his hateful words with affirmations and laughter. Pastor Worley's sermon represents rhetorical extremism. However, the message fits squarely into the agenda of the Christian Right. Unaffiliated with the Southern Baptist Convention (SBC), Pastor Worley came under their rebuke when popular media exposed the harsh content of his message. Nonetheless, Pastor Worley and the SBC share the common perspective that homosexuality is sinful.[29]

Hate-filled rhetoric falls on the ears of LGBTQIA folks as shameful abuse. It lingers and festers and can breed self-hatred, as Quincy experienced in his black church. Rhetoric similar to that spewed by Bishop Rader Johnson caused Quincy to question his preacher's method of interpreting the biblical text:

> *Quincy:* I think it is important that when one does "proper exegesis," um, one understands the historical context of the text. And, I think that is very ... I think Kelly Brown Douglas and others use the term "hermeneutic of suspicion," and so it's very imperative that you understand what was happening and what was not. And in reading that, you know, I'm not a New Testament scholar and I'm not a Hebrew Bible scholar, but I do know, from the little research that I have done and continue to do, is that "homosexuality" was a nineteenth-century invented term. And so, if we think about where that fits within the traditional biblical text, it doesn't. So, how do we begin to have conversations around what it means to be ah, not only human, but what does it mean to be sexual beings, right, and for sexuality to be fluid and not monolithic?

Quincy zeros in on the conundrum that Kelly Brown Douglas confronts in her chapter titled "Black Sexuality: A Pawn of White Culture."[30] Quincy's reference to the "hermeneutic of suspicion" is his signal that the lack of constructive conversation around sexuality generally gives rise to misinterpretation of texts, false prophecy, and misleading assumptions about LGBTQIA persons' capacity to relate to God. Distorting the gospel message is a technique used to garner sociopolitical control of faithful black people. In the next section I will review one such effort on the part of Southern Baptists to control black Baptists' messaging using monetary incentives.

Intentional False Prophecy Messaging

The Cooperative Program of the Southern Baptist Convention was launched in 1845. Its website reports that "the Southern Baptist Convention (SBC) has always had one mission—the Great Commission (Matt. 28:19–20). To fulfill its assigned part of this divine mandate, each SBC entity made special offering appeals to the churches. The method was referred to as the 'societal' approach to missions."[31] Beginning in the 1970s, the SBC began giving hefty "grants" to black preachers for community "uplift." The convention pledged to raise $75 million to fund this effort. Member entities of the Cooperative Program are eligible to receive funds to "support missionaries, train pastors, and other ministry leaders, provide relief for retired ministers and widows, and address social, moral, and ethical concerns relating to our faith and families."[32] This same paradigm was codified in a Republican executive branch campaign called the "faith-based initiative."

President George W. Bush, by executive order, created the Office of Faith-based and Community Initiatives to fulfill a promise to fund "compassionate conservatism."[33] President Bush is part of the evangelical wing of the United Methodist Church. While the denomination is part of mainline Protestantism, Bush shares many values with and has aligned himself with evangelical Christians around the nation.[34] The faith-based initiative was an effort to further conservative moral imperatives using government funding, and helped to solidify support from those in the black preaching tradition who were willing to serve as operatives in disseminating the rhetoric of the Moral Majority and others in the Christian Right.

Messaging against LGBTQIA persons was given top priority alongside planks opposing abortion and supporting the right to bear arms. In fact, conservative Christian groups sponsored "Justice Sundays" to promote the anti-gay, anti-abortion, and pro-gun agenda of the ultraconservative, hatemongering Family Research Council, which focused on assembling the conservative factions in the country to plan political action. The Values Voter Summits have strategically sought to configure the judiciary on the state and federal levels to serve their agenda—and they devoted millions of dollars to secure this vision.[35] As I listened to Mara's story, I felt the piercing sting of how this messaging was designed to make her run away from her church.

Mara: I left my church. Because I would have gone crazy if I hadn't. I didn't feel like I had a place there. I became a member of this church when I was nine. I was baptized on my tenth birthday. I was, I have been a Sunday school teacher, I have been a children's church teacher. I have directed adult choirs, children's choirs. I am a soloist; I love the church that I grew up in. I mean, everything that I did revolved around my church. I was there every Sunday. Like I said, I taught in the church. I sang in the church. If we had somewhere to go, I was front and center. I directed the choir. My life revolved around my church. If I wanted to do something with friends, I had to make sure first of all that I did not have a church engagement, especially if it was on a Sunday. It couldn't be on a choir rehearsal night because of course, I had to be at choir rehearsal. If it was a meeting that I had to go to, regarding teaching or whatever, I couldn't do anything because I had to be there for the meeting. I want to go back to that church, but I am still not there yet.

Mara's experience resembles that of so many others who grew up in the church. An unshakeable affinity grows up in you when your whole world revolves around church participation. The church is where much of one's sociality is formed. Parting from that is a painful process. Even more painful is traversing the road back to church once you have accepted your difference and resigned to walk in it as your truth. Going back to church environments that you know will oppose your ontological being causes stress and strife. The violent rhetoric that one anticipates in sermonic moments along with targeted denigration and feelings of inferiority can be a deterrent to full inclusion in many worship settings.

Framing the Theological Argument Against Equality

The theological attacks on same gender-loving persons stem from three major contentions. The core argument is that homosexuality is sin and therefore not sanctioned by the Bible. The other two arguments are offshoots from this main argument: the first is that God made Adam and Eve, not Adam and Steve; the second is that marriage is strictly limited to one man and one woman. Black church public theology typically views homosexuality as "unnatural" in keeping with "the old racist notion that Black people were cursed, immoral people without souls."[36] Consequently, as Marvin McMickle notes, the "theological view that homosexuality is sinful, and that the only legitimate sexual expression is towards the opposite sex in marriage" finds expression in black church public theology.[37]

Hebrew Bible, stories such as Genesis 13:13, deals with what preachers mistakenly interpret as forbidden homosexual desire: Deuteronomy 22:5, which discusses temple dressing practices; and Leviticus 18:22 and

20:13, which address men "lying with" men as with women, fuel the Christian claim that homosexuality is an "abomination." New Testament texts such as Romans 1:26, which references unnatural passions, and 1 Corinthians 6:9–10, in which Paul declares that male prostitutes and sodomites will not inherit the "kingdom of God," are used to justify condemnation of LGBTQIA persons.

There are two counterarguments that bear mentioning. First, marriage equality is a legal issue. Equal protection under the law for every human being is a matter of civil rights, which the US Supreme Court has now recognized in a landmark decision, *Obergefell v. Hodges*.[38] Second, religion and religious institutions do not have the right under the law to impose their faith convictions on the public in a manner that contravenes religious freedom. Moreover, the Bible is hardly the standard bearer for one-man and one-woman marriage given the plethora of polygamous unions represented therein. Solomon is described as having had 700 wives and 400 concubines.[39]

Parroting

Parrots are mockingbirds. They mimic the musicality of other birds and often police the spaces they occupy. They are socially awkward and resort to mimicry as a technology of superiority. In the context of black bully pulpit preachers, the same concept is theoretically at play when it comes to messages spoken regarding LGBTQIA persons.[40] Many black preachers parrot the claims of fundamentalist evangelical right-wing national leaders and have dispensed this very same vitriolic hate-talk disguised as God-talk to their congregations. For instance, Bishop Wellington Boone's messaging functions like a parrot for the Promise Keepers, a white evangelical movement. It aligns itself with Focus on the Family, led by Dr. James Dodson, and *The 700 Club*, led by Pat Robertson. Bishop Wellington Boone preaches hate for homosexuality, declaring that homosexuality will lead to the "ultimate destruction of society." In solidarity with white evangelicals, Bishop Boone encourages his congregation "to boldly affirm Uncle Tom." He opines that "the black community must stop criticizing Uncle Tom. He is a role model."[41] Bishop Boone stated in a sermon about "God's Purpose in Marriage" that

> simple-minded people know same sex doesn't work. Alright, glory to God. And I think it still would look funny if I kissed a man right in front of you, that's my age, tongue-kissing him right now; there's something about that that would be yucky right now. But yet, they are trying to say to us that's not yucky anymore. And God said, yes, it is because He said, I am the Lord your God, I change not. He doesn't change. Now, you might allow the tyranny of the masses to make you think that God has

changed His mind about what the word says but the word says this: let every man be a liar but let the word of God be true.[42]

LGBTQIA folks like Mileece are able to distinguish this hate-talk disguised as God-talk.

> *Mileece:* It's internalized homophobia is what it is. It's the need to ... it's a self-hatred ... it's like turning on yourself, inwardly turning against yourself. It's taking on all the hatred and saying, "This is okay." I was just kind of just there, numb and looking at ... checking this out like: "Look at this!" And see, I know that God is not ... I know what my relationship with God is; this is not what He's about. I knew that this was not Him. This was hatred, this was oppression, this was homophobia within your own church, within your own people. That's what that was about. I knew that was not God.

Mileece, operating in a mode of discernment, identifies the disconnect between church leaders and LGBTQIA persons. It is important to develop this gift to circumvent the horror and pain of the violent rhetoric, which can be paralyzing.

The black Detroit pastor Rev. Keith Butler, a leader of Word of Faith International Christian Center, joins Bishop Boone in his disparaging sermons about how queers threaten the family. In a sermon on January 23, 2009, Pastor Butler yelled:

> What I don't understand. Where are those cameras? And, I want to look right at the camera, whichever one, which one? Let me tell you something. What I don't understand about you Madame lesbian, why would you pick another woman that dress like a man, walk like a man, act like a man, hard like a man, but ain't really a man? [*pointing*] Got us talking about oh, that's the man, and that's the woman. If you want somebody that hard, get a man, just don't pick a thug. Git a easygoing man. That means he got more ways [*gesturing*] than a woman, but he a real man. [*yelling*] Homosexual, how you gone pick a man that try to dress like a woman, walk like a woman, talk like a woman, hold his hand like a woman, but you don't want a woman? I ain't figured that one out yet. I know the real answer though. The reason why you won't get married heterosexual, the reason why you are attracted to another woman, lady, and another man, man, is because you know the word says it's wrong and what sin does is just look at God and say I don't care what you say, I ain't going to let nobody tell me how to live. I am what I am and I am going to do what I do. Well, let me tell you it's wrong. You see why I got a few captives is because we either raising them, or we are one of them, or we condone what they do. But wrong is wrong. Tell your neighbor wrong is wrong.[43]

For those in the pews who are questioning their sexuality, the pressure of this rhetoric leads them to make life choices that are not true to their emerging or authentic selves. As Benjamin demonstrates, the violent rhetoric can burn a brand in one's mind.

> *Benjamin:* Um, I think things began to unravel, and I think going back I paid close attention to what people would say. Um, so, examples of that would be um the year that I graduated from high school and, um, traditionally our congregation would celebrate high school graduates in a service you know. Some part of the service would be highlighted in showing who our seniors were and giving us a certificate of some sort, and I was given a Bible, um, for graduation. But, I remember that Sunday that the pastor spoke about, um, not necessarily in his message, but in some commentary in the service, about "sissies [were] going to hell." Oh yes, [*chuckling*] it has always been with me you know, because in some way even then, I thought, "Out of all the Sundays to choose to say that, why are we doing it today?" You know, where does that come from? Now, I didn't say it was because of me. I think in hindsight it was. But I just kept saying, "Well, what context … what does it have to do with what we're doing?" You know? And you know, I'm trying to be … even had a little girlfriend. So, he couldn't have been talking about me. But, that stayed in my mind you know.

Benjamin, like so many LGBTQIA persons, began to question the message, the messenger, and the motivation for the message. As he reflected on the message about "sissies," he began to question himself. This type of questioning can lead people to the proverbial closet. Queer theorist Eve Kosofsky Sedgwick wrote of the proverbial nature of the closet that:

> the gay closet is not a feature only of the lives of gay people. But for many gay people it is still the fundamental feature of social life; and there can be few gay people, however courageous and forthright by habit, however fortunate in the support of their immediate communities, in whose lives the closet is not still a shaping presence.[44]

Consequentially, the parroting of white evangelical patriarchal hegemony in these messages by pastors like Benjamin's tracks with the hate-talk of Pastor Worley, the Moral Majority, *The 700 Club*, and many others, and most importantly assaults the faith and selfhood of LGBTQIA churchgoers.

Black pastor Rev. T. J. Graham of Tennessee, known for his protests against homosexuality, said in an interview with *Intelligence Report* that "God said man shall not lie with man as with woman nor woman with woman as with man," and in that same interview he continued his (im) moral rant to establish his allegiance to white supremacy by stating "if any Klansmen showed up at his rallies, he'd be 'supportive' of their presence.

After all, he said, 'This affects their families, too.'"⁴⁵ Often the racialization in such rhetoric is so despicable that LGBTQIA persons flee the church to avoid this persecution. Rev. Ken Hutcherson, a black former NFL player, contends that "doing God's work means excommunicating gay members of his church, rather than ministering to or counseling them."⁴⁶ According to the *Intelligence Report*, his "Mayday for Marriage" rally in Washington, DC, attracted 140,000 people.⁴⁷

Rev. James Meeks is a black member of the "Gatekeepers" network, an interracial group of evangelical ministers who launched a legislative campaign in Illinois called the Illinois Family Institute to promote "family values" and amplify the fearmongering that gay marriage posed a threat to the family. He was joined by Focus on the Family, the Family Research Council, Americans for Truth, and the Alliance Defense Fund, all major antigay organizations of the Christian Right. Rev. Meeks, as a former Illinois state senator, transmitted a prerecorded "robo-call" emergency message to approximately 200,000 African Americans in fourteen districts in advance of an Illinois state legislative vote on marriage equality, stating, "Please listen closely, your state representative in Springfield is under serious pressure to redefine marriage in Illinois. If marriage between one man and one woman is redefined to add same-sex marriage, our family structure, as we know it, is in serious jeopardy."⁴⁸ This is direct evidence of an attempt to control the sociopolitical influence of the African American faith community. Brian Brown, president of the National Organization for Marriage, revealed his intent in using Meeks for this messaging by stating, "Obviously [Meeks is] a very well known figure in the area. He's an African American standing up for the issue. We're very happy he was willing to make the calls and stand up for marriage."⁴⁹

Finding Strength in the Midst of Struggle

Confusing signals from the pulpit and politics lead to lifelong struggles for LGBTQIA persons. Despite their struggles, those I spoke with found ways to experience the Divine and to affirm the call to ministry. Their stories mirror my own. The fight to hold onto one's faith in the moments when the sermonic moment reduces you to nothing is a hard one. However, those who press forward understand the reward of knowing in whom they place their trust.

> *Benjamin:* I knew that I was called to preach, I knew that I loved church, and I still believe that it was my calling. But it was also my refuge because when I answered the call to preach, preached my initial sermon, I think my dad, and my mother; but, my dad specifically, who always could see this call, but identified it as being a "sissy baby," something; when I preached my initial sermon, you know, he finally gave me some peace.

You know, in his mind it was like "that's what's, that's what's wrong with him. God's got his hands on him, so I'm gone take mine off," right, and "let God," you know. So, in many ways it was freeing for me, and I just lived into those peaceful years as the preacher, you know. I also think, you know, consistent with that when I told my mother, I told my mother before I told my father, that I was getting married to a woman, and my mother looked at me and she said, "well, son, I never imagined you getting married" [*chuckling*]. So, you know, it was like, you done put all of this pressure on you and that's not even ... "who ... really? ... are you sure?" You know, so, I mean I sort of paid attention to that, you know, and kept going, you know. And, the reality of my story is that I was serving a congregation as pastor for eight years before even going to seminary. But, after being in seminary probably two weeks, I could clearly see that the call for me there was sort of this deconstruction of my theology and this reconstruction of my theology; and, it all was about my sexuality: "Hey, I can be a black man, I can be a Christian, I can be a preacher, and I can be gay!" I never imagined that I would become the poster child of being a gay preacher, um, but I think that's what happened.

Benjamin illuminates the conflict that emerges when family members have internalized the vitriolic rhetoric of pastors. Motivated by a solemn determination to keep loved ones from damnation and from societal ridicule, a father may seek to hypermasculinize a male child who appears to be effeminate. The determination leads the child to respond in kind and seek approval from that family member through specific life choices, which ultimately leads to conflicts that must be unraveled throughout the course of life. Benjamin points to the "dogged" strength, courage even, that it takes to follow the Spirit into a place of complete freedom to be one's authentic self. As a result, his example offers hope for those who feel trapped in a bifurcated existence seeking to live out a call within the confines of an imposed social identity. In his devotion to follow the Spirit, Benjamin found the liberty with which Christ makes him free from "the law of sin and death."

Bishop Harry Jackson, black pastor of Hope Christian Church in Lanham, Maryland, also partners with white preachers of the Christian Right to promote a message that "we are in a moral war ... a battle of epic proportions" and must condemn homosexuality.[50] As the only invited black preacher to the white evangelical Justice Sunday in Nashville, Tennessee, in 2005, Bishop Jackson claimed homosexuality "is going to cost black America if we don't stand [with white anti-gay Christians] against this."[51] In a column condemning homosexuality, Bishop Jackson wrote: "The gay community, with the help of the liberal media, has worked strategically on a P.R. campaign to make Americans comfortable with homosexuality. From the slightly effeminate male assistant to the first gay marriage ceremony on television, American audiences have watched homosexual themes creep into their lives."[52] This condemnation that comes from the pulpit distorts the powerful liberative intent of the gospel. Franshon's experience illuminates this phenomenon, and she illustrates how one can overcome this violent rhetoric when one recognizes, through discernment, the nature of the violent rhetoric and the ungodly motivation for it.

> *Franshon:* It was preached from the pulpit about you know, homosexuality is a sin and, and uh, why African American churches are so hostile towards homosexuality I have no idea. You can be a pedophile, an adulterer, a murderer, and all those things are okay; but as soon as you say you are gay, it's a problem. Oh yeah, I think every week I was called up there so they could cast the devil of homosexuality out of me [*laughing hysterically*]. And then one pastor told me, "It's not in you, it's around you, it's around you." So, I was like "Jesus." And then she invited me to her house and she ain't have no clothes on. I was like, "but you knew I was coming, right?" But, it's around me, you know … yeah right? But, it's around me! ?! But, anyway, um … So, it's like still not understanding the language, like I didn't have the language to put to it, but in my heart, I just knew God is way bigger than this.

Franshon's *knowing* stems from her own spiritual formation, apart from violent rhetoric, in which she connected with her *morphóŏ*. This concept connotes the formation of the presence of Christ in the person in a similar process to how babies are formed in the womb of their mothers. That connection allowed her to identify God as bigger than what violent rhetoricians spew.

Archbishop Alfred Owens, the black presiding prelate and senior bishop of the Mt. Calvary Holy Church of America, preached a sermon on April 6, 2006, at his church, Greater Mt. Calvary Holy Church, located in the nation's capital, in which he said, "It takes a real man to confess Jesus as Lord and Savior. I'm not talking about no faggot or no sissy." He then invited "all the real men—I'm talking about the straight men … You ain't funny and you ain't cranky, but you are straight. Come on down here and walk around and praise God that you are straight. Thank Him that you're straight. All the straight men that's proud to be a Christian, that's proud to be a man of God." One man, Zachard, who was present when this message was preached, expressed his feelings to me:

> *Zachard:* Okay so, initially, um, when Pastor Owens or Bishop Owens made that comment I was just in shock. I really didn't expect it. Um, I don't know what his sexuality is or if he has participated in homosexual activities in the past, but I felt like it was just unnecessary and it just seemed hypocritical. Um, I felt like he made a lot of people, you know, in that church that day uncomfortable. And he pretty much told some people that were in there, "You can't come down here and you can't," you know, "serve the Lord like everyone else." He kinda divided us, um, and I just feel like it was coming from hate. I don't think that someone

that serves the Lord would say something like that. And, it kinda just made me not want to go to the church, you know, anymore after that. So, um, you know, stuff like that from people that are bishops and preachers, and you know, people that are respected in the community—that stuff has weight; so, if they say stuff like that then their congregation is going to follow suit and have those same ideas. You know, young kids are gonna have those same ideas and treat members of LGBT in the schools, you know, in a negative way. So I feel like with his kind of power he needs to or he needed to have been a little bit more responsible with his words because he is a man that is highly respected in the community. Um so, it just made me not want to go to the altar, um, and I don't feel like, you know, if any preacher would say something like that, I would feel comfortable going; um, and, yeah, it was just full of hate, in my opinion.

As an openly gay man, Zachard was devastated at hearing this violent rhetoric in what was then his place of worship. It was the driving force for his decision to leave Mt. Calvary. Acknowledging that the violent rhetoric was filled with hate helped Zachard keep his faith intact, but he made a conscious decision to leave that congregation and move to higher ground.

A few years later, on January 3, 2010, the archbishop, Alfred Owens, mounted his bully pulpit with this same acerbic message, shouting, "Sex is only pleasing to God in the marriage bed, and the marriage bed is a man and … a woman. If marriage wasn't between a man and a woman, you wouldn't be here because two men doing it don't produce no kids, and two women doing it don't produce no kids! It's all about the family."[53] In response, two gay men, Jon Mack and his partner, Michael Garrett, who had been members at Greater Mt. Calvary Holy Church for one year, sought to expose this antigay hate-talk disguised as God-talk by taking their message of disappointment and woundedness to the local papers. They vowed to move their membership to an open and affirming church, Covenant Baptist United Church of Christ, pastored by Drs. Christine and Dennis Wiley in southeast D.C. Anthony Williams, then mayor of the District of Columbia, threatened to remove the good bishop from the prestigious InterFaith Council to which he had been appointed if he did not issue an apology for preaching such vitriolic rhetoric.[54] Bishop Owens remained "silent, refusing press inquiries."[55] The confusion that this rhetoric ushers in for LGBTQIA persons can create a void in their relationship with God and can cause them to refrain from church membership altogether.

Although some LGBTQIA persons reckon with the violent rhetoric and attribute it to conservatism, Quincy's experience led him to internalize that rhetoric in ways that made the experience of being an LGBTQIA person an experience of ontological sinfulness. The idea that one could be delivered from one's ontological being is ludicrous, yet it holds currency in many faith traditions that offer conversion programs.

Quincy: The church's doctrine is very conservative like many other churches where homosexuality is sin. I was always taught that it was sin. You can be delivered from it. And so, I knew that these feelings or these passions that I was experiencing was real, but I wasn't quite sure where it came from. And in many ways suppressed it, right, because that was the ethos of the church to not give into temptation. And so, I recall the preacher coming across the pulpit often times saying you know "hate the sin, love the sinner," which for me is ontologically impossible and theologically impossible.

While many advocate for the bifurcation of the sinner from the sin, as Quincy mentions, it is virtually impossible to parse that out in a theological formula that takes seriously the claim of Christ. The idea that God hates a particular kind of sin but loves the sinner has no substantive merit if Jesus Christ has conquered sin, death, hell, and the grave. Despite this, the rejection and condemnation fashioned through racecraft by the violent rhetoric of some black pastors establishes an existential anxiety experienced by many LGBTQIA persons.

Particularly in the economy of small-town life, being shunned, ostracized, and made to feel dehumanized generates extreme anxiety. This same anxiety causes an internal ambiguity that leaves people questioning their relationship with God. That is because there is a problem with the construction of a Christian tradition that seeks to objectify God. When God is treated like an object, there is the tendency to see God like we see other individuals; this dangerous limitation subjects the God concept to human frailty. Human beings therefore position themselves to speak on behalf of God about the things human beings do not want to tolerate! Consequently, everything that does not fit into the prescribed normative order of heteropatriarchy is pronounced anathema. God becomes an instrument in the hands of preachers to prescribe their (im)moral judgment, putting the divine seal of approval on human insecurities. It is one in a number of classic heteropatriarchal devices to dominate and control others. Quincy offers the example that happens often when one is notably gifted and given opportunity to share their gifts in the worship space but with a proviso that their homosexuality be closeted.

Quincy: The person that licensed me in the ministry. Um, and so, still allowing me to preach, still allowing me to function as a preacher; licensed me, but was very careful in making sure that I didn't get too far out there, too lost. And so, what that did was it caused me to turn on myself. So, then I started preaching messages of hate and messages of coming out and being delivered from homosexuality, yet having sexual encounters with men after, you know by the end of the week or by the end of the day or whatever the case may have been. Um and so, it wasn't until that I got to college that I really just started exploring what that meant.

So, in 2002 I remember praying to God for this deliverance. And uh, I remember saying to myself ... So, at this time I was "highly spiritual." I was listening to Juanita Bynum and she had these prayer services and I would just say, "Oh, I want deliverance." And every service that I went to it was you know, "Write down what you want to be delivered from, bring it up here, throw it in the garbage, throw it in the casket, throw it in the fire, whatever the case may be," and every time I wrote down the word "homosexual," I want to be delivered from homosexuality.

Quincy's desire to be delivered from homosexuality was born from a sincere desire to comply with what violent rhetoric had delineated as a prerequisite for acceptance by God. This rhetoric causes people to deny their authentic selves in favor of an acceptable ontology that is pleasing to the concept of an abusive God promulgated by the rhetorician of violence.

Gay Bashing, God Bashing, and Women Hating

Bishop Paul Morton, the former presiding prelate of the Full Gospel Baptist Church Fellowship International, preached a sermon explaining:

> God vs. Gays actually means God vs. Gay lifestyles. He loves gays. He loves the sinner. He loves all of us that fall short of the glory of God. It's not that God doesn't love people; it's the lifestyle that He hates. It really boils down to God bashing vs. Gay bashing. Bashing means slamming. And God slams the gay lifestyle. He's saying, "I'm God, and I change not. It's not a lifestyle I made for man."[56]

Quentin DeVaughan, a blogger who responded to Bishop Morton's sermon, merits quotation at length:

> Lifestyle simply means "the manner in which a person lives their life." So what exactly is "the gay lifestyle"? What do gays do that straight people don't? Is it clubbing? No. Is it smoking, drugging and drinking? No. Is it promiscuous, pre-marital or unprotected sex? No. Is it oral or anal sex? No! Is it infidelity? No. Lying, stealing, murder, gossip? No. So exactly what is it? Most of the gays and lesbians I know are upstanding, tax and tithe-paying, church going, law abiding citizens that are trying to live life the best way they know how; just like straight people. The one thing straight people *have* done is make a mockery of the "sacred institution of marriage" (check the divorce rate, domestic violence, etc.), but that's another subject altogether.[57]

DeVaughan's response to Bishop Morton points to the trite way LGBTQIA sexuality is treated. Morton's message serves no purpose except as a neon sign to the church of his personal intolerance. It does not speak for God. As Franshon demonstrates, when one is in a relationship with God, this hate-talk disguised as God-talk becomes see-through:

> *Franshon:* Because there was so much hatred in the church; and, and, and, and, so, here's the thing. I don't like being limited. You trying to control me and limit who I am and my understanding and my beliefs, and I felt very constricted and I don't believe I serve a constricting God. I just don't believe that. And so, um, it wasn't just the dogmatism or the ignorance, cause that's what I think it is. It's ignorance. It was that their ... and this has really informed how I do ministry too, by the way ... but, their, meaning the pastors ... were trying to impose their views on me. And, I don't think that's the purpose of church. I don't think that's the purpose of preaching. In my mind the purpose of preaching is to share with people what Jesus shared with people and provide them tools and resources to have a different understanding, to enable them to become who God created them to be. I felt like they were trying to control and manipulate me. And, I don't like that. Because, I don't think that's what ministry or being a preacher is about.

Franshon found the strength within to resist the message of violent rhetoric. She demonstrates what it means to be an overcomer. Her assessment of the role of the preacher and her assessment of the ministry of Jesus gave her the impetus to formulate a better vision for her life.

Gendered Rhetorical Violence

Pastor Jesse Lee Peterson of Los Angeles, California, heads an organization called the Brotherhood Organization of a New Destiny (BOND), which privileges the position of men over women and lays at the feet of LGBTQIA persons the complete annihilation of the black community. He remarks in his book that "black women are just plain mean." His rant regarding black women is eerily reminiscent of many heteropatriarchal diminutives used to describe women and relegate them to a position of social deviant. He goes on to support his idea about black women with reasoning that purports to explain why young black men become gay:

> Many of them swing between mean-spiritedness on the one hand and smothering their sons with what they wrongly perceive to be love on the other. The first response comes from bitterness against men—a bitterness that is understandable, though not excusable. As for the other, since mothers cannot provide the kind of masculine guidance that boys need, these moms try to protect their sons to the point that they end up feminizing them. The boys assume the mother's identity, which is

frequently that of an insecure, frustrated, and angry person. A boy in this situation ends up resenting his mother because she has smothered him instead of teaching him to be independent and responsible. The father is the one who teaches children to be risk-takers and to be confident and productive in the world. The mother's tendency to coddle actually emotionally cripples these young men.[58]

Pastor Petersen's message formulates a baseless provocation. The mere fact that he is a preacher espousing this view is reckless because he exercises an influence over his congregation that promotes hate. His bully pulpit instantiates a meritless mythological association of homosexuality with dysfunctional family dynamics. Yet, his rhetorical effectiveness causes irreparable harm to folks who try to live into it with little ability to find a place of solace with themselves.

> *Benjamin:* Sissy, fag, um, punk. Um, and those are not my terms, but those were the terms that my father would use when he could see something in me that he wanted to deter me from. He was like, "You ain't gonna be a punk, I'm gonna make sure you're not a sissy." "Son, that's not the way you hold your hand, ah, you're supposed to stand up straight; why you, why you fold your arms, why you cross your legs?" All those kinds of things pointed towards my sexuality. So, I was always … I grew up sort of just keenly aware that something was different about me and it was obvious to others. And, in many ways I think my siblings, the older three as well as the younger three, served to protect me. So, I found myself being sheltered. And I know that my mother did a good job of sort of pulling me back and saying, "You stay with mom, you stay here, they are going to do this, but you stay here." But, my dad on the other hand would say, "No, we are going to play baseball" or "We're going to play football across the street." I mean he made me go out for every sport, you know, that was represented in school. I hated P.E. course, you know, all that dressing out in front of the other boys, all that kind of stuff, just drove me crazy. I was a nerd. So, I paid attention to books and read a lot. Um, I liked to cook with my mother, and um, knew that I had gifts of ministry, knew that I loved church a lot and felt like I was called to preach. So, I started preaching at an early age—fourteen years old.

When Benjamin says, "all that kind of stuff, just drove me crazy," his words ring true for me. The words of the preacher should never have that effect. That signifies a dysfunction in the motivation and intention of the preacher. The rhetoric of the preacher should bring you to a place of comfort and conviction. The comfort comes when you know that you are a part of God's family. The conviction comes to help you understand your role in that family. Your role does not emanate from the "outward appearance."[59] God is seeking your heart to be in line with God's justice and love. Preachers violate the mandate of preaching when their rhetoric causes you to question your humanity in a way that overrides your self-esteem. Moreover, the words of the preacher often bleed into family dynamics and infect how parents relate to their children in ways that alter the trajectory of their children's lives.

> *Benjamin:* Yeah, I tried to please my father. "I'm not going to be a sissy, I'm going to be a powerful preacher," you know, and so, I think uh, I probably overplayed masculinity through preaching. Ah, because I really did want to be pleasing to my father. And the whole business of being gay was not an option for me, you know. Um … But, my dad, he was tough about this whole business of being a man. I got married, have a daughter, and now have grandchildren, you know. Obviously had to come off of that and get a divorce and had to come out openly um, as a pastor, 'cause I was married serving a congregation so, just trying to live into the … what would be considered the "normal" role of a preacher being married to a woman and you know, having a family and living in a house and the people in the city respect you and voilà, you've reached success.

Benjamin's lived experience is representative of the harm that preachers invoke from the pulpit, which trickles down to family dynamics that both confuse and damage LGBTQIA persons and the folks that they love. LGBTQIA persons who try to live into the *pro forma* heteronormative projections for their lives often find themselves needing to walk away from years of family life created by the illusion that they could overcome their authentic selfhood. In turn, the folks that they genuinely loved while living out someone else's narrative of heteronormativity, and the children and even grandchildren that are among them, can also be harmed. The confusion that ensues hurts all involved and indicates the ways in which an ethics of care must figure into the discourse more prominently. In the following section, I will further outline and define how this ethical mandate unfolds.

Ethical Considerations—Who Defines Me?

I can remember so vividly as a child in the late 1950s and early 1960s attending womanless weddings where men, often the preacher and the deacons, dressed up as women and carried out a full wedding ceremony in a local black church. It was done in "fun"—thus the colloquialism "funny" began to attach to transgender persons. But, at that time, the ritual was a relic of a past long gone in which the Akan people of Africa would act out a famous folktale in which gender roles were changed as a means of social leveling. The ritual demonstrated that all persons of the community were regarded with respect and dignity.[60] The narratives of early enslaved Africans reveal the same consistent theme: everyone in the community was valued. Survival depended on everyone being valued.[61] However, in the North American context, it is highly probable that the womanless wedding originated from "post-Civil War minstrelsy and reinforced white southern fears of the unity of the black male and white female through joining the blackface male and the transvestite bride on stage. Minstrelsy and vaudeville most certainly made gendered and racial impersonation an acceptable form of entertainment by the 1880s."[62] Consequently, the characters from the hegemonic imaginary took the stage to make fun of transgender people and LGBTQIA persons in general. As historian Craig Friend explains regarding minstrel shows, "Mammy, Sambo, and Joe were done in blackface, and the dialog was written in racist 'Sambo' dialect."[63] Blackface served as a platform for mockery and division. This mechanism is demonstrably similar to what bully pulpit preachers do to LGBTQIA persons from the pulpit. The womanless wedding I experienced in my hometown, adapted most likely from white southerners, is another example of how the homophobia of black preachers derives from the white culture's mockery of blackness in the form of whiteface mimesis.

As Christian ethicist Cheryl Sanders asserts, the familiar scripture "do unto others as you would have them do unto you,"[64] known as the Golden Rule,

> framed as a general guide toward empowerment for liberative praxis, … would be rendered something like this: as you would that others should do to you—whatever your sex, race, class, sexual preference, or however you measure your status in relation to those others—do so to them. In short, treat others as you would like to be treated if you had to trade places with them.[65]

Christian social ethics places the onus on everyone within a community to see themselves in the face of the other. In so doing, the sociality of Christian interconnection is built on mutual appreciation for the humanity of the next person. With that as a foundational premise of human relationality, the distinction between who is in and who is out dissipates, as do any claims that God hates certain groups.

Resisting the essentialism that the patriarchal domination of conservative evangelical piety projects onto the black LGBTQIA body through the rhetoric proffered by the black preaching tradition, Townes notes:

> Our sexuality is who we are as thinking, feeling, and caring human beings. It is our ability to love and nurture. To express warmth and compassion. It is not only our gonads. Heterosexism encourages the objectification of our bodies—male and female. One of its strongest underlying premises is that the emotion expressed in same-sex relationships is only that of pure sex. Too often we do not see or want to discover the care and nurture that lesbians and gay men can and do have for each other. We must raise some

exacting questions about an ethic that insists that homosexuals should either try to engage in heterosexual relationships unhappily or remain celibate. An ethic is suspicious when it allows some to impose on others obligations that they are unwilling to accept for themselves.[66]

Only when all of humanity is given the same respect will the ability to see LGBTQIA persons as valuable to communal life emerge as an ethical standard. Forming this ethical standard requires a more serious look at how the law has functioned as a progenitor of a hegemonic system stuck in plantation values.

Moral and Spiritual Freedom

According to womanist theologian Delores Williams, confronting the "non-liberative thread running through the Bible" warrants "a womanist hermeneutic of identification-ascertainment that involves three modes of inquiry: subjective, communal and objective."[67] Constructing a black systematic theology that responsibly takes into consideration the plight of the truly marginalized in the black community requires recognizing the plight of black women as the victims of prolonged oppression, an experience that parallels the story of Hagar in the Bible. Black women are the "oppressed of the oppressed." But, have black theologians identified so closely with "Israel's liberation that they have been blind to the awful reality of victims making victims in the Bible?"[68] The question points to a void present in black church public theology as it relates to any marginalized group. In light of the experiences of black queers with the black preaching tradition, there is a need to reevaluate what is most important to a liberative black public theology. A public theology that condemns people to death and destruction is neither productive nor life-giving. I contend that black LGBTQIA persons, too, are the "oppressed of the oppressed" when addressed by some black church public theology.

The ways in which morality is invoked in the pulpit represents the principal issue facing black queers in the context of the black preaching tradition. Invariably, this is because their very existence is too often named as immoral.

Helen: My paternal side of the family is National Baptist. Um, some of them have branched off into American Baptist; but, National Baptist, very stoic and very patriarchal, very sexist, um, they kind of shifted away from that since then, but when I was growing up that was the theme. And then, my paternal side of the family is Church of God in Christ—holiness, Pentecostal, so that's a whole other breed. But both of them had some stuff in common, you know: no sex outside of marriage, babies out of wedlock is a sin, ah, if you're having sex, it's supposed to be between a man and a woman, if you're having sex with somebody of the same sex or gender, then you are going to hell. And we are going to use these scriptures to tell you why you are going to hell. Um, and that was the extent of it. Um, so it was very negative from jump.

Black preachers reveal the theological content of their faith through their sermons. Personal biases often shape a preacher's selection of scripture. As Delores Williams notes, this practice "consign[s] the community and black theological imagination to a kind of stalemate that denies the possibility of change with regard to the people's experience of God and with regard to the possibility of God changing in relation to the community."[69] Even as I anticipate the counterargument that God does not change, as Bishop Paul Morton argues above, it is important to note instances where God *does* change in scripture, such as with the daughters of Zelophehad in Numbers 27, in the extension of Hezekiah's life in Isaiah 38, and in the decision in Exodus 32:14 to spare the children of Israel despite many declarations that they would die. The Bible does not present a static God. God is dynamic. "God is still speaking."[70] Moreover, believers are compelled to change in the face of new and more clearly established revelation from the Spirit of God. This is a function of one's relationship with God. Know God for yourself.

Covenants

According to Mark 10:9, "What God has joined together let no man put asunder."[71] Here I use the archaic translation of this scripture regarding marriage to illustrate how absurd it is to think that anyone, especially a black preacher who purportedly represents a covenant-making God, could hinder the union of human beings in covenant love to one another. After all, it was the institution of slavery that ripped covenant partners of enslaved Africans away from each other and shattered their family units. In light of this historical dynamic, black preachers should celebrate the freedom to covenant for all of humanity. In most instances, enslaved Africans were not permitted to marry. That fact alone should dissuade any black preacher from denying anyone the privilege of such a legal arrangement. The masters' tools desecrated our houses. Audre Lorde's famous pronouncement that "the master's tool will never dismantle the master's house," urges a reordering of our priorities toward a theology of embodiment, which makes radical inclusion a by-product of an even more liberative stance. After all, radical inclusion, I would argue, merely makes one a "permanent guest"[72] in the master's house. Real freedom to build one's own house comes in a Christological understanding of the work of Christ on the cross for everyone. M. Shawn Copeland gives voice to such radical inclusion through an interpretation of the significance of Jesus of Nazareth:

Jesus of Nazareth is the measure or standard for our exercise of erotic power and freedom in the service of the reign of God and against empire. He is the clearest example of what it means to identify with children and women and men who are poor, excluded, and despised; to take their side in the struggle for life—no matter the cost. His incarnation witnesses to a divine destiny seeded in our very flesh. Jesus signifies and teaches a new way of being human, of embodied spirituality. Through his body marked, made individual, particular, and vivid through race, gender, sexuality, religious practice, and culture, Jesus mediates the gracious gift given and the gracious giving gift. His incarnation, which makes the Infinite God present, disrupts every pleasure of hierarchy, economy, cultural domination, racial violence, gender oppression, and abuse of sexual others. Through his body, his flesh and blood, Jesus of Nazareth offers us a new and compelling way of being God's people even as we reside in the new imperial order.[73]

This is a Christology of inclusion, which asserts that Jesus of the Cross opened a freedom to all of humanity to live, move, and be. Copeland's formulation of a theological gateway for LGBTQIA bodies to enjoy the embodiment of Christ offers queers of color hope in the face of the gloom and doom often encountered in the black preaching tradition. The freedom to enjoy the full complement of what it means to be human is given to all through the finished work of Christ.

Freed from Judgment

The realization that Christ's finished work on the cross absolves all from judgment and condemnation requires theological thinkers to embrace a counternarrative—one in which death-dealing rhetoric gives way to life-giving affirmation. Mercy Amba Oduyoye argues that such an affirmative approach changes the task of theologians and preachers: "Theologians throughout the world who felt a call to speak more relevantly to their age and generation freed themselves from traditional dogmatic and systematic theology and focused on life issues. Instead of telling people what questions to ask and then furnishing them with the answers, theologians began to listen to the questions people were asking and then seek answers."[74] Preachers must listen to the cries of the people. The people who have been marginalized because of their "otherness" deserve to be heard.

We need progressive trifocals to acculturate America. Trifocals correct vision in three fields: near, middle, and far distances. By analogy, clearer focus on the work of Christ and its import engenders a greater appreciation for the human beings who are near to us, sharpens our willingness to center Christ's love for all people, and allows us to see far into the future when all of humanity is redeemed from death and destruction based on our witness of this good news. Race, ethnicity, gender, and sexuality converge in our complex society, with people's identities generating social and spiritual implications. It is simply no longer sufficient to think in terms of "man and his God." Rather, there is a socio-theo-political demand for complete inclusivity for every person in every aspect of American life, including those who practice various religions and who do not fit traditionally heteronormative identifiers in public and private life. A transformative public theology, where a counternarrative focused on life-giving affirmation informs a new way of thinking about and practicing the same old things, fosters an interrelationship between theory and praxis.

Staunch biblical literalism may be countered with sound theological reasoning and responsible methodological approaches to interpret the Bible for the present moment. In effect, the black preaching tradition must seek to "rightly divide the word of truth" such that the truth of Jesus as a complete liberator and as the one who embodies all freedom is applied to all of humanity. In the next section, I employ the theories of Audre Lorde and Luce Irigary to more succinctly define the parameters of spirituality and sexuality that support this freedom for all of humanity.

Encountering Freedom

Wading through the waters of violent rhetoric from the bully pulpit often involves throwing off the parasites of shaming, badgering, and mocking. Feminist lesbian author and poet Audre Lorde and French feminist philosopher, psychoanalyst, psycholinguist, and cultural theorist Luce Irigaray provide the scaffolding for building a strong spiritual and sacred core that helps LGBTQIA persons survive the treacherous waters of indifference so that M. Shawn Copeland's process of "enfleshing freedom" becomes a reality.[75] Shaming, badgering, and mocking LGBTQIA people in the sermonic moment is a misuse of the power of the pulpit. The response of LGBTQIA persons to such sermons is varied. Some people endure this volatile rhetoric week after week. Over time, it influences one's psyche. Others walk away from the church to seek other avenues for spiritual fulfillment. Some grow bitter and denounce God and the church. In order to encounter freedom from the dregs of the bully pulpit, LGBTQIA persons must develop what Copeland calls "embodied spirituality." Embodied spirituality, as Copeland argues, entails following:

> A healthy appropriation of sexuality is crucial to generous, generative, and full living. A fully embodied spirituality calls for the integration of sexual energies and drives, rather than repression or even sublimation ... A reclaimed notion of eros offers one way of thinking about such interplay ... Eros as embodied spirituality suffuses and sustains depth or

value-laden experiences and relationships ... Eros enhances our capacity for joy and knowledge, honors and prompts our deepest yearnings for truth and life, and validates our refusal of docility and submission in the face of oppression. Eros steadies us as we reach out to other bodies in reverence, passion, resisting every temptation to use or assimilate the other and the Other for our own self-gratification, purpose, or plan. Eros empowers and affirms life.[76]

Sexuality is integral to our spirituality. Despite the ancient Greek practice to see love in a divided manner—that is, as *eros* (intimate love), *agapé* (God's love and love for God), *philia* (friendship), or *storge* (typically between parents and children)—love is not only multidimensional, but interrelated. All aspects of love are implicated in the spiritual makeup of a person. Our spiritual development and maturity depend on all facets of love being operative.

Audre Lorde offers a healthy and practical understanding of Eros in her claim that the erotic is power. It is the power "of sharing deeply any pursuit with another person. The sharing of joy, whether physical, emotional, psychic, or intellectual, forms a bridge between the sharers which can be the basis for understanding much of what is not shared between them, and lessens the threat of their difference." Lorde's point has theological value in that Lorde identifies Eros as igniting our life force, which springs forth as a "kind of energy that heightens and sensitizes and strengthens" our life experience.[77] Freeing the mind and the body to pursue life requires a theological turn that places theism outside the body politics of Western Protestantism. Lorde helps to frame this turn by concluding "that deep and irreplaceable knowledge of my capacity for joy comes to demand from all of my life that it be lived within the knowledge that such satisfaction is possible, and does not have to be called *marriage*, nor *god*, nor *an afterlife*."[78] Lorde hints toward an embodied spirituality in which Eros powers the mind and body to transcend the physical, where difference rules, into a place of spiritual joy, where differences are shared.

Philosophical Implications

Luce Irigaray, a French feminist philosopher, explained sexual difference in *The Way of Love*, her 2002 monograph in which she posits the need for dialogue between the sexes. Focused primarily on heterosexual love, Irigaray's contention is that Western culture completely masculinizes sexual subjects in a vortex of polarizing masculine subjectivity. She argues that the "wisdom of love" as a modality for communication between human beings who are different relies on "a philosophy which involves the whole of a human and not only that mental part of ourselves through which man [*sic*] has believed to distinguish himself from other kingdoms." Love must be "cultivated" in light of the relationality between the two parts of the human, the one and the other—male and female.[79] This task involves acknowledging that there is no universal language capable of effectuating this communication. This "interaction ... calls for a relation between subjective and objective where the one could never assume nor integrate the other because the one and the other are two." As such, "the Being of each of its parts and of their common world no longer belong to a traditional ontology." The two "interpenetrate and transmute each other such that the dichotomy between them no longer exists."[80] They are ever "becoming." Irigaray proffers a feminine subject as the mediator of difference. In effect, she proposes a mere substitution of gendered subjects, female instead of male, in establishing interpersonal subjectivity, which is no less totalizing than a masculine subject and which superimposes masculinity as the consummate dominant frame, thereby "othering" the feminine. However, by containing her analysis to heterosexual beings, Irigaray's philosophical conceptualization invites the shift that Audre Lorde invokes. Lorde and Irigaray differ in two ways with respect to the understanding of difference. First, Lorde situates difference in desire whereas Irigaray situates difference in gendered embodiment. Second, Lorde sees the "female plane" not as a gendered philosophical location but rather as an original, creative wisdom, like God-consciousness. In this way, philosophy and theology have a reunion. Instead of "male models of power," Lorde proposes a "bridge" whereby the erotic serves as the engine for creativity, joy, knowledge, feelings, love, capacity, and most assuredly meaning, lessening the threat of difference in all human spaces.[81]

Western philosophy fails to give requisite attention to "the relations of speaking between subjects," as Irigaray amply points out. At the core of Irigaray's depiction of a theo-philosophy of love is the notion that a new speech emerges from the silence between the two where "their language-house finds itself questioned, even abandoned, in order to uncover the still mute domains of Being."[82] This leads to a "gesture of reciprocal recognition" that serves as an opening for the two (male and female) to interrelate with one another.[83] The exchange highlights another problem of Western philosophy. In its historical construction, humanity has given deference to the masculine. Arguably, there is a default setting to the "things of the world" in contrast to a preoccupation with the "Being of another subject."[84] "To consider this relation as a co-belonging of man and woman in the constitution of human identity requires rethinking what being-in-relation itself implies." Language, through variegated speech, then becomes a tool (*techné*) for producing meaning in much the same way that art brings forth meaning.

> To experience this co-belonging implies leaving representative thought and letting oneself go in the co-belonging to Being which already inhabits us, constitutes us, surrounds us. It presupposes, in fact, dwelling "there where we truly already are." ... In order to have access to it man has to leave his own world, or rather to partly open its limits. It is not in his

house, including that of language, that he will find out how to enter a new historical era, a new speech. The feature referring to the specificity of man has to change place—passing from the relation to things to the relation to the other.[85]

To this analysis, Lorde forecasts a limitation, which the erotic, as conceived by Lorde, eliminates. Co-belonging intimates an interdependence whereas the erotic frees. No longer will fear "externally define us," but we follow the path to inward power.

Black Preachers and the Way of Love

Black preachers must change their theology as it relates to LGBTQIA persons as we move toward a more inclusive society. This calls for a tangible love that transcends the boundaries of the two to a new ground of understanding where each participates without presupposition.[86] This is *the way of love*—to envelop the differences between the sexes, genders, and orientations in a communication not bound by differences and yet reverent of them. The goal is "to construct the possibility of an intersubjective relation between masculine and feminine subjects that is founded on love, and, more specifically, on a particular formulation of love that could provide the basis for a new socio-political order."[87] It is the task of the philosopher to provide this framework. To challenge the traditional role of philosophy—and specifically the Hegelian approach—one must "free philosophy from the exteriority of History itself."[88] Theology must make room for a God who is involved with human interaction. Reconceptualizing the meaning of love within Christian communities requires extending unconditional love to bisexual, transgender, queer, questioning, and same gender-loving people. Love—not hate—is the true vehicle for negotiating difference. Some pastors make an effort by befriending the LGBTQIA person but not accepting their sexual preference. As I heard Quincy's reflection on his relationship with his pastor, I thought about the importance of pastors understanding their roles in guiding their parishioners without doing harm. When people are looking for genuine love, it is harmful when their authority figure attempts to compartmentalize their authentic selfhood. Quincy identifies the interpersonal conflicts that arise when one is made to feel that some aspect of their humanity is rejected not only by God but by their pastoral figure:

> *Quincy:* I did not have a father growing up in my life. So around 2002 I adopted one of the persons whom I consider to be a father in the ministry to me. And, I remember sharing with him that I was gay. And, I remember him saying to me, he said you know, "I do not agree with the lifestyle; but I will cover you, and I will treat you like my son." And, he has done that even to this day. Um so, going through the church in which I grew

up in, as I became older my pastor used to always say to me, "You have to bolt the door because if you don't bolt the door then the spirit is going to overtake you and you are not going to be able to recover. The spirit of homosexuality."

The requisite love, however, is irreducible. God's love is not subject to the sameness that characterizes much of Western philosophical discourse on love; rather, it is the love that gives currency to the irreducible differences between the sexes. This love reframes Western philosophical notions of relationality. By reappropriating relationality, shifting from a construction based solely on desire and dependent on possession, submission, and confinement to one grounded in celebration of difference with fluidity and respect for the other, mutuality and respect can overtake hatred. The object of this love is not hierarchical in the sense of master and servant; instead, the two selves are embodied equivalents. Irigaray would say that love is measurable when there is an appreciation for both embodied selves whereby neither is displaced by the presence of the other and both are valued in the exchange. Moreover, she states,

> God, in this sense, really represents the transfer of the other into the beyond. As invisible, he [sic] acts as guarantor of alterity as such. God is waiting for our encountering and entering into relation with him or her. God is a beyond regarding our discoveries and homologations, cultivations and fabrications, reductions to the One and to the same, where energy of or for the other is used without recognizing their irreducible emergence.[89]

Lorde rescues Irigaray's use of desire by recognizing desire as a progenitor of erotic power such that one's desires are part and parcel to "erotic knowledge." As Lorde explains,

> Our erotic knowledge empowers us, becomes a lens through which we scrutinize all aspects of our existence, forcing us to evaluate those aspects honestly in terms of their relative meaning within our lives. And this is a grave responsibility, projected from within each of us, not to settle for the convenient, the shoddy, the conventionally expected, nor the merely safe.[90]

Lorde's conclusion is that safety is found in authenticity. Lorde contends that one's erotic knowledge is the place where power is centered. As such, the capacity to "enflesh freedom" is generated first by the capacity to be free in one's mature sexual expression. Taken together, Lorde and Irigaray urge an understanding of love that values diversity, embraces alterity, and is fluid in its negotiation of desire to the extent that it serves the purpose of erotic power.

Spiritual Formation

It was only at the point that I gained the courage to be myself, that I pursued, for myself, the Spirit within. Theretofore, I had faced a tension between my own need to participate and the need that my psyche perceived, albeit subconsciously, to emerge as an independent individual whose self-worth and self-identity remained intact despite rejection. Being effectively exiled from the gatherings of other women because of difference created a moral dilemma overcome by the personal discovery that "Jesus loves *me*, this *I* know." Jesus as the Christ[91] in my life sustains my ability to claim oneness with the Spirit of God. In consequence, no amount of rejection could or can permeate my existence. Gathering with people who think you are a sinner destined for hell can be replaced with gathering in community where the love of Jesus is felt by all.

The acts of women in relationship should "embody women's love for one another" whether we connect for a potluck, for a girls' night out, or for intimate love.[92] In Renee Hill's words, "mutuality among women—sisterhood—is a bedrock of power for survival and transformation in the Black community. Perhaps it is because of the potential power of mutuality that it is discouraged (or perhaps destroyed) by forces in society including means such as lesbian-baiting and the promotion of male-identified consciousness."[93] Through my personal orientation, I have identified the rhetorical control mechanisms employed to keep women like me in their place within the context of my black church experience. Sneers became the dividing lines for those of us who did not fit the prescribed definition of womanhood. Stones were cast to separate us from the pack. The wounds those stones produced are not easily healed. When people decide they cannot be your friends because you are "not right," it burns a brand into your psyche that eats away at your self-esteem and slowly kills your spirit. This is a death not easily overcome. Eventually, and inevitably, the lesbian-baiting and male-identified consciousness worked like a tag team to exile young women like me. Fear led to broken friendships.

People in my hometown did not want to be associated with Lillie Ruth because she was "funny." The same held true for me. This speaks to the lack of Jesus as the Christ in the life of those who would engage such rules of separation. I suggest that my own experience—and that of Lillie Ruth—demonstrate how black church public theology has departed from the basic message of good news. Those who would mock and scorn others for being sexually diverse do not exemplify the full formation of Jesus as the Christ in their lives. This rhetoric demonstrates a lack of Christian maturity, or *morphóō*. The black preaching tradition needs to get into *formation*. I suggest that a raised consciousness is needed to measure the theological claims of the black preaching tradition against its historical intolerance of sexual diversity. Moreover, I contend that an optimal psychological intervention to aid this process must be based on an Africentric worldview—a worldview that draws on African perspectives, that accords everyone the same respect, places no strictures on anyone's access to the divine, and receives all as a part of the human family. This paradigmatic shift should start with the black church in the formation of the beloved community.

Managing Devaluation

As Traci West so eloquently states it, "Either way, lesbians are relegated to a devalued status as children of God, and their femaleness is not reflected in this image of God."[94] Consequently, faith communities that single people out because they are lesbian, gay, transgender, bisexual, or queer make the tenets of their faith exclusionary. Their faith claims exclude those who do not conform. Mara evaluates the effect of such a message:

> *Mara:* Always. You always take stuff like that personal. I took it personal because that was my personal life. That was what I was going through, that was what I was fighting through. Well, God made us all. I took it personal because no matter what, I still felt like I am doing something wrong. Sinful. And I say sinful because it wasn't wrong to me; it was the most natural thing to me. It was, it is extremely natural to me. So, um, so for me, no it was not wrong. But from my teachings, it was sinful.

As she wrestles with the message that excludes her, Mara settles upon a revelation of her own—God made us all. This revelation helped her separate teachings that would exclude her from her knowledge of a God in whose image she was created. Excluding people from the church masks the true intent of Christ's liberative ethos with divisiveness. It sanctions the same kind of disparity felt by blacks that ultimately ignited the fire that became the civil rights movement. In the 1960s, the scorn and dejection black people experienced formed the impetus for protest. The same holds true for the treatment of sexually diverse people who experience rejection, ridicule, and retort in the black preaching tradition. Our protest is to expose the lack of full formation of Jesus as the Christ in the life of the black church, beginning with the sermonic moment. Mileece was able to see how sharing her narrative gave her a sense of pride and healing when she reflected on her past experiences and shared how she reached a peace within:

> *Mileece:* Um, I'm glad to have talked about this. I've never really expressed what I experienced before, like I have today. Maybe I needed to do this. This might be a part that needs a little healing ... some healing. So, I'm glad for an opportunity to participate in your study. Maybe I

did need to get this off of me. It's just, um, we've been so oppressed and abused and hurt, yet we do this to our own people. How can you be so hateful towards us? We're, we're African American people; we're people of African descent. But, we're separate because "you're gay and you are straight and you're going to hell, and you're wrong." How can we oppress people when we have been so abused throughout centuries, even until today? You know, the church is powerful in the black community. It really is. And, some people I know have been in their churches since they were kids; thirty, forty years in one church getting that same kind of teaching. And so, that sinks into their spirit and that's what they know to be true. That's some slavery shit, right there. That's where white folks used to go to "pic-a-nics" and they have fun seeing the people hung and beaten. Same people. Post Traumatic Slave Disorder, that's what I call it. We are a beautiful people, but some of us are very hurt and still hurting others. I think I will find another church home. I'm not against church at all. It's the people in the place. It's not the church, it's the people in there that are abusive. That's not what God is about. That's human, that's just the people. It, it doesn't turn me against God because I know that that's not God. It doesn't turn me against the church because all churches are not like that. Just certain ones are. Which, I won't let them uh, scar me so much that I won't go to church again; no, I would not let them have that effect on me because I know it is wrong. That kind of behavior is wrong, not who I am.

Mileece identifies the punitive nature of the violent religious rhetoric and the lengths to which preachers went to engage with her physical body as a sight of terror. Her characterization of these acts being "some slavery shit, right there," is congruent with arguments made throughout this chapter and the next regarding bullying and the punitive nature of a Christian social ethics designed to "change" a person from sinner to "delivered." It is a forced marriage. Moreover, Mileece experienced what she called "Post Traumatic Slave Disorder," something Dr. Joy DeGruy describes as "Post Traumatic Slave Syndrome."[95] The amazingly similar characterizations from two separate individuals, one who has studied it extensively as a sociological phenomenon and one who has experienced it firsthand, serve as mutual validation. Mileece's ability to detect the ungodly nature of this rhetoric, appropriate her own self-defining belief system in light of her faith convictions, and emerge capable of discerning the difference between the voice of God and the voice of people motivated by their own prejudices serves as a stark reminder of the importance of cultivating an "ear to hear what the Spirit is saying to the churches."[96] In this way, it becomes virtually impossible for violent rhetoric to transmute your spiritual resolve that knows you belong to God, you are loved by God, and your ontological being was created in God's image.

Faith Formation

Christ being formed, as an ontological concept, envisages the breath and Spirit of Christ in the lived experience of all who hold that confessional Pauline declaration, "Christ lives in me."[97] The Christ-embodied self loves unconditionally. That love produces, according to Renee Hill, communal concern "where self-love becomes important in the transformative work."[98] My childhood experience brings this into clearer focus. When I was a child, I saw something in the people who made up my social location. I experienced their love and concern. I could tell those who were for me, and I could tell those who were against me. I thought I could tell the love of Christ. But, as 1 Corinthians 13:11 (NIV) states, "When I was a child, I spoke like a child, I thought like a child, I reasoned like a child; when I became an adult, I put an end to childish ways."

Jesus as the Christ is an embodied phenomenon. As I grew into my own sexual identity, I was no less deserving of the love of my community of faith, but my deviation from the sexual norm caused church folks to withdraw that love for superficial reasons. That love, rather than being unconditional, was conditioned upon my conformity to certain external standards. Those standards became the artificial markers of my morality, when, in fact, the judgment employed to oust me, both literally and figuratively, pronounces judgment on the black preaching tradition when measured against an Africentric worldview. A tradition that would reject me as abnormal on the basis of morality offends the very law it seeks to uphold. When preachers stand in the pulpit and pronounce judgment on LGBTQIA people in the name of God, they do so believing that God condemns people for their sexuality. The paradox is that no one escapes the tension inherent in their existential reality. The church, and specifically church leaders, are in no position to point fingers. People who are hurting need to know that God accepts them. I advocate for an Africentric worldview that privileges an experiential knowledge of reality, leads to happiness and peace, maximizes positivity, and respects the unity of all human beings with the Divine. I contend the tension is resolved when a holistic unity of spirit and matter results in oneness with the Divine. When we socialize all human beings to this reality, there is less room for the ideological prisons that push people to leave their places of worship or, more tragically, to suicidal ideations.

Notes

1   "N.C. Pastor Charles Worley: 'Put Gays and Lesbians in Electrified Fence to Kill Them Off,'" posted by Corpus Callosum, YouTube, May 21, 2012, http://www.youtube.com/watch?v=w2839yEazcs</> (accessed July 5, 2024).

2   Ibid.

3 "President Obama Endorses Gay Marriage in Emotional Interview with ABC," posted by orangecountyfldems, YouTube, May 9, 2012, http://www.youtube.com/watch?v=qecdYEAby5I</> (accessed July 5, 2024).

4 Marvin A. McMickle, *Where Have All the Prophets Gone?: Reclaiming Prophetic Preaching in America* (Cleveland, OH: Pilgrim, 2006).

5 Ibid., vii.

6 Ibid.

7 Marriage equality was upheld as constitutional by the US Supreme Court in *Obergefell v. Hodges* on June 26, 2015.

8 "James Meeks—The Crime of the Century," posted by Wheaton College Billy Graham Center, YouTube, August 24, 2016, https://youtu.be/G_r3fZQlaD0</> (accessed July 5, 2024). Bishop Meeks thanks his host for inviting him to preach all over the world as affirmation of his acceptance by white, Evangelical Christians as he delivers a sermon for a conference.

9 "Preacher Wants to Imprison Gays/Lesbians—Let Them Die," posted by Neuroticy2, YouTube, May 25, 2012, https://www.youtube.com/watch?v=Bwfnbz_9AZM</> (accessed July 5, 2024).

10 Ibid.; and "Pastor Advocates Electric Fence for Gays," posted by CNN, YouTube, May 22, 2012, https://youtu.be/UtHgUaSyOy8?si=-OClccxx62w_VSGW</> (accessed July 5, 2024).

11 "Preacher Wants to Imprison Gays/Lesbians."

12 Between 1877 and 1950 more than 4,000 African Americans were lynched in the South. "The Trauma of Lynching," Equal Justice Initiative, January 25, 2017, http://eji.org/history-racial-injustice-trauma-of-lynching. More than 100 of those lynched during this time frame were residents of North Carolina. Lisa Sorg, "New Report Documents More than 100 Lynchings in North Carolina, Several in Chatham County," *Indy Week*, February 11, 2015, https://indyweek.com/news/archives-news/new-report-documents-100-lynchings-north-carolina-several-chatham-county/</> (accessed July 5, 2024). The motive for the lynchings was to terrorize African Americans as a form of social control. James Weldon Johnson, "Lynching: America's National Disgrace," *Current History* 19, no. 4 (January 1924): 597. The deposition testimony of Governor William Holden of North Carolina, January 5, 1871, "relating to crimes of the Ku Klux Klan against citizens of North Carolina, 1869–1871," documents "a colored woman drowned in a mill pond in Orange County, because she had been 'impudent' to a white lady! This is the only charge." https://ccharity.com/contents/historical-reports/papers-related-crimes-committed-ku-klux-klan-north-carolina-1871-1800/statements-depositions-and-other-records-submitted-gov-william-w-holden-relating-crimes-ku-klux-klan</> (accessed July 5, 2024). While I am unaware of other direct evidence to support sexual orientation as the express basis for a specific case, there is evidence that alleged "deviant sexual behavior" was often a motive. Given the history of bogus rape charges hurled at black men, it is conceivable that sexual orientation would have been a motive for multiple lynchings. According to A. Phillip Randolph, "Most Anything in the South May Be the Occasion of a Lynching," *Truth about Lynching: Its Causes and Effects* (New York: Cosmo-Advocate,

1917), 8. Cynthia Skove Nevels reports that lynching was conducted by some immigrants as a means of social acceptance in *Lynching to Belong: Claiming Whiteness through Racial Violence* (College Station: Texas A & M University Press, 2007).

13 Harvey Young, "The Black Body as Souvenir in American Lynching," *Theatre Journal* 57 (2005): 640–41.
14 Riley, *This Here Flesh*, 15.
15 Lorde, *Sister Outsider*.
16 Barbara J. Fields and Karen E. Fields, *Racecraft: The Soul of Inequality in American Life* (New York: Verso, 2014), 198.
17 "The Preachers: Mini-Profiles," *Intelligence Report*, Southern Poverty Law Center, Spring 2007, https://www.splcenter.org/fighting-hate/intelligence-report/2015/preachers-mini-profiles</> (accessed July 5, 2024).
18 Aaron Rupar, "'Values Voter Summit Features Attack on 'Faggots,' Claim That Gay Rights Inspired 'From the Pit of Hell Itself,'" *ThinkProgress*, September 26, 2006, https://archive.thinkprogress.org/values-voter-summit-features-attack-on-faggots-claim-that-gay-rights-movement-inspired-from-the-pit-3d3e33108ae3/</> (accessed July 5, 2024).
19 "The Preachers: Mini-Profiles."
20 Lance J. Rips, "Circular Reasoning," *Cognitive Science* 26 (2002): 768.
21 Mignon Moore, *Invisible Families: Gay Identities, Relationships, and Motherhood among Black Women* (Berkeley: University of California Press, 2011).
22 Fields and Fields, *Racecraft*, 137–38.
23 Ibid.
24 Ibid., 202–03.
25 Greater Bible Way Temple of the Apostolic Faith, Elder Rader Johnson, March 20, 2010, https://youtu.be/CVNcg9K9b00 (accessed November 26, 2021).
26 Deuteronomy 31:8; Matthew 28:20; Psalms 139:8 (NIV).
27 Lorde, *Sister Outsider*, 110–13.
28 "Preacher Wants To Imprison Gays/Lesbians," 4:49–8:24.
29 Jerry Pierce, "Baptist Leader Condemns Anti-Gay Diatribes," *Baptist Press*, May 24, 2012, http://www.bpnews.net/37894/baptist-leader-condemns-antigay-diatribes (accessed July 5, 2024).
30 Brown Douglas, *Sexuality in the Black Church*, 11–30.
31 "The Cooperative Program," Southern Baptist Convention, http://www.sbc.net/cp/ (accessed July 5, 2024).
32 Ibid.
33 "The Spirituality of George W. Bush," *Frontline*, PBS, http://www.pbs.org/wgbh/pages/frontline/shows/jesus/president/spirituality.html (accessed July 5, 2024).
34 Ibid.
35 Brentin Mock, "Bishop Harry Jackson," *Southern Poverty Law Center Intelligence Report*, Spring 2007, https://www.splcenter.org/fighting-hate/intelligence-report/2015/bishop-harry-jackson (accessed July 5, 2024).

36 Horace L. Griffin, *Their Own Receive Them Not: African American Lesbians and Gays in Black Churches* (Cleveland, OH: Pilgrim, 2006), 3.
37 Ibid., 57.
38 *Obergefell v. Hodges*, 576 U. S. 644 (2015).
39 1 Kings 7:8; 11:1–3 (NIV).
40 Christopher GoGwilt and Melanie D. Holm, eds., *Mocking Bird Technologies: The Poetics of Parroting, Mimicry, and Other Starling Tropes*, online ed. (New York: Fordham University Press, 2018).
41 "The Preachers: Mini-Profiles." This message also appears in Bishop Boone's book, *Breaking Through: Taking the Kingdom into the Culture by Out-Serving Others* (Nashville, TN: Broadman and Holman, 1996).
42 "'God's Purpose in Marriage' by Wellington Boone," posted by Sojourn Church Carrollton, TX, YouTube, July 22, 2014, https://youtu.be/w07CFxpxm5k</> (accessed July 5, 2024).
43 "Rev. Butler's View on Homosexuality," posted by butlerk1402, YouTube, January 23, 2009, https://youtu.be/RECqduOz568</> (accessed July 5, 2024).
44 Eve Kosofsky Sedgwick, *Epistemology of the Closet* (Berkeley, CA: University of California Press, 2008).
45 "The Preachers: Mini-Profiles."
46 Ibid.
47 Ibid.
48 "Rev. Meeks Sends Gay Marriage Emergency Message against Legislation," *Chicago Sun-Times*, November 27, 2013, https://chicago.suntimes.com/politics/2013/11/27/18625834/rev-meeks-sends-gay-marriage-emergency-message-against-legislation</> (accessed July 5, 2024).
49 Ibid.
50 Mock, "Bishop Harry Jackson."
51 Ibid. "The Preachers: Mini-Profiles."
52 Ibid.
53 Lou Chibbaro Jr., "Couple Walks out During Anti-Gay Sermon," *Washington Blade,* January 14, 2010, https://www.washingtonblade.com/2010/01/14/couple-walks-out-during-anti-gay-sermon (accessed July 5, 2024).
54 "Bishop Alfred Owens," Crooked Crosses, https://crookedcrosses.wordpress.com/crazies-for-god/bishop-alfred-owens</> (accessed July 5, 2024); Chibbaro, "Couple Walks Out."
55 "Mayor Slams Bishop Owens," *Washington City Paper*, May 19, 2006, https://www.washingtoncitypaper.com/news/loose-lips/article/13033130/mayor-slams-bishop-owens (accessed July 5, 2024).
56 "Is This Your Pastor?: Bishop Paul S. Morton," Operation: Rebirth, accessed June 24, 2016, archived version available at https://web.archive.org/web/20161118033028/http://www.operationrebirth.com/archive/paulmorton.html (accessed July 5, 2024).
57 Response from Quentin Devaughn, http://www.operationrebirth.com/yourpastor.html (accessed July 2, 2016).

58 Jesse Lee Peterson, *Scam: How the Black Leadership Exploits Black America* (Nashville, TN: Nelson Current, 2003), 173.
59 1 Samuel 16:7 (NIV).
60 Naana Jane Opoku-Agyemang, "Gender-Role Perceptions in the Akan Folktale," *Research in African Literatures* 30, no. 1 (Spring 1999): 116.
61 Cheryl J. Sanders, *Empowerment Ethics for a Liberated People: A Path to African American Social Transformation* (Minneapolis: Augsburg Fortress, 1995), 4. Sanders is often cited as being antiqueer because of her ethical stance at the inception of the womanist methodology in a roundtable discussion with other black female scholars: "Christian Ethics and Theology in Womanist Perspective," *Journal of Feminist Studies in Religion* 5, no. 2 (Fall 1989): 83–112.
62 Craig Thompson Friend, *Southern Masculinity: Perspectives on Manhood in the South Since Reconstruction* (Athens, GA: University of Georgia Press, 2009).
63 Ibid., 225–28.
64 Matthew 7:12 (NIV).
65 Sanders, *Empowerment*, 4.
66 Emilie M. Townes, *In a Blaze of Glory: Womanist Spirituality as Social Witness* (Nashville, TN: Abingdon, 1995), 81.
67 Delores Williams, *Sisters in the Wilderness* (Maryknoll, NY: Orbis, 1993), 149.
68 Ibid., 151.
69 Ibid.
70 This is the motto of the United Church of Christ.
71 Mark 10:9 (KJV).
72 This phrase was inspired by a conversation I had with Dr. Stephen Ray during the spring of 2015 when he was on sabbatical from Garrett Evangelical Seminary and took up residence for a semester as a visiting scholar at Chicago Theological Seminary. Dr. Ray inspired me to think about building our own theological house as LGBTQIA persons by looking within for liberty and freedom from the tyranny of the bully pulpit.
73 M. Shawn Copeland, *Enfleshing Freedom: Body, Race, and Being* (Minneapolis, MN: Fortress, 2010), 65.
74 Mercy Amba Oduyoye, *Hearing and Knowing: Theological Reflections on Christianity in Africa* (Maryknoll, NY: Orbis, 1986), 3.
75 Copeland, *Enfleshing Freedom*, 64–65.
76 Ibid.
77 Lorde, *Sister Outsider*, 56, 57.
78 Ibid., 57.
79 Luce Irigaray, *The Way of Love*, trans. Heidi Bostic and Stephen Pluháček (New York: Continuum, 2002), viii.
80 Ibid., 11.
81 Lorde, *Sister Outsider*, 53–59.

82 Irigaray, *Way of Love*, 47.
83 Ibid., 88.
84 Ibid., 88–89.
85 Ibid., 90.
86 This is so with one clarification. Irigaray states, "I am not you and you will forever remain the other to me, such is the necessary presupposition for the entering into presence of the one and the other, of the one with the other. The search for a link requires the respect for the strangeness of the one to the other, the recognition of a nothing in common calling into question the proper of each one" (ibid., 168).
87 Ibid., 105.
88 Ibid., 94.
89 Ibid., 156–60.
90 Lorde, *Sister Outsider*, 57.
91 Kelly Brown Douglas, *The Black Christ* (Maryknoll, NY: Orbis, 1999), 111.
92 Renee Hill, "Who Are We for Each Other?: Sexism, Sexuality and Womanist Theology," in *Black Theology: A Documentary History*, vol. 2, ed. Gayraud S. Wilmore and James H. Cone (Maryknoll, NY: Orbis, 1993), 348.
93 Hill, "Who Are We," 345–51.
94 I believe this excerpt speaks to the entire LGBTQIA community, including those like me who identify as bisexual. Tracy C. West, "Visions of Womanhood: Beyond Idolizing Heteropatriarchy," *Union Seminary Quarterly Review* 58, nos. 3–4 (2004): 134.
95 Joy Degruy Leary, *Post Traumatic Slave Syndrome: America's Legacy of Enduring Injury and Healing* (Portland, OR: Joy Degruy, 2005).
96 Matthew 11:15 (NIV); Revelation 2:7a (NIV).
97 Galatians 2:20 (NRSV).
98 Hill, "Who Are We," 349.

3

Whiteface and the "Face of the Other"

> *It is a peculiar sensation, this double-consciousness, this sense of always looking at one's self through the eyes of others, of measuring one's soul by the tape of a world that looks on in an amused contempt and pity. One ever feels his twoness,—an American, a Negro; two warring souls, two thoughts, two unreconciled strivings; two warring ideals in one dark body, whose dogged strength alone keeps it from being torn asunder.*[1]

Considering black public theology and the struggle for freedom, justice, and equality for blacks in America leads naturally to the contributions of W. E. B. Du Bois. Reflecting upon his early years as a child growing up in the hills of New England, Du Bois saw himself as a *veiled subject*. Born in Great Barrington, Massachusetts in 1868, in some sense the veil was a protection in which Du Bois could freely define and identify himself separated from the nauseating glare and stare of the white children around him who made him feel the depth of his difference. Du Bois's idea of "double consciousness" is an apt starting point for this chapter as I explore the ways in which blacks navigated their "twoness" after the abolition of legalized slavery. In whiteface, some black preachers attempted to mime the ideology, attributes, and behaviors of white people. As "the other," blacks were treated as aliens and animals by those in the dominant culture. This chapter will reveal the deep ideological divide between those who sought the respectability of white people and those who sought to define freedom for themselves and those similarly situated despite lynching, domestic terrorism, and all manner of indignities over the following century. It is this "twoness" that reverberates in the rhetorical violence so determined to follow the same patterns of behavior to either harm or annihilate LGBTQIA persons.

Doublemindedness

The Bible declares that double-minded people are unstable in all of their ways.[2] Du Bois wrote *Souls of Black Folk* in 1903, an immensely unsettled time for the formerly enslaved. Everyone was thinking about how to move forward with a semblance of freedom. There was a commonality of oppression, but as designations of class and status began to separate the formerly enslaved one from the other, a war for survival ensued. By the time Du Bois's *The Negro Church* was completed, the reputations of the formerly enslaved had been contrived. The men were considered by the white normative gaze to be rapists, and the women were lewd and lascivious. The "warring souls" had to devise a plan to overcome this stigmatization. However, as we will see, some key initial efforts to forge such a plan, aided by black preachers, reflected white, Victorian values. Whiteface represents the failed conception of adopting another's values in order to find acceptance. Whiteface stands against the face of "the other" on the "color line."[3]

As Nell Painter, in her book *The History of White People*, points out, Peter Camper in 1792 drew a chart comparing the faces and skulls of an orangutan, a "Negro," a Kalmuck, a European, and *Apollo Belvedere*.[4] Though Camper was known to be a proponent of human equality, his work was used together with Protestant clergyman Johann Kaspar Lavater's book *On Physiognomy* and the work of anthropologist Samuel Morton to cement the ideal of "white beauty."[5] These positions on physiognomy were later adopted by those in psychological circles, both researchers and therapists, to substantiate Negro inferiority. That historical sidebar notwithstanding, whenever African Americans have been confronted with systemic racism, our collective will is to fight against it. How that fight takes shape is the question of the day.

Minstrelsy as a Trope of Black Church Public Theology

What Audre Lorde commemorated in a poem entitled "A Litany of Survival" offers the perfect posture for people who have been ostracized and silenced by hegemonic cultural practices. Lorde declares: "We were never meant to survive."[6] The irony of Lorde's poem is that it presents yet another *coup de poing*, a warring of belonging. Lorde's theoretical framework describes perfectly the existential anxiety that marginalization produces. The practices of derision that undergird the posturing of colonizer against colonized produce feelings of alienation and exclusion among marginalized people. Out of Lorde's theory comes a prophetic voice for survival that offers "dreamers" an alternative to the death traps of hopelessness and despair while concomitantly acknowledging the (im)possibility of survival. This voice turns what appears to be a hopeless situation into a course on survival equipped with a map for the journey:

A Litany of Survival

For those of us who live at the shoreline
standing upon the constant edges of decision
crucial and alone
for those of us who cannot indulge
the passing dreams of choice
who love in doorways coming and going
in the hours between dawns
looking inward and outward
at once before and after
seeking a now that can breed
futures
like bread in our children's mouths
so their dreams will not reflect
the death of ours:
For those of us
who were imprinted with fear
like a faint line in the center of our foreheads
learning to be afraid with our mother's milk
for by this weapon
this illusion of some safety to be found
the heavy-footed hoped to silence us
For all of us
this instant and this triumph
We were never meant to survive.
And when the sun rises we are afraid
it might not remain
when the sun sets we are afraid
it might not rise in the morning
when our stomachs are full we are afraid
of indigestion
when our stomachs are empty we are afraid
we may never eat again
when we are loved we are afraid
love will vanish
when we are alone we are afraid
love will never return
and when we speak we are afraid
our words will not be heard
nor welcomed
but when we are silent

> we are still afraid
> so it is better to speak
> remembering
> we were never meant to survive[7]

In the first verse of the poem, Lorde addresses those who are marginalized, referring to them as those situated "on the shoreline" at "the edges of decision." She next identifies their existential reality: "crucial and alone." Many of our slain indisputably reached that shoreline. In her appeal to the humanity of the marginalized, Lorde characterizes them in terms of their limited ability to choose how and whom to love. Nonetheless, she proclaims the hope that lies within by acknowledging that LGBTQIA persons, like all people, are negotiating life with a fear of extermination. She speaks to their existential anxiety but also to the hope that dreams produce. This is the window from which the prophetic voice must speak. The people I interviewed described the impact of rhetorical violence on their families. Mileece encountered abuse from several communities:

> *Mileece*: That's about people don't want to voluntarily go into a place, a building, and be abused. People don't want that. Why would you want to put yourself in that? You're paying tithes just like everybody else, you're serving just like everybody else, your time, your talents, your tithes. Why would you voluntarily want to go someplace where you're not appreciated, you're tolerated? You want to be welcomed and loved in a church. Because the church is a lot like a family also; people have church families. But if you've suffered church hurt, it's like, "Let me keep going back to this abuse?" Naw, people … they'd rather find another outlet, or another way to express themselves and to receive spiritual feeding than in a church building.

The confusing signals from the pulpit can morph into lifelong struggles whereupon some feel they are not meant to survive and, consequently, literally commit suicide. Despite their struggles, participants in the study managed to find ways to experience the Divine and to affirm the call to ministry.

Participants also found ways to cope and to commune with their own sense of authenticity. Shedding the role of the "Great Pretender" proved a worthy spiritual discipline. Doing the hard work of freeing oneself from the entanglements of other people's judgment and exuding the courage to speak truth to power provided mental relief.

> *Quincy:* I wrote a letter to my old pastor, which probably had to be the most difficult letter that I had to write, but it was a very freeing experience. To this date, I have spoken to the pastor many of times, but we have never discussed that letter. I basically told him about my, my

evolution, my theological evolution, coming into myself. I told him about how his language was very, is very dangerous. Um, I told him about how he used to tell me to "bolt the door," whatever that meant, and how it was going to destroy my ministry; and sixteen years later, I'm still preaching. Um, I told him about reexamining his position about what it means to love and to love authentically. Um, and also to be aware of those persons in his congregation, many of whom are gay, you know, and struggling, and to think about what type of rhetoric, um, you are putting out there in your messages, particularly with sermons that have nothing to do with anything sexual. Um, so, something to that effect. Um, and I never asked him about if he read the letter, what were his thoughts about the letter. It was just like, for me, I needed to get that off my chest. And it was like a release. I was releasing hurt, frustration, a burden.

Quincy points to the very significant phenomenon of pretense that exists in black church culture. His childhood pastor suggested that he could keep his gayness locked away. This pastor recognized the call on his life, the mastery of his preaching ability, his giftedness, and his sincerity in service, but the pastor could not accept his ontology. As Quincy evolved, he became more courageous and was able to overcome the pretense. However, very few people can pivot to that place of confidence and faith. In the process Quincy learned some valuable lessons about authenticity. It is important to weigh the choices one faces against one's own sense of self-worth, self-motivation, and self-identity. Being open with one's sexual identity can sometimes be in tension with the basic need for safety, affirmation, and support.

Participants articulated new conceptions of the Divine as they emerged from their reflections on the rhetorical violence they endured. They discovered the infinite nature of God.

> *Franshon:* Yeah, God is bigger than this little box that sometimes I think some, some, some ministers want to put God in or that the faith community wants to contain God in this little box. And, I think God is pervasive. Like, I think God is massive and I think God can handle things. I think God can handle our sexual orientation [*smiling*]. I think God can handle us questioning God. I think God can, God is ... God is big and tough; you know what I mean? And, God can just handle whatever struggles we have, or whatever questions we have, or whatever thoughts we have, or whatever feelings we have God can handle it because God is way bigger than those things.

Franshon brings the theo-ethical inquiry full circle as she unfolds her sojourn from an innocent child absorbing the Bible like a meal, to a curious young adult, to one fully embracing her self-identity in the face of oppositional forces seeking to deliver her from her authenticity and cast out of her the thing that she holds as sacred. Franshon demonstrates the importance of seeking a personal relationship with God. Key to this discovery is Franshon's willingness to listen to and follow the voice of God, which she learned to hear despite the deafening sounds of negativity. Franshon took the necessary steps to remove herself from the distractions and to equip herself with concentrated study, which enabled her to frame her liberative narrative. When Franshon discovered the magnanimous nature of God, she could articulate a concept of God that was much more encompassing than the boxed-in view of God presented to her in childhood and young adulthood. She was able to push past a colonizing concept of God to a relational dynamic filled with wonder and hope in a God much bigger and much more creative than her initial teachings revealed. Franshon was able to seek resources through higher education, enabling her to communicate through a ministry of her own.

Participants acknowledged the deep wounds that marked their ontological discovery of difference. The sharp acts of correction by close family members dealt indelible blows to their psyches. Despite those hurts, an indomitable faith led them to resources for renewal.

> *Helen:* On one of the *Ricki Lake* episodes there was a black woman, um, you know, she wanted to come out to her family. At the time, you know, I didn't have full knowledge or language or understanding about what any of this meant, but she said, um, you know, "I think I might be gay." And so, I, in turn, took to my diary, which I used to write in all of the time, and wrote, "I think I might be gay." I was all of like ten years old—did not fully understand what that meant—but she talked about how she was attracted to women. And I was like, "Well, I like boys and girls," that's how I rationalized it. And so I wrote it in my journal, went on about my day, and a few days later my mom found it. And so we went home and she made me read from the diary and then proceeded to ask a bunch of questions like, um, "Do you want to go to hell? Do you want God not to be pleased with you?" She prayed over me, like, made me rip the pages out, burned them, watch them go down the toilet. Um, and so, from then I was pretty much scarred. Um, and my mother and I have never talked about it until this day and I am thirty. Um, but that stifled me in a lot of ways. Ah, from then, I stopped writing. To this day, if I do write, I take my journal with me everywhere because I'm like I never want anybody to be able to find it. But, then it made me question like, "But, I didn't ask to be made like this; this is just who I am. So, did God make me like this only to torture me, or what?" Um, so it wasn't until I got to college that I started finding other resources, um, whether it was in people that I met or in literature, in different texts or reading the Bible differently.

Helen understood her selfhood in terms clearly inapposite to her family, her church, and her idea of God. The teachings of her church ignited a holy curiosity in her that would not be satisfied until she encountered

God, who drove her to seek, and she then found a holy community filled with acceptance, guidance, and support. Upon removing herself from her home environment, she was able to find a place where she could feel comfortable, nurture her relationship with God, and embrace her own ministry. In so doing, she carefully reflects on a trauma she experienced with her diary as an innocent child who was seeking to understand her own sexuality at the intersection of religion and family. In the reflection is a peace that comes from having located a community of believers who embraced and nurtured her authentic self, a self she wishes to present to the world.

Finding an affirming community is important for many LGBTQIA persons, whether they are believers or not. The fact that Helen sought to leave her home environment but still "walk out" her faith speaks to the mandate that every person seek a loving community. In this respect Benjamin, Franshon, Quincy, and Helen share experiences that model faithful reliance on the Holy Spirit. Driven by their passion to relate to God, they all went away to school, pursued Master of Divinity degrees, and followed the voice of God in their lives. Such exploration generates a strong sense of belonging to something larger than the narrow picture of God drawn for them in their conventional church settings.

Black Church Theology as Accommodation

Much black church public theology has been inclined to denounce the Black Lives Matter movement in form, if not in substance. This is in part because the movement was initiated by sexually diverse individuals and has adopted a position privileging those traditionally marginalized such as lesbian, gay, bisexual, transgender, and queer people. The decision by the Black Lives Matter movement to privilege LGBTQIA persons because they are marginalized from mainstream policy making and legal protection places the movement at odds with most black preachers, who follow the "family values" agenda of the white, fundamentalist evangelical Christian Right to whom they are beholden. Building multi-million-dollar edifices with the help of the Right's financing arm, sitting in coveted board positions, and appearing on evangelical television precludes preachers from speaking truth to power regarding the "open season" on black bodies.

Audre Lorde would urge the emergence of holy anger within the prophetic voice.[8] Anger that brings about constructive, systemic action toward justice must dominate the discourse. "We need to talk about what we do to each other, no matter what pain and anger may be mined within those conversations."[9] Lorde's dialogue with James Baldwin in 1985 in the aftermath of twelve murdered black women in Boston spawned the writing of *Need: A Chorale for Black Woman Voices*. "As aggressive acts of white racist violence" escalated against black bodies, Lorde declared war.[10]

> It is time to pump up the volume again around this wasteful secret and not hide from it under a cloak of false unity, not turn away from it, believing it will be solved by somebody else. Black women will no longer accept being slaughtered like sheep on the altars of Black-male frustration. On the other hand, we do not want to have to blow away Black men in our own self-defense. So, Black women and men must devise ways of working together as a people to end this slaughter.[11]

The "secret" to which Lorde refers involves the deadly wounds inflicted within the black community. Baldwin and other men in the audience tried to hush the voice of black women in the face of the "cascading violence" being hurled upon black women's bodies.[12] The black men wanted the black women to be silent regarding the women's experience of black-on-black crime so as to more prominently pronounce the atrocities committed against black bodies by whites. In response, Lorde broke the silence. Her holy anger rose up to resist.

> Dead Black women haunt the black maled streets / paying the cities' secret and familiar tithe of blood / burned blood beat blood cut blood / seven year old child rape victim blood / of a sodomized grandmother blood / on the hands of my brother blood / and his blood clotting in the teeth of strangers / as women we were meant to bleed / but not this useless blood / my blood each month a memorial / to my unspoken sisters falling like red drops to the asphalt / I am not satisfied to bleed / as a quiet symbol for no one's redemption / why is it our blood / that keeps these cities fertile?

> I do not even know all their names. / My sisters deaths are not noteworthy / nor threatening enough to decorate the evening news / not important enough to be fossilized / between the right-to-life pickets / and the San Francisco riots for gay liberation/ blood blood of my sisters fallen in this bloody war / with no names no medals no exchange of prisoners / no packages from home / no time off for good behavior / no victories. no victors.[13]

Lorde recognized the tendency of the "prophets" to recoil. Her description of the bloodshed is reminiscent of the multiple ways in which the lives of black women, particularly when lost to violence, are *ungrievable*.[14] Reference to the "tithe" of blood suggests that there is something owed to the city like a tax paid in blood. This bloodshed demands a costly response, which requires the voice of one motivated by holy anger. The blood, for Lorde, cannot redeem male privilege. Lorde determines that the correct response to the shedding of blood is unmitigated confrontation. The confrontation that comes from freedom fighting is not designed to be violent. In fact, the peaceful protesting of Black Lives Matter proponents reflects the kind of confrontation that Lorde speaks of. Nonetheless, many black preachers chose to denounce Black Lives Matter protest efforts as violent in order to align with their white counterparts.

Audre Lorde and the Black Lives Matter Movement

Lorde's analysis brings us to the other reason some black clergy avoid the Black Lives Matter movement: they maintain that it tends toward violence. Lorde's description of shed blood is memorialized in the dictum of black pastors who "draw blood" with their words, sacrificing peaceful protest upon the altar of whiteface mimesis. Pastor Jesse Peterson describes the Black Lives Matter movement and other black leaders as the "race hustlers."[15] He characterizes the movement as "evil" and "wicked" and "worse than the KKK." His rationale is that they are "all into keeping black Americans angry and demoralized." He points to several marches where participants chanted, "What do we want? Dead cops. When do we want them? Now!" and "Pigs in a blanket, fry them like bacon!" Peterson, president of BOND—the Brotherhood Organization of a New Destiny, a nonprofit religious group dedicated to "Rebuilding the Family by Rebuilding the Man"—claims that Black Lives Matter incites violence that leads to cop killing.[16] Lorde would counter that it is Peterson who draws the blood. And as her poem points out, it is important that the leaders of Black Lives Matter, three black women who embrace their difference as lesbians, speak up and out as modern-day prophets regarding injustice.

Fanon and the Black Lives Matter Movement

Pastor Peterson mischaracterizes #BlackLivesMatter. The recorded chants were isolated incidents produced by parties disassociated with the movement, though presumably they were angry about the same senseless and murderous police brutality.[17] Notably, Frantz Fanon, Martinican, revolutionary psychiatrist and philosopher, in his magnum opus, *The Wretched of the Earth*, contemplated strategic violence as the only effective act of resistance to defeat prolonged mental and physical bondage and to bring about lasting political liberation. Decolonization, according to Fanon, cannot be achieved without violence. Social structures do not change voluntarily. In order for the marginalized to move to the center, those in the center must be shifted, and that shifting invariably involves violence because no entity likes to give up its privileged position without a fight, according to Fanon.[18] Fanon was interpreting the effects of colonial rule, which involved ruthless violence on the human psyche, as he encountered Algerians in his psychiatric practice. Fanon served as head of the psychiatry department of Blida-Joinville Hospital in Algeria from 1953 to 1956. Through his psychoanalysis and socio-philosophical approach he identified the effects of prolonged colonization on the colonized of Algeria.[19]

Anatomy of Racecraft in the Black Bully Pulpit

Considering the work of sociologist Karen E. Fields and her sister, historian Barbara J. Fields, in *Racecraft: The Soul of Inequality in American Life*, I deemed it important to offer a sermonic exemplar to demonstrate the specific ways that violent rhetoric shows up in a bully pulpit. Lilly Grove Missionary Baptist Church, in Houston, Texas, is a megachurch with an annual budget of $3 million as of its financial report for 2021. Its membership grew by 148 persons over the course of six months in 2020.[20] Terry K. Anderson, the church's pastor since 1990, is a nationally renowned black evangelist. He was licensed and ordained in 1977 and attended Bishop College, Dallas, Texas; Louisiana State University, Pineville, Louisiana; Union Theological Seminary, New Orleans, Louisiana, and Houston Baptist University in Houston, Texas. Pastor Anderson presents a fascinating example of how whiteface minstrelsy operates in black church public theology and is representative of the phenomenon of anti-LGBTQIA black preachers.

Pastor Anderson preached a message titled "What Must the Church Do about Same Sex Marriage" to his congregation in 2012.[21] It had received 193,312 views at the time of my transcription.[22] This message was chosen because it was posted as a public video on the church's YouTube channel, it contains highly explosive and derogatory language toward LGBTQIA people, and it pans the crowd on the Sunday morning that it was recorded so that the congregational reactions to the message are easily reviewed. Effectively, the video captures the process that the Fields identify in describing how racism is obfuscated by race such that, in the case of black bully pulpit preachers, racist messages are used to denigrate black LGBTQIA persons. Pastor Anderson's sermon exemplifies how the rhetoric of right-wing evangelical fundamentalism has invaded black public theology through racecraft—an *invisible ontology* that grips people with a mechanism of control so powerful that it compromises sound reason and that deploys hatred through vitriolic speech acts. The message provides a clear picture of the plantation's success in controlling the black preaching moment and ensconcing divisiveness within it.

Anderson commences the excerpted message by making the claim that God can change "our condition." After noting that he has been dubbed "intolerant," the pastor continues with a diatribe against same-sex marriage. For Pastor Anderson, "the gays" threaten the family and are on their way to hell. To illustrate this point, he deploys numerous examples laced with slurs to describe same-sex attraction and characterizes all LGBTQIA persons as irreparably sinful. In the message, Pastor Anderson recites portions of Romans 1 and with a comparison to heterosexual attraction refers to the Song of Solomon. Framed as a social justice issue, same-sex marriage dominates the message. Pastor Anderson also tacitly claims that heterosexual marriage must be deployed more flawlessly in order for the church to have any legitimacy in its message against same-sex marriage.[23] In this sermon, Pastor Anderson named himself "a prophet" and declared that he has the "voice of God in [his] mouth." But where is his prophetic voice? Despite this pronouncement, he elicits the prayers of the congregation and the unction of the spirit to "temper his speech" so that he is "not offensive in a hurtful way." I contend that he missed that mark. At one point in the sermon, he confessed that the congregation made him "say" certain things.

Yet, in the political victimization of black folks, Pastor Anderson promotes a "family values" agenda preoccupied with regulating sexual orientation. Pastor Anderson's God is more concerned with the gender identity of married intimate partners than whether "justice rolls down like a mighty river and righteousness like an ever-flowing stream."[24] In liberationist public theology, there is no substitution for prophetic witness that focuses on how God's justice requires a commitment to proclamation that seeks the elimination of oppression.

Amos and Anderson

The prophet Amos was concerned with hollow displays of piety and religious devotion in the face of suffering and death. Martin Luther King Jr. invoked the prophecy of Amos in his "Letter from a Birmingham Jail" to call clergy to action against the injustices experienced by black Americans during the civil rights movement. Contrastingly, Pastor Anderson's eschatological vision is of an angry God whose intolerance of diverse sexual orientations requires persons who Anderson claims are created in God's image to conform to humanity's image of what is acceptable. Note the constricting nature of his exegetical application to what purports to be one of the creation stories from Genesis, though the particular pericope is not mentioned in the sermon: "I've come to tell you that you are made in the image of God. He made you male *or* female." The rigid formulation of physiological binaries precludes the known spectrum of human physical differentiation, such as intersex persons,[25] all of whom were also created in the image of God, a fact one would presume he would admit given that elsewhere in the sermon Pastor Anderson declared his God to be sovereign. Some of those I interviewed also experienced this kind of rhetoric in the midst of attempts to exorcise them.

> *Mileece*: Pastor decided that they needed to pray for us to have the lesbian spirit prayed out of us. So, I'm following my girlfriend. I think if I wouldn't have been with her, I wouldn't have been there at all. So, they decided that we needed to be prayed for; the lesbian spirit, the gay spirit needed to be prayed out of us; "you need to be delivered from the,

from the gay, the demon, the devil." So, they bring us to the front of this little storefront church and they um, actually touch us, pushing … I mean violently touch us, supposedly laying hands on us; but, it was violent, actually pushing, shoving, and calling out the devil in us. And one of the men said "oh, I like this, this is getting good … " as if it was some kind of show, some kind of freak show. And when I heard that I said, "no, this is not for me, why am I in this place with her?" And she, my girlfriend, still insisted, at the time … she said that this was the right thing to do … My girlfriend at the time thought that this, this was okay. I said, "I am not going back there anymore; you can go, I am not going." I said, "how does this make you feel that we are being paraded around like some kind of witch-hunt or something?" She still didn't buy into it; she still didn't see anything wrong with it. I left the place, she stayed, and eventually we separated. And now, she's in the pulpit; but she says that she's not preaching homophobia and hatred. I don't know, I have never heard her. I won't go.

In *Our Lives Matter: A Womanist Queer Theology*, Pamela Lightsey contends that "how we see ourselves in relation to God's creation has something to do with how we see ourselves in relation to each other. Black people's response or lack of response to oppression is part of the ongoing historical saga of our country." This is evident in Benjamin's reflection of his pastorate.

Benjamin: And I think the other part to my story and probably the last component of it is that serving a congregation that you actually do begin to do the theology that you are learning. The person that you are, you're beginning to wrestle with, they become a part of the wrestling match. And that certainly was what happened in my relationship with the church that I served in Colorado. That um, I mean, I never imagined that I would become the poster child of being a gay preacher, um, but I think that's what happened. Because I came out openly you know. My ministry started drawing me into these spaces where I could see the face of Jesus Christ in different ways. And, one of the ways, serving in Colorado that I could see the face of Jesus was when "Referendum I" came out and that was for legal protections for same-sex couples. They couldn't get married at the time, but, you could get … we would get … the State was trying to get legal protections for them. So, in the event one of the partners would become ill the other could come and tend to them, could get, you know … be a part of the will, all of these pieces. And you know, and I just thought you know "that is so cool." I mean, you love somebody, you know, and I just don't remember thinking, this is about me. I just remember thinking, you know people should be able to love who they need to love and want to love, you know. And so I got behind that as a professional, as a clergy person, and became a spokesperson for that. And there was much fallout in my congregation about that, you know, to the point that the congregation or members of it were saying to me, "We don't want to be a gay church," whatever that is. "And, now you got all these gay people coming to this church and, um, we want to know from you what is the future of this congregation?" And I had had some itchings about, you know, you serve a congregation for so many years and your work is done. You know, it's time to move on, and I never went to that church thinking that I was going to be there permanently and so, after sixteen years it seemed like the time that we had come to the crossroads. And so part of leaving that was not to just leave them and say, "Well, I'm out," but I needed to say, "Let me tell you who I am, you know, who you have loved, who you will need to continue to love: people that look like me. And we've come to this crossroads, and much of it is because of my sexuality or what is perceived as my sexuality and certainly my beliefs around it. Um, and so I need to tell you that I am gay, you know, and that, you know, this is who I believe God is calling me to be." And that just didn't work.

Pastor Anderson's worldview, however, is cemented in a catechesis that regards "sin" as disobedience to "the rulers." Consequently, he defines "family" in the narrowest terms and identifies that limited conception of family as a mandate from God: "What God calls family is a man, a woman, and their children." Neither Pastor Anderson nor his God can see any other construction of family. This may explain why, in this sermon, all others are anathema and relegated to abject poverty, rejection, and derision. Additionally, in this sermon, sin is literally whatever the preacher says it is, whatever he delineates as disobedient to the rulers—master and mistress.[26] For instance, sin is *being* gay, and sin is engaging in same-sex sexual relationships. All LGBTQIA persons are ontologically sinful in Pastor Anderson's theology. Moreover, the practice of same-sex love is deemed sinful: Pastor Anderson defines sin as "missing the mark," which ostensibly means having sex with a same-gender person. His identification of the "right target" is tied to his anatomical and sexual fixation on Adam and Eve. Pastor Anderson frames his argument in terms of cisgender black males, explaining that as long as a black man is "aiming at the right target," which for Pastor Anderson is a woman's vagina, he is not headed to hell, provided the folks in the church "pray for him."[27] This hypocrisy breeds disdain for the church.

Anderson and Solomon

As mentioned previously, Solomon, the son of David, whom Pastor Anderson invokes, is noted in scripture as having had 700 wives and 400 concubines. Pastor Anderson's close identification with Solomon is not simply tied to Solomon's ostensible gender preference; rather, Anderson explicitly advocates for multiple heterosexual sexual partners as well, in complete contradiction to the "family values" of rigid adherence to heterosexual marital monogamy he purports to advocate. Theoretically, then, the sexual escapades with multiple partners to which Pastor Anderson refers are also overcome by the prayers of the saints. That is to say, same-sex lovemaking invariably sends you to hell; however, if you are a heterosexual preacher like Pastor Anderson, you simply need the prayers of the saints as you *deal* with your issues of lust for women.

Couching the theology of sexuality in terms of "God's natural order," Pastor Anderson characterizes sexual promiscuity as sinful or not sinful based on the sexual orientation of the people engaged in it. A double standard is invoked for Pastor Anderson's presumed sexual exploits that is not available to the LGBTQIA person. That is, a woman, in Pastor Anderson's estimation, is a possession to be objectified, even by God: "If God made anything better than a woman, he kept it for himself." Consequently, any configuration that deviates sexually from a female-made-for-male construct is "sinful" and "just as sick" as bestiality.[28] Pastor Anderson suggests that engaging in same-sex love is the same as having sex with multiple partners, a lamb, a goat, a dog, or a mountain lion. In many instances, this rhetoric is internalized by LGBTQIA persons and redirected at others.

> *Quincy:* Um, so before I came out, it impacted me in a very negative way, because it really taught me how to not really like myself. So, I was very disingenuous. Um, I was using language that was almost used against me, against other people. That was very hurtful. So, it was like a rehearsed narrative; you hurt, so you get up and you do the same thing. So, it was almost hypocritical; well, it was hypocritical.

Interestingly, in describing his own sexual prowess Pastor Anderson described himself in the third person as beast-like: "He is USDA prime, 100 percent all man who loves women." His is a slave mentality that self-identifies as property that can be sold to the highest bidder. Pastor Anderson parrots the language of the auction block, repurposing it in a theological shroud that amounts to hate-talk disguised as God-talk. While perhaps a fine Mandinka warrior was displayed bare on the auction block and examined from head to toe, the crowd of potential buyers gawking at his genitals, fondling them for their breeding potential, Pastor Anderson is perched on the bully pulpit, on display to the tithe-paying congregation who gazes at him longingly. The phrase "USDA prime, 100 percent" also signifies an allegiance to American exceptionalism, which teaches one to idolize phallic symbols and privileges male sexual organs as supreme. In the Turnerian sense, it is a dominant symbol.[29]

Anderson and Bestiality

Pastor Anderson's appeal to bestiality is designed to shame LGBTQIA persons and attempts to reduce them to animals. However, in so doing, he also reveals his own ideological biases that reflect a kind of *mind slavery* wedded to self-hate and chained to a view of himself as beast. His "prime" status affords him the coveted ability to drive a Mercedes-Benz S63 and to strut around like the gangster in William DeVaughn's 1974 song, "Be Thankful for What You Got," despite the song making the rather different point that people should be thankful for what they have, even though most do not have elaborate cars. Additionally, the disgust associated with Pastor Anderson's characterization of LGBTQIA sexual relations, particularly the false claim that LGBTQIA persons are child predators, causes those in his congregation to despise LGBTQIA persons, even those in their immediate families, and engenders violence against them. It also alienates LGBTQIA persons within that congregation, often leading them to dissociate from church participation or to crumble under the pressure to "change" such that they may subjugate themselves in false identities and submission to the psychological torture of "conversion" therapies.[30] The cheers and snickers of the congregation during the sermon's diatribes against LGBTQIA persons, along with loud, obnoxious call-and-response affirmations of those assaults demonstrate the communal process of degradation that this kind of preaching orchestrates.

Blood Sacrifice

Pastor Anderson subjected the LGBTQIA persons who were present for this sermon to shame, ridicule, indignation, ignominy, embarrassment, chagrin, humiliation, and disgust. LGBTQIA persons, designated as animals, become through such ridicule the metaphorical "blood sacrifice" for the master and mistress who signify Adam and Eve in the garden. Sacrificing LGBTQIA persons purifies the heterosexuals in the congregation to live free from their sexual sins. LGBTQIA persons are offered up as "the scapegoat." The term "scapegoat" is employed in the Girardian sense: "Persecutors always believe in the excellence of their cause, but in reality *they hate without a cause*. The absence of cause in the accusation (*ad causam*) is never seen by the persecutors."[31] Mileece relates it to the experiences of her ancestors during enslavement:

> *Mileece:* You know what, I compare it to a beating. It's compared to slavery to me. It's equal to the kind of oppression that we suffered as a people. But, then later on I learned that hurt people, hurt people. I learned that later on. Because of the abuse that we've suffered as a people, we project onto others, to our own people. We push that, all that abuse that we've suffered, we put that on our own people.

JoAnne Marie Terrell opines that animal sacrifice was prominent in ancient Near Eastern cultures that influenced Hebrew Bible authors.[32] It is implied in the story of Adam and Eve when God required their expulsion from Eden.[33] It is also implied in the flight of the Hebrews from Egypt. In the

Enuma Elish, the Babylonian creation epic, not just animals but human beings are sacrificed to honor the "gods." Even the Yahwistic story indicates "God" seeking after this. However, sacrifice is resignified in Hebrew culture in a way that is not evident in other Near Eastern cultures. Employing no curse upon the people but rather cursing the ground, God acts *in love* to protect them. Animal sacrifice is God's instrument of cultic purity because God is the only one who has jurisdiction over blood.[34] In many Christian theologies, the concept of blood sacrifice aims to resolve the tensions created by the law of sin and death by offering a scapegoat, such as a lamb or goat, to be sacrificed in the place of the sinner.[35] In so doing, the sins transferred onto the sacrificed animal would supplant the sinner's punishment of death. In the New Testament, Jesus is referred to as the "lamb who takes away the sins of the world" as a sacrifice for all.[36] This Western Protestant theological construct, particularly as espoused by Pastor Anderson, emphasizes sin as death but makes little provision for an escape from this death.

Despite many references to select sections of the argument set forth by Apostle Paul in Romans 1 and with wholesale disregard for the culminating conclusion that Paul reaches in that chapter, pastors like Anderson defile the nature of blood sacrifice and risk committing an even worse offense—the scattering of the flock, a phenomenon we discuss more critically in the next chapter. Pastor Anderson's theology, comingled with human sacrifice, signifies a distinct break with the New Testament. To this point, Terrell suggests that the idea of blood sacrifice requires specific analysis:

> This analysis mirrors the primacy of right relationship, mutuality and themes such as relational Christology (Thistlethwaite, 1991), Christ as community (Brock, 1988; Williams, 1993) and community relatedness (Cannon, 1988) in feminist and womanist theologies, yet deeply ingrained bias against women existed in the enactment of Hebrew sacrificial rites. Priests instructed men to bring their offerings to God and instructed the women to bring them to the priest. A *she*-goat or an ewe-lamb was to be offered for idolatry and "private sins" because "a female is in all species more defective than the male, and there is no greater sin than idolatry, and no kind more defective than a she-goat" (Maimonides).[37]

It is no wonder that noticeably absent from Pastor Anderson's shallow theological stance in this sermon is any understanding of what it means for Jesus to be Christ.

God's Rule

Kelly Brown Douglas argues that the meaning of Jesus as Christ eludes those who fail to accord Jesus a role as "the bearer of God's rule, the mediator of God's salvation."[38] Jesus as Christ commands a respect for the work of Christ while he walked the earth. It requires an appreciation for his life and his ministry. Jesus's ministry to the poor and downtrodden exemplifies the character and tenor of God's rule. Christ's actions toward and love for the marginalized are central themes of this Christology, and it is imperative that this love be replicated in the lives of all those who claim Christ as Lord and Savior so that Christ's example is evident in their lives and, as Douglas states, "Christ can be seen in the faces of others."[39] Contrastingly, the faces of "the gays" in Pastor Anderson's family have no human attributes. In his sermon, they were talked about as though they were not human, calling into question the pastor's most basic ethics of inherent human dignity. Christian social ethics matter. Interestingly, the ethical is best undergirded by the philosophical. In the story of Jesus there is a direct nexus between the atonement and the requisite compassion one must have for others. The French philosopher, existentialist, and phenomenologist Emmanuel Levinas offers an applicable theory for this nexus based on "ethics as first philosophy."[40] Levinas introduces the phenomenological concept that "the surpassing of phenomenal or inward existence does not consist in receiving the recognition of the Other, but in offering [him] one's being. To be in oneself is to express oneself, that is, already to serve the Other. The ground of expression is goodness."[41] The goodness that Levinas refers to comes in recognition of the face of the other.

The "Face of the Other"

Emmanuel Levinas, a Lithuanian Jewish philosopher, wrote an essay titled "Ethics as First Philosophy" in 1961.[42] Seeking to differentiate between a totalizing Western Protestant ontology and one that offers freedom, Levinas established a metaphysics of the Infinite whereby the intersubjective relationality of one human being to another did not depend on reducing the one to the sameness of the other. The human condition, according to Levinas, is one of "radical multiplicity."[43] This means that each human being is uniquely designed; no two human beings are exactly the same. Levinas broke with the traditional understanding of human subjectivity proffered by Martin Buber because it supported a totalization of all humanity as reducible to the same. Rather than an ontology that regards the uniqueness of every human being, Buber's "I and thou" construct, by Levinas's assessment, could not appreciate the alterity of the other unless it reduced the other to the likeness of the same. This, in Levinas's estimation, leads to imperialistic attitudes about existence. As a Jew, Levinas had a keen understanding of how such a totalization of humanity corralled all of humanity into a homogenized collection that could be manipulated by the state.

Levinas served in the French Army at the height of the Nazi Party's rise to power. When he was captured and placed in a Nazi concentration camp for officers, his immediate family was murdered by the Third Reich, and his wife and baby daughter narrowly escaped the same fate. His time in confinement sharpened his understanding of how a totalizing ontology operated as a tool for Nazi control. His friend and colleague Martin Heidegger, with whom he would separate ideologically as a result of Heidegger's allegiance to Hitler, catalyzed his philosophical turn. Central to his theme of ethics as first philosophy is the idea that "metaphysics precedes ontology."[44] Levinas argued for a formulation of intersubjective relationality that embraced the uniqueness of every human being:

> A calling into question of the same—which cannot occur within the egoist spontaneity of the same—is brought about by the other. We name this calling into question of my spontaneity by the presence of the Other ethics. The strangeness of the Other, his irreducibility to the I, to my thoughts and my possessions, is precisely accomplished as a calling into question of my spontaneity, as ethics. Metaphysics, transcendence, the welcoming of the other by the same, of the Other by me, is concretely produced as the calling into question of the same by the other, that is, as the ethics that accomplishes the critical essence of knowledge. And as critique precedes dogmatism, metaphysics precedes ontology.[45]

By this, Levinas advances his own critique of Western philosophy in that the "reduction of the other to the same" governed the ways in which human beings were understood. The danger in this understanding is that the other is never embraced for the distinctive attributes they possess; rather, "the neutralization of the other who becomes a theme or an object—appearing, that is, taking its place in the light—is precisely his reduction to the same."[46] Levinas is not authoring a traditional ethics, but an ethics that undergirds philosophy.

I maintain that Levinas's thought is instructive for a Christian social ethics that appreciates the uniqueness of every individual fashioned in the *imago Dei*. In the case we have been discussing, Pastor Anderson treats every individual as though that person must conform to a particularized existence dictated by sameness. The sameness to which he relegates each individual is not simply bound by gender but also makes invisible the identity of each nonconforming individual such that they are reduced to nameless and faceless objects. This provides insight into Pastor Anderson's heartless and hurtful descriptions of LGBTQIA persons. In his totalizing treatment of their existence, LGBTQIA persons do not merit human or intersubjective relationality. As such, when he looked out into the congregation, Pastor Anderson did not *see* "the gays." He only saw a concept or an appearing that he negatively objectified. Levinasian intersubjective relationality functions to bring the face of the other into clear focus. Levinas made the very face of the other the site of meaning for the interchange between the one and the other. In simple terms, relationality is born of an appreciation for, an awakening by, and a compelling of the face of the other. According to Levinas, when you see the face of the other, that face beckons you "to do no harm."

Do No Harm

Theologian Stephen Ray admonishes the prophetic voice against "using a marginalizing cultural discourse (*Negro* pathology) to explain and rationalize a situation of oppression."[47] Ray cites theologian Reinhold Niebuhr's "discursive economies" with caution because the prophetic work addressing the social condition of the oppressed can so easily be tainted by implicit bias. Niebuhr's rhetoric actually induced condemnation as a result of how he characterized the plight of the oppressed.[48] Most notably, theologian James H. Cone said, "Niebuhr saw justice as a balance of power between groups, whether classes, races, or nations, he saw it always in a state of flux, never achieving perfection in history."[49] Niebuhr's realism drew criticism because it failed to directly confront oppression. Analogously, Ray's admonition is instructive in the critique of black church public theology, because it reminds preachers that there are consequences to espousing rhetoric that harms. Ray argues that "the continual debasement of a people by the imputation of some inescapable moral imperfection can result in assaults against their very survival if the liminal cultural space they inhabit is demonized and deemed expungable."[50] The treatment of LGBTQIA persons in the black preaching moment is an example of this phenomenon.

Most LGBTQIA persons who grew up in the church desire to "work out their soul's salvation" in the context of the black church. However, their "difference," in Ray's analysis, is seen "as defilement" by many in the church. As a result, they are demonized, named as "sinful," and put outside of the gate like the lepers.

> *Quincy:* I started having complications with my home church. And um, by this time, the pastor had said to me, "You can no longer preach here because of your theological stance and, um, your sexuality. You just can't; I just can't have you preach anymore." So, other pastors in the city started finding out; of course, preaching engagements went out the door.

Ray contends, and I agree, that this naming is itself the "sin" of "sin-talk."[51] Sin-talk for Ray is as much sinful for what it says as for what it fails to say but which "ought" to be said. Quincy faced this sin-talk and suffered immensely with disruptions in his God-given ministry. In his assessment of "the Jew" in Dietrich Bonhoeffer's "treatment of 'the Jewish Question,'" Ray notes that Bonhoeffer "essentializes Jewish difference." I make the same claim of Pastor Anderson's treatment of "the gays" in this sermon. The reduction of all LGBTQIA persons to criminals or animals proffers a racialized and gendered essentialism that mirrors the post-Civil War characterization of blacks as overly sexual beings. Just as "the Jewish presence was understood to be so corrosive that its very existence threatens the destruction of society," so Pastor Anderson frames the existence of "the gays" as a threat to "family values" and thus to the church and society.[52] This rhetoric obscures the good news of the gospel to LGBTQIA persons. Using Anderson's example, black church public theology therefore usurps the prophetic tradition that characterized the struggle for liberation in the mid-nineteenth to mid-twentieth centuries. Any black preacher who follows this ideology is complicit in the damage it causes. And, as Audre Lorde admonishes, "your silence will not protect you."[53] The words of James 3 are instructive. It reads in part, "not many of you should become preachers/teachers, my brothers and sisters, for you know that we who teach will face stricter judgment."[54] Preachers and teachers are cautioned by this passage to operate in wisdom and meekness. In that pericope successful ministry is described as a peaceable endeavor that resists the urge to curse people but rather hastens in blessing people. James characterizes the work of preacher and teachers as kind, merciful, and gracious. The ethos of such a ministry avoids falsehoods and seeks truth. Where black church public theology participates in "the cultural production of evil," its message of hate and condemnation causes some to flee to a safer space.[55]

> *Mara:* Definitely. But you know what, now this is the funny thing about the church, the church, especially back then, in the '70s and the '80s. So, men, gay men were more accepted, but because of their talents. They were accepted because of their talents. They could play, they could sing, they could direct, they could bring a church to their feet with song and so everybody overlooked the fact that they were gay. So, the women who were gay were not easily identified. Because they didn't come to church dressed like they do now. They dressed like women. Like, if you met me on the street, today, you would probably never say oh, she's a lesbian, because that's not what I present. Not that I wouldn't, but that's not how I present myself. This is what I had to come to realize going back to my scripture: No matter what anybody preaches from a pulpit, no matter what anybody says to me about my sexuality, no matter how people feel about me being a lesbian, He made me. God made me. He made me. And He knew. And, I don't think He is going to send me to hell because I'm loving somebody, be it man, woman, whatever.

However, if "culture" can produce evil, it can also produce good. As the survey responses collected during my research demonstrate, there are black churches that do not speak dangerously at all on the issue of sexuality and there are others that do not speak negatively against LGBTQIA persons with messages of hopelessness and doom. And, just as importantly, there are black preachers who are shifting their rhetoric. For instance, Quincy talked about his experience with the megachurch pastor E. Dewey Smith, who was initially quite hostile toward LGBTQIA people.

> *Quincy:* I graduated Wilberforce 2007, and I started attending Emory University in Atlanta, Candler School of Theology. So, here I was in this mega city, didn't know anyone, and it was just like beautiful men everywhere, and it was just like, "I'm in heaven" [*laughing*]. I hit the jackpot uh, and so, um, I started meeting people and still on the down-low or closeted you know, because I attended a ministry, "House of Hope," where Pastor Dr. E. Dewey Smith is the pastor and, uh, was there from 2007 to 2010. Well, to fast forward a few years in 2010 I started having a theological shift, I started having a sexual orientation shift, and what I mean by that is I started feeling like I can no longer deny who I am as a gay person, as a Christian man, and as a clergy person. And so, I remember Dewey standing one time and preaching a message, and it was around healthcare reform. I remember him making a statement concerning the health of men. And, I remember him saying that men need to go get checked out, and you know, have a doctor stick his hand up your rectum. And uh, I remember, you know, people kinda looking like "what?" And then, of course, that led to him stating the next statement, which was "well, unless you like it." So, then, that just down spiraled to homosexuality. So, I remember my head spinning, and I remember asking myself questions or raising questions around who give or who gave you the authority to make these types of statements. "Who is it that gave you the authority to condemn those of us who are gay?"

Since Quincy's time in Georgia with Pastor Smith, Smith's rhetoric has changed significantly. Smith moved closer to the margin in a message he preached at the Mt. Calvary Holy Church, the church pastored by Bishop and Lady Owens mentioned in Chapter 2. Smith's message made clear that "you can't evangelize and antagonize at the same time," referring to how Christians should respond to people with "sexual identity problems."[56] While sexual identity is identified here as a "problem," the pastor's theological reassessment is much less harsh. The spiritual shift in his message is born of divine intervention.

In the words of Howard Thurman: "The movement of the Spirit of God in the hearts of men often calls them to act against the spirit of their times or causes them to anticipate a spirit which is yet in the making. In a moment of dedication, they are given wisdom and courage to dare a deed that challenges and to kindle a hope that inspires."[57] In fact, a small percentage of the respondents in my research study felt loved and affirmed in their church. The experiences of the much larger percentage of respondents, however, point to a need for a new theo-ethical philosophical paradigm. The deeply embedded tendency toward homophobic theology is evident in the writings of twentieth-century theologians.[58] Quite possibly, the popular phrase "God loves the sinner but hates the sin" emanates from a protracted history of homophobia within Western theology.[59] The root cause of the vitriolic rhetoric promoted by the preachers examined herein can be deconstructed through spiritual and wholistic practices that engender growth and maturity. I argue for a queer theo-ethical philosophy moored to intersubjective relationality. Relying upon an ethical mandate while concomitantly dislodging the spirit to flow freely through the prisms of human materiality, Levinas points the way forward for healing and restoration of those who have endured violent rhetoric. Intersubjective relationality presupposes an exchange between human beings that fundamentally regards the humanity of the other. That regard not only accepts another's humanity, but it also vows to do no harm, according to Levinas and Ray. When this theo-philosophical ideal is at work, there is no human constitution—male, female, gay, straight, queer—through which the Spirit of God will not flow.

In this chapter, I reviewed the formation of whiteface mimesis in the social process of blacks in general and black preachers in particular navigating the relative ideological war. Beginning with W. E. B. Du Bois, I characterized the tensions along the path toward freedom for blacks in light of the need for racial uplift and freedom from tyrannical lynching, segregation, and other racist tactics in order to highlight the necessity for historical contextualization of a womanist black public theology that centers black LGBTQIA worth and dignity. Using Pastor Terry K. Anderson as an exemplar, I connected the internalized whiteface mimesis with black church public theology. Next, I analyzed the impact of whiteface mimesis on LGBTQIA persons during the preaching moment. Informed by Audre Lorde, Luce Irigaray, Stephen Ray, and Emmanuel Levinas as theorists, I expanded the notion of intersubjectivity to include the face of the other giving deference to difference. Finally, I called for prophetic voices to combat the attack on the poor and the oppressed and specifically demonstrated the ethical and philosophical imperative to do no harm, especially from the pulpit. Through my interviewees, I demonstrated the spiritual conundrum created by violent rhetoric and simultaneously provided examples from their truth-telling that helps LGBTQIA persons embrace the *imago Dei*. The impact of rhetorical violence leveled against LGBTQIA persons from the black bully pulpit is more deeply explored in the final chapter.

Notes

1 W. E. B. Du Bois, *The Souls of Black Folk* (Chicago, IL: A. C. McClurg, 1903), https://www.bartleby.com/114/ (accessed July 5, 2024).
2 James 1:8 (NIV).
3 Frederick Douglas, "The Color Line," *North American Review*, 1881. The phrase was made famous by W. E. B. DuBois in *The Souls of Black Folks*.

4 Painter, *History of White People*, 65.
5 Ibid., 65–66, 191.
6 Audre Lorde, "A Litany for Survival," in *The Black Unicorn: Poems by Audre Lorde* (New York: W. W. Norton, 1978), 31–32.
7 Ibid.
8 I coined the phrase "holy anger" from Ephesians 4:26 (NRSV).
9 Audre Lorde, *Need: A Chorale for Black Woman Voices* (New York: Kitchen Table, Women of Color Press, 1990), 5.
10 Ibid.
11 Ibid., 5–6.
12 "Cascading violence" is a phrase used by Dr. Marsha Foster Boyd in the tenth anniversary C. Shelby Rooks lecture at Chicago Theological Seminary on October 17, 2017. Dr. Boyd used the term to characterize the phenomenon of violence against black bodies.
13 Lorde, *Need*, 10–11.
14 Butler, *Frames of War*, 42–43.
15 Rev. Jesse Peterson interviewed by *Tea Partier*, https://www.youtube.com/watch?v=430ijbr2bNE (accessed December 9, 2016).
16 Further information about Peterson can be found in Chapter 2 of this book.
17 Mark Lamont Hill and Cornel West, interview, "Fox News vs. Black Lives Matter," on *CNN's Reliable Sources*, September 6, 2015, https://cnnpressroom.blogs.cnn.com/2015/09/06/marc-lamont-hill-on-fox-news-narrative-of-black-lives-matter-its-very-different-than-the-narrative-they-had-when-the-tea-party-had-people-with-racist-signs-and-had-obama-looking-like-a-monke/ (accessed July 5, 2024).
18 Frantz Fanon, *The Wretched of the Earth*, trans. Richard Philcox (New York: Grove, 1963), 51–52.
19 Frantz Fanon, *Black Skin, White Masks,* trans. Richard Philcox (New York: Grove, 2008), vii.
20 Lilly Grove Missionary Baptist Church, "Financial Statement Notes and Clerks Report," May 31, 2021, https://www.lillygrove.org/images/uploads/May_31_2021-YTD__Financial_Statements.pdf (accessed March 5, 2024).
21 The relevant portion of the sermon was published on YouTube by lillygrovembc on April 15, 2012, though the video is no longer available on the platform.
22 See my full transcription in Appendix B.
23 See my full transcription in Appendix B.
24 Amos 5:24.
25 I acknowledge that gender is a contested category among queer theorists. See Judith Butler, *Gender Trouble: Feminism and the Subversion of Identity* (New York: Routledge, 1990); Butler, *Bodies That Matter: On the Discursive Limits of "Sex"* (New York: Routledge, 1993); and Butler, *Undoing Gender* (New York: Routledge, 2005). See also Melissa M. Wilcox, *Queer Women*

and Religious Individualism (Bloomington, IN: Indiana University Press, 2009); and Wilcox *Queer Religiosities: An Introduction to Queer and Transgender Studies in Religion* (Lanham, MD: Rowman and Littlefield, 2020).

26 This trope is dealt with more explicitly by Derrick Bell, "The Rules of Racial Standing," in *Faces at the Bottom of the Well: The Permanence of Racism* (New York: Basic Books, 1992), 109–26; and later by Michael Eric Dyson, *Race Rules: Navigating the Color Line* (New York: Vintage, 1997), 84.

27 "What Must the Church Do about Same Sex Marriage? (Matthew 13:24–30)—Rev. Terry K. Anderson," posted by Lilly Grove Missionary Baptist Church, YouTube, April 15, 2012, https://youtu.be/SfpVPydcNrQ?si=vNSGwGUSjG7re_ja</> (accessed July 5, 2024).

28 In many respects Pastor Anderson's verbiage confirms an explanation offered by Butler in *Gender Trouble*, in a section entitled "The Compulsory Order of Sex/Gender/Desire," where she states, "The presumption of a binary gender system implicitly retains belief in a mimetic relation of gender to sex whereby gender mirrors sex or is otherwise restricted by it" (10).

29 Patterson, *Slavery and Social Death*, 37. Symbols in this context take on worshipful religious meaning.

30 For an edited volume on the dangers of conversion therapies, see Douglas C. Haldeman, ed., *The Case against Conversion "Therapy": Evidence, Ethics, and Alternatives* (Washington, DC: American Psychological Association, 2022).

31 René Girard, *The Scapegoat*, trans. Yvonne Freccero (Baltimore, MD: Johns Hopkins University Press, 1986), 103.

32 JoAnne Marie Terrell, *Power in the Blood? The Cross in the African American Experience* (Maryknoll, NY: Orbis, 1998), 19. See also Renita J. Weems, "The Hebrew Women Are Not Like the Egyptian Women: The Ideology of Race, Gender and Sexual Reproduction in Exodus 1," in *Ideological Criticism of Biblical Texts* (Atlanta, GA: Scholars Press, 1982); Christian Eberhardt, *The Sacrifice of Jesus: Understanding Atonement Biblically* (Eugene, OR: Wipf and Stock, 2018); and Eugene F. Rogers Jr., *Blood Theology: Seeing Red in Body- and God-Talk* (Cambridge, UK: Cambridge University Press, 2021).

33 "Sacrifice is perhaps the most evident element of reconciliation with God in Israelite temples. Although the Bible records the sacrifices that two of Adam and Eve's children offer, the Bible does not directly record Adam and Eve ever having offered sacrifice. There is, however, an indirect mention of what could have been a sacrifice by Adam and Eve, as well as ample extra-biblical traditions supporting the notion that the offering of sacrifice began with Adam and Eve. One hint that the Bible gives concerning sacrifice and Adam and Eve is the coats of skins given to them by God. The coats of skins most likely came from a sacrifice that would have been offered immediately after, or as part of, their expulsion from the Garden. This sacrifice must have been offered either by Adam, or by the Lord." James L. Carroll, "The Reconciliation of Adam and Israelite Temples," *Studia Antiqua* 3, no. 1 (2003): 89, https://scholarsarchive.byu.edu/studiaantiqua/vol3/iss1/8 (accessed July 5, 2024).

34 JoAnn Marie Terrell, Lecture in TECH510, Womanist and Feminist Christology, Chicago Theological Seminary, May 8, 2013.

35 Hebrews 9 (NIV).
36 John 1:29–32 (NIV).
37 JoAnne Marie Terrell, "Blut/Menstruation (Blood/Menstruation)," in *Worterbuch der Feministischen Theologie*, ed. Elisabeth Gössmann (Gutersloh: Gutersloher Verslaghaus, 2002), 89–91.
38 Kelly Brown Douglas, *The Black Christ* (New York: Orbis, 1999), 111, quoting from Richard A. Norris, trans. and ed., *The Christological Controversy* (Philadelphia: Fortress, 1980), 3.
39 Douglas, *Black Christ*, 113.
40 Sean Hand, ed., *The Levinas Reader* (Oxford: Basil Blackwell, 1989), 75–88.
41 Levinas, *Totality and Infinity*, 183.
42 Ibid.
43 Levinas, *Totality and Infinity*, 220.
44 Ibid., 42.
45 Ibid., 43.
46 Ibid.
47 Stephen G. Ray, Jr., *Do No Harm: Social sin and Christian Responsibility* (Fortress Press: MN, 2002).
48 Ray, *Do No Harm*, 75.
49 James H. Cone, *The Cross and the Lynching Tree* (Maryknoll, NY: Orbis, 2011), ch. 2.
50 Ibid., 74.
51 Ray, *Do No Harm*, 24. Ray borrows this phraseology from a personal conversation he had with Serene Jones, the former president of the American Academy of Religion.
52 Ray, *Do No Harm*, 78, 81.
53 Lorde, *Sister Outsider*, 41.
54 James 3 (NRSV).
55 Townes, *Womanist Ethics*, 159.
56 L. Dewey Smith at Greater Mt. Calvary Holy Church, YouTube, https://youtu.be/a0UfBD5Tuuk (accessed December 24, 2016). It should also be noted that through the work of organizations like Many Voices, "A Black Church Movement for Gay and Transgender Justice" situated in Washington, D.C., black clergy have begun to embrace a more inclusive message. See www.manyvoices.org</URI> (accessed July 5, 2024).
57 Howard Thurman, *Footprints of a Dream: The Story of the Church for the Fellowship of All Peoples* (Eugene, OR: Wipf and Stock, 2009), 7.
58 James B. Nelson's claim points to Karl Barth's homophobia as he discusses four possible theological stances toward homosexuality: (1) a rejecting-punitive position, which bears a punitive attitude toward homosexual persons, (2) a rejecting-nonpunitive stance, (3) qualified acceptance, and (4) full acceptance. Barth adopted the second stance, rejecting-nonpunitive, in his *Church Dogmatics*, which claims that because humanity is "fellow-humanity," the

same-sex arrangement is "physical, psychological and social sickness, the phenomenon of perversion, decadence and decay." This Barth described as idolatry. Despite Barth's obvious prejudice, Nelson notes, he "hastens to add the central theme of the gospel is God's overwhelming grace in Jesus Christ. Hence homosexuality must be condemned, but the homosexual *person* must not." James B. Nelson, "Homosexuality and the Church," *Christianity and Crisis*, April 4, 1977, 63–69.

59 Nelson, "Homosexuality and the Church," 63–69. Nelson refers to Karl Barth, "The Command of God the Creator," in *The Doctrine of Creation*, vol. 3, part 4, of *Church Dogmatics*: "From the refusal to recognise God there follows the failure to appreciate man, and thus humanity without the fellow-man (CD, III, 2, p. 229 ff.). And since humanity as fellow-humanity is to be understood in its root as the togetherness of man and woman, as the root of this inhumanity there follows the ideal of masculinity free from woman and a femininity free from man. And because nature or the Creator of nature will not be trifled with, because the despised fellow-man is still there, because the natural orientation on him is still in force, there follows the corrupt emotional and finally physical desire in which—in a sexual union which is not and cannot be genuine—man thinks that he must seek and can find in man, and woman in woman, a substitute for the despised partner."

4

"Wounded Healers" Wound People

Theological Foundations of Black Preaching: The Slave Catechism

Adriana Cavarero, an Italian feminist philosopher, offers an important analysis of the "Word," or *logos*, that informs my conceptualization of sermonic speech acts. Cavarero distinguishes between the word as speech and the "Word" as voice. She notes:

> For the most ancient phase of the Hebrew religion, God is voice, or also breath, not speech. Speech, according to the ritual formula "word of God," is what God becomes through the prophets who lend him their mouths, in such a way that the divine *qol* is made articulate language, or the language of Israel. The prophet "does not make God speak, but at the moment in which he opens his mouth, God speaks." The word of God thus makes itself "perceptible in the *medium* of human language."[1]

To the extent that a messenger, purporting to speak for God, substitutes his or her own speech in the place of God's voice, the message becomes distorted and no longer represents "a Word from the Lord."[2] Rather, it simply becomes a word from the messenger, whose prejudices and myopic views influence the hearer in ways that are not "God's ways."[3]

Proclamation is an essential key to believing. This is made evident in Apostle Paul's letter to the Romans, which emphasizes the importance of the preacher in shaping the faith of the believer:

> For, "Everyone who calls on the name of the Lord shall be saved." But how are they to call on one in whom they have not believed? And how are they to believe in one of whom they have never heard? And how are

they to hear without someone to proclaim him? And how are they to proclaim him unless they are sent? As it is written, "How beautiful are the feet of those who bring good news!"[4]

Interestingly, cultivating an ear to hear the "good news" depends, in large measure, on the message and the messenger. In the "Great Commission" (Matthew 28:18–20), the church is charged with a precise mission: to spread the good news. This good news is invariably disseminated through culturally specific reasoning and interpretation of Scripture. The culture that influenced the black church in North America is a complex of intermingled ideologies adapted from centuries of domination, mimicry, archetypal repression, patriarchal hegemony, and idolatry too often deceptively disguised, in part, as a worshipful fulfillment of the depth and meaning of the Great Commission. But I wish to appeal to a critical, independent mindset that operates with courageous discernment to speak truth to power in these religious settings.

Bible scholar Mitzi J. Smith offers an understanding of how the Great Commission, or *missio dei*, was understood in the nineteenth century.[5] She notes that missionaries saw their responsibility to teach, preach, and convert the "poor," "heathen," "brutish," or "savage" "Negroes, or African slaves," whom they *othered*. They strategically used the Bible to reinforce and sustain a message of domination over the enslaved with social constraints that ensured docility and conformity. These Southern slaves were largely missionized to accept an inferior status and to revere their masters, and a system of laws instantiated this hierarchy. The mission field became the crucible through which a certain Christian conservatism formed among the slaves. The twenty-first-century remnants of that Christian conservatism are evident in the rhetoric of some black preaching and teaching when it promotes a hate-filled homophobia. Smith further explains how "white missionaries and slave masters, from an overwhelming desire to preserve the institution of slavery, theologically and rhetorically conceptualized and taught the slave to understand himself as a dichotomous being with a soul to be saved and a body to be enslaved, thereby inflicting trauma on his *psyche*."[6] She uses the slave catechisms as evidence of this point.

> Slave catechisms served as a vehicle for converting slaves to the Christian faith. They were designed for oral instruction since it was forbidden to teach slaves to read, by law or in practice, in most southern states. The instructor or catechist of the slave student (the catechumen) was ideally the slave master or someone sanctioned by him, such as his overseer, his wife or children, a hired white preacher or missionary, and in rare cases, a black man with an exceptional gift unspoiled by a meticulous sense of and contentment with his place in slave society.[7]

As a tradition in black church public theology, catechesis is still a prevalent practice in the ordination of ministers in many contemporary evangelical black church traditions. It serves the same purpose as it did in the nineteenth century to ensure that the proper message is pronounced and that the minister holds a strict understanding of the Scriptures that does not deviate from what was taught by previous generations. The catechizers usually give the preacher material to study for several weeks, and the catechumen is expected to regurgitate that content before an audience who looks on as the process unfolds. When the catechizer is convinced that the person being catechized is ready for ordination, they are said to have passed the catechism. This affords the newly catechized the opportunity to go and spread the "good news" on behalf of the church.

The "good news" in the Gospels of Matthew and Mark proclaims that Jesus's finished work on the cross liberates believers and covers them from the punishment of "sin." In contrast, black public theology often highlights the presence of sin rather than freedom from the effects of "sin."[8] As a consequence, there is a slavish commitment to identify what is or is not "sinful" behavior and then to condemn that behavior. In this problematic framework, sin is attached to LGBTQIA people, defined in terms of nonheterosexual or same-gender human sexual orientation and behavior that, according to this distorted expression of black public theology, causes the human subject to be separated from God and condemned to hell. Freedom from "sin," which is the indelible good news, is lost in translation. The process of liberation has been converted to a ball and chain for those whose lives and behaviors have been categorized by humans as "sinful." This is a theological fallacy, which I seek to critique.

The Challenge of Personal Identity

Tadhi's narrative helps us understand how to embrace a personal identity that goes against the norm. Tadhi's childhood experiences growing up in a religious family, the product of a teenage pregnancy, provide him with a unique perspective on how the natural visibility of one's sexual identity is suppressed when loved ones operate in a protective mode. The protective mode is the veil that often covers hate-talk. It is the shroud that makes an aura of protection the license to condemn people to hell. This testimony reveals how damaging it can be when someone's authenticity, their truth about themselves, is dismissed under the guide of protecting them.

> *Tadhi:* I just don't buy that a person doesn't know one's sexuality. Even if it's your mom or your grandmother, there must be some kind of "I wonder?" But, because of our faith tradition typically that denigrates people, no one wants their loved one to be denigrated and, uh, abashed. And so, um, you know, there is just that sense in which, you know, the structure of the church, a small congregation, everyone knew everyone's business in some ways, at least those things that, unlike sexuality, there's just certain things you wouldn't even talk about in the church. But, you

know, my mom was a teenage ... had me when she was young ... so she conceived me when she was sixteen, had me when she was seventeen. And so, there is just a lot there. You don't discuss sexuality, but yet it's in your face. And, um, you know, I think that too has to do with a sense of what it means to not want one's ... not to desire a loved one to suffer in the world, dominant world, trying to orchestrate and trying to map scripture onto a kind of, you know ... political text, uh, corporate text that says my son or my daughter is equally positioned to take on the world. Um, but the moment sexuality gets thrown in there, it can be a problematic, especially if it's, you know, same-sex or the Quare terminology I use, you know.

Tadhi points to the interconnection between the church and state that seems to drive the discourse, or more accurately the lack of discourse, on sexuality in black church theology. There is an ever present sense of legalism, which operates to rigidly enforce particular interpretations of biblical texts without context or interrogation. The ostensible goal is to be "right" or to "protect" those being condemned so as to prevent their suffering in the future. Tadhi's naming of the "black hermeneutic of poverty" also asserts that the cycle of poverty is perpetuated by the way the "state apparatus" rewards the Black community with that which simulates success but which is, in fact, carefully designed social conditioning. The irony is that the church functions as the progenitor of this hermeneutic.

Tadhi: Um, so, until I was sixteen, or actually seventeen, I was a part of that church. I was very much a part of teaching vacation Bible school, I read the scripture, I learned all of the books of the Bible, the King James Version, of course; didn't really we were very, very traditional in a very pattern of reading scripture in a kind of black hermeneutic of poverty—a black hermeneutic of poverty of understanding that even though you lived in poverty, the place you cohabited, which was Community Arms Apartments, which the church actually was a part of founding the place, uh, through a contract through the State of California. And so, you had all of these interesting ways in which, you know, it was political to not say things in church, but yet you were receiving government funds for your church and then the apartment complex you lived in was a part of the church and, um, so ... and the housing ... the development piece was beautiful, I mean it was landscaped every day. I remember coming out of the apartment complex, I didn't know I was poor. I mean we had what would be gardeners every single day of the week. I'd wake up to the sound of lawn mowers knowing that the landscape was going to be beautiful and, you know, we had clean clothes ... fresh ... we ate ... there was the Coleman James Learning Center filled with the summer youth employment program. My grandmother, who was a part of Community Baptist Church, she ran the summer employment program, employing, um, teenagers across, you know, the San Gabriel Valley. There had to be at least, I would say anywhere between fifty and one hundred students, I call them, right, going to, um, different places for professional development. I learned how to type or improve my typing; I learned secretarial skills.

On its face, Tadhi's environment seemed ideal. Under the surface there was a concerted effort on the part of his immediate family, his church family, and his community to suppress the reality of life in poverty. Consequently, under the canopy of poverty, the uniqueness of one's sexual difference was subsumed in the larger picture of gaining basic skills to survive. Contextually, one had to conform to the minimal norms that provided a way out and avoid standing out as a unique individual.

Theological Fault Lines

From its inception, black preaching traditions have exhibited clear lines of demarcation that reflect the origins of the rhetoric critiqued in this work. The theology that guided black preaching coming out of slavery was influenced by two primary modes of communication: (a) conformity and (b) contempt. Some conformed to the plantation mentality, embellishing that basic line of reasoning over the centuries to hold people in bondage, valuing men over women and relegating "others" to a place outside the safety of God's reach. Others held contempt for plantation efforts to control the message of the Bible and to relegate enslaved Africans to a place of inferiority; this group has evolved to recognize the importance of a theology of inclusion, acceptance, and love for all of God's people.

In 1995, Chicago-based United Church of Christ pastor-scholar Jeremiah A. Wright published a sermon titled "Good News for Homosexuals" in *Good News! Sermons of Hope for Today's Families*, and that sermon inspires the framing of this argument. Wright's vision of hope gave voice to sentiments that were quite unpopular during that era. He outlined arguments from the biological, psychological, biblical, and theological realms to conclude that the *missio dei* is about "good news" that brings hope to all of humanity from a God who "loves the world." Wright laments, "I have been the ministerial outcast among many of my colleagues for some fifteen years because I refuse to believe that my God loves only some of his world." In effect, Wright refuses to be boxed into biblical interpretations that limit the love of God. In so doing, Wright also critiques the preaching culture, which does engage in such delimited preaching. As he explains, "Culture is often wrong. Culture was wrong about slavery. Culture was wrong about women. Culture was wrong about Africans and Indians, and culture was wrong about Christ. I refuse to limit my God, to lock God into little cultural prisons, no matter how comfortable those prisons may feel."[9] Dr. Wright's position amplifies the message of the interviewees presented thus far. Culture has adjudged these

LGBTQIA men and women wrongly. As such, there has been an erosion of the faith of our ancestors, most of whom understood how God values God's "good" creation, God's humanity, and who stood up for the dignity of all against oppressive and repressive regimes.

The Psychological Impact of Slavery on Black Church Public Theology

In the early 1980s, psychologist Reginald L. Jones edited a volume, *Black Psychology*, in which leading black psychologists helped to shape the field of racial identity studies in psychology. In 1991, the second edition was published; in it, black psychologists deduced the need to use an Africentric perspective when counseling black people. The contributors in that second volume leaned heavily upon Africentrism—the influence of Africa and African cultures, ideas, and worldviews on the attitudes and behaviors of black people. Racial identity within the context of Western knowledge production was deemed insufficient to characterize black people.[10] Na'im Akbar was a contributor to the third edition of that volume. His contribution to the idea of Africentrism in psychology focuses on developing mechanisms for deconstructing ideological holds on one's capacity to freely think and be.

Na'im Akbar's *Breaking the Chains of Psychological Slavery* argues that the period of enslavement of African people left a psychological wound. Akbar observes that individual behavior can be "influenced by collective factors, which are historically remote."[11] He claims that "a full appreciation of the uniqueness of people can emerge from an appreciation of such factors." With this, Akbar suggests that data demonstrate the impact of the extended, universal suffering of enslaved Africans. Akbar then looks at religious imagery dominated by white perspectives to decipher the impact of slavery and the extent to which religion shapes one's worldview. He concludes there are myriad ways that these influences have shaped African Americans' worldviews, with the overwhelming impact being the "damaging influence on the psychological and spiritual development of human beings."[12] Supporting this contention is Akbar's belief that during slavery whites sought to give the Divine androcentric features resembling themselves. This caused some enslaved Africans to worship white people.

Akbar contends that the psycho-social functioning of some African Americans is directly attributable to this pseudo-spiritual indoctrination. I do not mean to suggest that this acceptance of white indoctrination was born of rational thought so much as it was deemed a rational choice given the circumstances. Popular culture offers demonstrable proof of this. For example, in *Roots: The Next Generation* (1979), LeVar Burton, playing the young Kunta Kinte, is asked his name by the overseer. He repeatedly replies "Kunta Kinte," and each response is met with the crack of a whip against his back, lashes leveled by his fellow enslaved African at the command of the overseer. However, at some point in the ferocious beating, once his back is filleted like the lattice top on a fruit pie, he realizes that saying his name is "Toby," the name his "mistress" chose for him, will stop the beating.[13] Saying his name is "Toby" did not mean that it was his name, but just that he understood that saying so would make the beating stop. This kind of experience was all too common for enslaved people.[14] Likewise, some speech acts are not spoken because the speaker believes them but because the utterance alone signifies alignment with the oppressor. Similarly, some of the enslaved Africans embraced the slave catechism wholesale.[15] They saw it as a rational understanding of the Bible based on what was presented to them by slaveholders through select itinerant preachers and missionaries sent to the plantations to Christianize enslaved Africans. Others simply said what it took to alleviate oppression. The number of enslaved Africans given permission to preach on the plantations is evidence of this. In some instances, they preached to mixed audiences of both blacks and whites because the message they promoted had been approved by the plantation owners as sufficiently effective in achieving its ultimate goal: to save the soul and keep the body in bondage.[16]

There is a nexus between enslaved Africans' pseudo-spiritual indoctrination and black church public theology in which LGBTQIA persons are vilified. Those enslaved Africans who denounced the slaveholders' Christian-inspired control mechanisms rebelled against white domination. The extent to which the rhetoric of the black preaching tradition differs in tenor and tone from the prophetic voice can be traced to the ill effects of indoctrination on the black psyche. Engaging the notion of racecraft, described as an "invisible ontology" akin to witchcraft that refers to "mental terrain" and "pervasive belief," the ideology of indoctrination takes on a magical quality through spiritual activity.[17]

Akbar contends that slavery was so intense and prolonged, spanning three centuries, that its aftermath can still easily be felt almost 160 years since its legal abolition.[18] The level of vitriolic rhetoric, violence, and total depravity with which many people were treated has a lingering and identifiable effect on the collective psyche of the formerly enslaved Africans and their progeny. For Akbar, the identifiable mannerisms are clown-like behavior, parroting speech, internalized inferiority, color discrimination, and community division.[19] More importantly, the scars of prolonged mental bondage over the course of three centuries often interrupt human flourishing. Wounded people wound people.

Historically, there is a definite correlation between psychological bondage and physical bondage as well. The physical violence and the mental violence endured by enslaved Africans, according to Akbar, are equally devastating:

> As cruel and painful as chattel slavery was, it could be exceeded only by a worse form of slavery. The slavery that captures the mind and imprisons

the motivation, perception, aspiration and identity in a web of anti-self images, generating a personal and collective self-destruction, is more cruel than the shackles on the wrists and ankles. The slavery that feeds on the mind, invading the soul of man, destroying his loyalties to himself and establishing allegiance to forces which destroy him, is an even worse form of capture. The influences that permit an illusion of freedom, liberation, and self-determination, while tenaciously holding one's mind in subjugation, is the folly of only the sadistic.[20]

The cruelty described is responsible for producing in the enslaved a self-loathing that leads to divisive behavior. I am focused specifically on the divisiveness within black preaching where LGBTQIA persons are consistently mocked, derided, and condemned from the pulpit. The concept of *mind slavery* signifies an existential reality where some persons are disparaged and outcast to preserve the purity of others.

Black bully pulpit preachers tend to denigrate LGBTQIA persons as diseased because of their personal dis-ease in the presence of LBGTQIA persons. They ridicule LGBTQIA persons from the pulpit and make hurtful remarks that make LGBTQIA persons cry out, in effect, that they are "unclean." LGBTQIA persons are treated as outcasts in black church public theology. For instance, in 2014 a young male attending a Church of God in Christ (COGIC) worship service appeared in a YouTube video. The scene begins with the preacher urging the congregants who are gathered at the front of the meeting hall, saying, "He is delivering you now, whatever it is you need God to do, He just told you it's done right now." At the altar, the preacher says to the gathered, "Anything you ask God to do, God says it is done." The young man is asked by the preacher, "What did you come here for, what did you come down here for, what do you want God to do for you?" The young man replies, "To get delivered more." One can only presume that his first "deliverance" did not take. The preacher then asks the young man to "turn around and tell those people." Whereupon the young man takes the microphone handed to him, turns to face the congregation, and denounces his "homosexual lifestyle." He shouts a decided pronouncement, which crescendos to the top of his voice: "I am not gay no more, I am delivered, I don't like mens no more, I said I like womens, womens, womens, womens … I am not gay, I will not date a man, I will not carry a purse, I will not put on makeup. I will, I will love a women [*sic*]."[21] This is done in the face of browbeating preaching that required the man to make these declarations to the congregation while the preacher exhorted him to "come out from among them" and "break every yoke." Here, the leprosy effect distinguishes those who are worthy to be in the camp from those who are unworthy. Only those who denounce homosexuality or "uncleanness" can enter the ark of God's safety.

Akbar refers to "the ghost of the plantation," a phrase he borrowed from speeches by Warith Deen Mohammed, a prominent black Muslim imam.[22] This ghost haunts the psychological and social processes of African

Americans, particularly that brand of black church pubic theology that holds as sacred the "master's" account of God, sin, and acceptance. These theological foundations of "the faith," when mimicked from an enslaved mentality, are like the "overseer" cracking the whip on those who refuse to be a "good slave for master."[23]

In the King James Bible, the version used principally by those laboring under *mind slavery*, based on my fifty years of observation, the term "master" refers to Jesus Christ. Similarly, slave owners required enslaved Africans to refer to them as "masters," and the person in charge of the slaves for the day-to-day operation of the plantation was known as the "overseer." In the COGIC structure, and perhaps in others, one of the official offices is that of the "overseer." These are simple examples of how the conditioning of the mind by white people led some enslaved Africans to see so-called "masters" and "overseers" as "God," a model that has continued in transmuted form in black church public theology.[24] Mara's reflection, mentioned above, on her experience in the 1970s and 1980s mirrors my own.

Mara's sense of connection to God flows from her own understanding of a God who made her in God's image. Her own identity sustains her capacity to identify and to be identified. This takes on a dimension of independence that creates space for her spiritual growth. Remaining in an environment that fails to foster one's spiritual growth is useless.

Homophobia in Muslim Faith Traditions

Citing Islam as a basis for his act, Omar Mateen, the shooter in the June 16, 2016 Pulse nightclub massacre, who killed 49 people and wounded 53 others, allegedly also struggled with his own sexual identity.[25] Arguably, Mateen may have been suspended emotionally between acting out a hate forcefully nurtured by a radical, violent interpretation of Islamic religious doctrine and law. Hate-filled religious rhetoric toward the LGBTQIA community was spoken by Sheikh Farrokh Sekaleshfar, an imam and Muslim scholar, at the Husseini Islamic Center near Orlando, Florida, days before Mateen's attack. Visiting from Iran, the imam, whose speech was video-recorded, stated, "Death is the sentence, I mean look, it's nothing to be embarrassed about this. Death is the sentence, but we have to have that compassion for people. With homosexuals, it's the same. Out of compassion for them, let's get rid of them now."[26] This imam is calling for LGBTQIA genocide.

One California pastor, Roger Jimenez, actually condoned the Pulse Nightclub massacre in his sermon the Sunday morning of the murders at Verity Baptist Church in Sacramento, California:

> As a Christian we shouldn't be sad at the death of fifty sodomites ... because the Bible teaches that the sodomites are all, every single one of them, a predator ... Are you sad that fifty pedophiles were killed today?

"Um, no, I think that's great. I, I, I think it helps society, you know, Orlando, Florida, is a little safer tonight ... You know, the tragedy is that more of them didn't die ... You know ... I'm kind of upset that he didn't finish the job!" Because these people are predators, they are abusers, they take advantage of people, and look, as Christians we need to take the stand that it is not our job to sit there and say "oh, this is a tragedy," or "oh, this is something we mourn." Look, the Bible paints the picture that these are wicked people; these are evil people ... Why would I try to reach someone that God has given up on? ... If we lived in a righteous nation, with a righteous government, then the government *should* be taking them. There's no tragedy. I, I wish the government would round them all up, put them up against a firing wall, put a firing squad in front of them and blow their brains out. If we lived in a righteous government that loved God and loved children and wanted to protect them, that's what we'd do.[27]

Dangerously engaging what mirrors the ideology of genocide, it comes as close as any rhetoric in the postmodern era to calling for a version of "ethnic cleansing." Coupled with the religious Right's agenda that is actively pursuing a "Christian America" and the power nodes in Washington, DC, that are boasting of political control over every branch of government, this message advocates *death squads*. "Firing walls" and "firing squads," rounding up undesirables, and "finishing the job," all in the name of God, are the currency of a sinister theocracy. If history is a witness, what happened to the Jews in the Shoah could be on the horizon for LGBTQIA persons in America.[28]

All over the world there are imams, preachers, pastors, priests, and clerics who follow this irrational line of thinking and thereby incite people to commit horrific crimes against LGBTQIA persons. Talk show host and MSNBC news commentator Rachel Maddow hosted David Bahati, the Ugandan lawmaker who went so far as to sponsor a "Kill the Gays" bill in October 2008. Bahati is also a member of The Family, a US-based antigay Christian fundamentalist group. In his role as member of parliament in Uganda, he sponsored the bill calling for life imprisonment for any homosexual and the death penalty for "aggravated homosexuality." He said the bill stemmed from his deep desire to "protect the children." Maddow opened the show with a reference to the "slippery slope" fallacy to guide her listeners through the destruction that such irrational thinking breeds. In the aftermath of so much insidious rhetoric on the global stage, the LGBTQIA community is under constant attack, both mentally and physically, around the world. Bahati's legislation is a direct result of American "Christian" missionizing in Uganda.[29] The danger of such ungodly rhetoric is that someone would actually be killed simply because they are gay. Nevertheless, utter shock came when several pastors either preached on the Sunday morning after the attack or took to YouTube upon learning of the tragedy to record videos celebrating the murders and lamenting that the attack might be used to support gun control measures.

Spiritual renewal is spawned in each individual when a step is made toward reordering the symbiosis of mind, body, and spirit. When mind, body, and spirit are perceived as one, the binaries that dominate Western thinking fall away. One is at once a living, breathing cocreator with the Divine. Restoration is achieved when with every breath one is reminded that it is the breath of life without which one cannot live. That connection to life is the Divine. I assert that wholeness in mind, body, and spirit results in the projection of God-ness in the face of every living being. This axiom was never more prominent than when I interviewed three lesbians of the Muslim faith. I met all three in Chicago while I was matriculating in a PhD program at Chicago Theological Seminary. Two of them, Patricia, and Sadiqua, were part of Affinity where our group, "40+," regularly met and supported each other. It was important to me to obtain non-Christian voices. In *Homosexuality in Islam: Critical Reflection of Gay, Lesbian, and Transgender Muslims*, Islamic Studies scholar Scott Siraj at-Haqq Kugle notes: "The Qur'an encourages solidarity with the oppressed and this is an essential component of its message."[30] In light of this powerful statement about Islam, I wanted to understand the experiences of my Muslim comrades who are LGBTQIA.

Breaking the Chains

All three of the brave Muslim women discussed below point to the need for a psycho-social-theological revolution to eradicate mind slavery. Just as Na'im Akbar emphatically rebuked the "slave mentality" by using arguments from within a black nationalist framework, Patricia, Sadiqua, and Zipporah found agency to dispel that same slavish framework when applied to LGBTQIA persons in Islam. Kugle contends "solidarity with the oppressed" is a hallmark of Islam because "it is inseparable from the divine charge to act with justice and responsibility."[31] Acting with justice and responsibility in Islam has a direct focus toward those who are oppressed. "The Qu'ran calls those who are oppressed *al-mus-tad'afun fi al-ard* or those who are made weak and held down. The Arabic phrase is very subtle. The oppressed are 'deemed weak' by others who grab power for themselves, but they are not actually weak."[32] This applies when persons are "held down" by oppressive ideologies that condemn them for their sexual orientation. This points to the need for LGBTQIA persons to consistently reevaluate the life-giving and life-sustaining aspects of our belief systems, no matter the context. In some faith traditions this is known as discernment, which enables a person to extract the life-giving content from the death-dealing content in any sermon, speech, or communication. It also prepares a person to follow the voice of reason, as in the case of Franshon, mentioned earlier, who heard womanist religious scholars emphatically and compassionately tell her to leave the place of worship where she was not being affirmed in her call to ministry. As Bishop Valeriano Melendez, who guided the Pentecostal faith community to which I belonged, put it: one must develop the spiritual discipline to *eat the meat without choking on the bones.*

Conversations with Patricia, Sadiqua, and Zipporah, Muslim members of my Affinity group, helped to frame my theo-ethical philosophy for LGBTQIA persons impacted by homophobic violent rhetoric. They focus on their sense of community, family, and social justice in their reflections. Their lived experiences point to a need to shift both metaphysics and ethics, emphasizing an underlying intersubjective relationality that recognizes the all-inclusive nature of being for all sexual beings. Each of them offers examples of the unique fluidity they embraced to meet and be met as human subjects wherever they are. The focus on the human subject does not depend on a particular faith tradition. Rather, a healthy psycho-social approach to queer public theology engages in an analysis of belief systems, a spiritual self-assessment, ritual practices, and community involvement.

Homophobia and One's Sense of Community

Patricia: A group of us came together. We were all part of AWA, which was African American Women's Association, um, and the founder of that was Lisa Pickens and her then partner, Karen Long, at the time. But we all met; she used to, you know, have the gatherings at her house and because of things that were going on in the community; the lack of presence and not even presence, but lack of acknowledgement on the Southside especially centered around Bud Billiken Parade and all of that. Um, everyone came together from you know, different black women centered LGBT organizations and we came and founded Affinity. Um, we were all sitting at the table one day at Lisa's house, and there it was. We came up with the idea; we did a lot of things as one of the youngest, not one, but the youngest member, founding member of Affinity, I spoke at like youth conferences all over Chicago. Um, but it was an awesome, an awesome experience. When you take away um Minister Farrakhan, when you take away all the big heads of the NOI [Nation of Islam], um, there was something that we had that was called MGT—and it was Muslim Girls in Training, and every Saturday we all came together. All the girls, all the women came together from MGT to the Vanguards. The Vanguards were, you know, we were the military kind of part of the Nation. But, the sisterhood was definitely there and it was just like Affinity. And no one actually came out and said that they were gay, but we didn't have to; you know it was just you were amongst the sisters and it wasn't about the men. You know we talk about the men sometimes, but it wasn't about that. And, it's so reminded me of Affinity. So, yeah when it comes to the

Nation, you know being gay was not, um, was not in, but behind closed doors you were just who you were. And a sisterhood was a sisterhood.

Despite a profound sense of family among the women with which Patricia was in communion, she still witnessed the violent impact of homophobia within the Nation of Islam. The Nation of Islam, founded by Wallace Fard Muhammad in 1930, is the longest lasting black national Muslim organization in North America and beyond. Forming the Nation in order to organize and instruct African Americans of their heritage, "Fard proclaimed himself a prophet whose mission was to prepare black people for the Armageddon and to free them from white oppression in America." The organization grew exponentially and was later led by Elijah Muhammad, one of Fard's devotees. Under Elijah Muhammad's leadership, Patricia joined the Muslim Girls' Training Class, which was the sister group to the Fruit of Islam (FOI) boys' group.[33]

Patricia: You know there was this time where one of the girls was dating, I think they were actually engaged, to one of the FOI—the Fruit of Islam members. And he was abusive and we all knew it. Like, it was just clear, and the brothers were supposed to talk to him, all this, that, and the other. Turns out, he was gay. So, it was just like, once I realized that … and, he committed suicide. That was the other key thing. That's when everything came out and I was like "Oh, my God." Like this is … And I had to make the decision then if I was going to be out, you know, as a gay woman or if I was going to continue to hide you know who I was. Um, and I was like, I can't do this. So, behind closed doors it's fine when it doesn't eat away at you. But, for some, "behind closed doors," it became very ugly. So, you know but, I don't know if it was different for men than it was for women. I don't know if it's because when we think of sisterhood and togetherness we're kind of more free in our expression of it whereas you know, FOI, we're the military, you know you had to be a man and you know all of that, so I don't know if for him it was a struggle because he couldn't really, I know it was a struggle because he couldn't really be him. But he couldn't even be free to be just an intimate, loving black man with other black men. And, at the end of the day it's like wow, I can hug my sisters all day and there's no tension between it, there's nothing crazy, but for black men it was just different.

The teachings Patricia received from the Nation of Islam prohibited same-gender love. Yet, Patricia found solace in the fact that, for women, there was an understanding emanating from the leadership that the closeness that women naturally brokered made them susceptible to such relationships. This closeness offered a respite from the racist college environment during her formative years.

Patricia: I was at Monmouth College in Monmouth, Illinois, and experienced racism like you wouldn't believe. It was a horrible experience. I was there for a year and a half, and I left there hating white people, couldn't stand them to save my life. And I was like, "Okay, I need to be with some people who hate them just as much as I do," and I found the NOI. And, at the same time I found a woman that I fell in love with tremendously. So, it was funny that the two would kind of come at the same time, it was really funny ... I was with the Nation for three years, three long years. But it was, you know, at one time I used to defend the Nation of Islam all of the time because there was a statement that Minister Farrakhan had said one Saturday at MGT. He used to come and give lectures every now and again at MGT. And so, he was talking about homosexuality and so he was saying I can understand why women would be with the other women because we develop this kinship towards one another and then for me it was like he understood it wasn't about sex, it wasn't about any of that; everybody be like, "Oh, you know the Nation, homophobic, Minister Farrakhan hates, hates, hates." I'm like if you all could just hear what I heard; like it's not that he was saying he was for it; he was just saying he could understand it, and that's all I am asking. If you can understand why you know I love women the way that I do, whether or not you agree with it or not, it doesn't matter to me. But, you at least understand it.

This example reveals how sometimes deep contradictions between the homophobic experiences of some men in Islamic settings and the experiences of some women represent patriarchal hegemony that can give rise to hatred and often violence against LGBTQIA persons.[34]

Patricia: NOI did not necessarily deal with native Muslims. We studied the Qur'an just like everyone else, but we did not exist with them and so, I have always lived in that separate place ... But, when you think of Islam globally, that whole Orlando thing kinda threw me for a loop. Especially when it came out that he was gay or had boyfriends and it was just like "here we go again with" ... and then we found out that he was a little, well I don't want to say a little abusive, but he was also abusive, and it's like how, how do you reconcile that? Like, these things keep coming around, and I'm not sure that it exists in black lesbian relationships um, and I don't hear about it as often so I know there's ... even if it's not physical there's still something where you know, you gotta, you're fighting and that aggressiveness comes out somewhere, somehow, um, but, at the end of the day, it's just when I think of the prayer in Islam, it's one of the most calming things ever. I'll still say the prayer today, it's just one of those things where it just feels like everything just centers and falls into place. Um, and I don't know how to ... you know in Arabic, you know on the floor with the rugs and you know they start off Allahu

Akbar. And so as soon as you say that for me it's just an instant, you know, Bismillah al-Rahman al-Rahim,³⁵ it just all like brings you right here because it's all about … and being a performance artist, it's all about voicing that connection to self as well. Um, and I don't know how to magnify that or bring that out to other people and explain how beautiful Islam is … to explain that at the end of the day it's not about Minister Farrakhan and the NOI; at the end of the day it's not about whatever is going on in Iran, Iraq, you know Pakistan, it's not about all of those men, it's about that one God and your connection to that one God. And so, it's like okay, "Where is your connection to that?" Despite what everybody else says your religion is, "What do you believe your religion is?" And then, "How do you kinda work inside of that?"

Patricia developed a personal connection to the sacred ritual in Islam. No matter what was said against her sexuality, she formed a true connection to "the one God," an intimacy in which her belief system was rendered impermeable. She also points to the importance of holding one's difference as sacred. She believed that it was enough if they could "understand why" she loves women; she did not need them to approve of her acting on that desire. Self-proclamation of both the Divine and her holy desire enabled her to separate religious content from faith. In the end, her faith in Allah, the one God, who is for her the Greatest, sustains her selfhood. Patricia also shared with me her experience in the Yoruba tradition, which I describe later in this chapter. Patricia's move to Yoruba practice was a natural one for her, given her poetic ingenuity. Yet, she carries with her in that ritualized practice the prayers she learned while actively participating in the Nation of Islam.

Homophobia and One's Sense of Family

Internal struggles over sexual identity presented Sadiqua, referred to earlier in her life as "Comfort," with an ultimatum. Her decision was not easy, but she made it with conviction. Her declaration was met with opposition by the folks she encountered both within and outside of her family. Kugle points out that people like Sadiqua "suffer in their vulnerability but actually have great strength and resilience. God is on their side. They hear God's message clearly because of their condition of vulnerability, suffering, and oppression."³⁶ Sadiqua experienced a prolonged period of internal tension before deciding that she must stand up for herself and what she believes. Kugle describes the experience of people like Sadiqua, explaining that their "endurance, pain, and patience render them open to hearing God's voice and accepting God's message when Prophets come. In standing up against their oppression they enact God's will in the world, to the surprise of those who are accustomed to wielding power and thinking themselves gods."³⁷

Sadiqua: I basically hid it for a decade from everybody, but I couldn't do that anymore. It was driving me crazy because I was in love, and I didn't want to keep pushing her in the closet and under the bed. And then these people say they love me all day but then they won't love this. So, I battled but then I'm like it's got to go down. You know and it was a battle, but I was willing to do it. And then the more I started to see my family … cause that's the first thing close to me … my family, behave, my Muslim friends, the people at the mosque, the TV people, strangers; they all began to change … well maybe that was my perspective of change of the people around me. And I said, "really?" This is all a farce. I really … it's like … this is a farce. I was taught to … Five Pillars of Islam and be good and love and trust your brother and care for him and don't be dwelling in usury and take care of the elderly people and orphans and little folk, you know? Even, you never raise your voice to a sick person. So, how could somebody stand over me and be ready to tear me down, and I just got out of the hospital? I know, everybody gets a story that their family gave them. You coulda had my story, I coulda got yours. But I think God gave me freedom of choice; despite what everybody says … now I know I am pushing against a machine.

Growing up in an orthodox Muslim environment taught Sadiqua values that were brought into conflict when her brother accosted her at her most vulnerable moment. For Sadiqua, her orthodox Muslim environment differed from the NOI in that the tradition taught her to believe in the eternal, omnipotence of God whereas NOI taught a more corporeal concept of God.[38] After she announced to her family that she was a lesbian, her brother remained largely silent. However, when she needed him most, he attempted to demonize her, causing lasting emotional hurt.

Sadiqua: I went into surgery, surgery, major surgery. I get out, he drives me home, 'cause I'm gonna be in the bed for quite some time. And, it was just like, okay, "now I got you." 'Cause I couldn't do anything. The only thing I could do is listen. And he had this duffle bag of Qur'ans and beads and prayer books, you know, everything, you know, just like a duffle bag of religious stuff he's just gonna get it up out of me, exorcise me, if I may say. And, I'm like "what are you doing?" You know. He's like "now, what is all this gay stuff that you are?" … And, I'm like "now?" My whole wound, I was having a hysterectomy, is hanging out. I'm on my back, you know and I'm like "are you kidding me?" "Naw," like, he thought it all out; like, "we fitting to fix this." And I'm like "now?!" "Okay!" Cause you know, if I'm strong and on my feet, you don't have a chance; but I'm weak, and I'm on my back. I couldn't do a thing. I was angry, but I was dying, and I was very hurt because he was literally trying to beat me over the head with his books, and prayer rugs, and beads, and reading … like "do you know blah, blah, blah, blah, blah, blah" … and the venom, he was so ... and I'm like "stop this, get out of here!" I saw a look in my brother's face like he was going to kill me. And it frightened me. I mean when he looked at me with such rage that I mean I'm frightened because I know how this can be. And he changed to me, because he had got under a different imam and this guy was making him, I thought, a big radical. And ah, he's like, "you gone stop this." And I'm like ... so it was tough, and I had to call my stud friends, my "myn" to protect me. And I said, "you all git here because my brother is here, and I don't feel safe and git him outta here," you know.

Sadiqua's sense of family was reconfigured as she reached out to her same-gender-loving family for assistance, support, and comfort. In a moment when she feared utter annihilation, Sadiqua summoned the strength to reach out for the family support that she could count on for survival at a time when her personhood was invisible to her biological family.

Sadiqua: And he was like "if they come here" ... you know. I'm like, "you better git outta here." So, I, I had to send him home emergency like, like quick and put him on a plane, and I don't think you ... I was like "I never want to see you again." You know, "you are here to help me heal and look what you are doing." And I, in my heart of hearts, I thought he was gonna hurt me, and I've never said these words out to another person, um, but I am so glad that I had my community, my masculinity, my womyn to protect me. And they were there lickety split. And um, it was a lot of ... that was one of the things that occurred.

From a deep hurt, Sadiqua decided to leave Islam. Her childhood memories of the goodness of the faith were overshadowed by the reality of a "radicalized" brother and the anger she felt from his violent reaction to her sexuality based on so-called religious teachings. It points to the breakdown of intersubjective relationality based on dogma.

Sadiqua: I felt disappointed because I thought our kinship, our siblingship was stronger than that. And he changed, 'cause that's not what grandma taught us. None of that no more. Every time we talk it was like you know, a proverb, a psalm. And then when I was able to be strong, I gave it to him and he was putty. But, he hurt me. And I was like, you know, he can't out anything me. So that ... I think ... so my feeling was anger. And I know anger hovers over pain; because I was hurt. So, I was angry 'cause I couldn't get up and whip his ass. That's the main deal, 'cause I'm older than you. That's the anger. The hurt was it's me, Saqa ... that's what my brothers and sisters call me. Put this stuff down. And, I wanted to come here and find this cat that he was listening to and give him something. We come from something stronger than that, so there was a mental change. Allah was good and pure and loves you and pray and be good, good,

good. And I say when did it get muddied, and sullied by the dogma of religion. I know God because of what my experience is. So I said ... that's when I kinda ... I said okay, "I'm letting the storybook, the dogma, the all of that of the religion go ... of any religion, of all religions and just believe in what is the Creator—the mountains, the trees, the grass, me." I have seen miracles ... what I would describe as miracles ... things happen and there's no explanation for it. I have seen them in my life. And it's only one explanation for it, and so that's why I would say when people say "well, are you a Muslim or a practicing Muslim?" We would joke, which the joke is Musla ... non-practicing ... we drink, fornicate, smoke, and carry on. But, I just say, you know, I am a spiritual person with a private relationship. That's it.

Sadiqua recalls a childhood ensconced in homophobia. However, her own self-identity yielded a different existential reality. Islam taught that homosexuality results in consequences, but the consequences for men and women differed according to Sadiqua. That distinction allowed Sadiqua to find the healing balm after the horrendous experience with her brother.

Sadiqua: There is passages in Islam, "Two men lay with one another; castrate them and cut both of their heads off." That's the law when it comes to gay, period. And I think people get stuck on that and they're like "kill 'em all," Orlando, what, what what ... those guys? First of all, that is the law, and that's exactly how its written for gay men. Castrate them and cut their heads off. There's no talking about it, there's no healing, no fixing it—done and done. But, for gay womyn, that's not what it said. And this is what I had ... it took some time for us to speak again ... and I had to show him that I knew ... 'cause he wanted to tell me what he knew ... We read the same book, we grew up the same way. I'm not making excuses for what I'm doing or how I want to live my life ... but it's "if two women lie together, separate them and lock them in the house" ... this is, I assume, the parents ... "separate them until you can find suitable husbands for them." That was it.

Though Sadiqua and her brother have mended their relationship, the scars are still visible. She has found the wisdom and guidance to interact with her brother on her own terms. More importantly, she has found the agency to name and own her sexual identity.

Sadiqua: And, uh, he has softened a bit. Because after we made up, um, he was gonna lose me. And, I don't have to do anything to you. It's a privilege and a gift to have me as your sister or friend or whatever in your life and he knows that. And I'm like, "You was gonna lose me." And I'll say, "You know you can come by, but don't come over with all that book in your hand stuff." "Well, you know I am a Muslim first." I say, "Then be that, but you can come over here as my brother and just be easy and eat some chicken and stop with the, you know, 'cause you can't tell me about my life at this age. I hear you, I respect you, but, um, my partner is sitting right there, and it's rainbows in my house." I'm studying more of just ... about more African traditions, um, which I'm falling in love with.

Sadiqua endured the ultimate tension when her brother used a vulnerable moment to spout off Islamic dogma to malign her sexuality. Her reaction is indicative of the struggle of LGBTQIA persons to be visible to the ones who claim to be ministering to their souls. This person that she grew up with, whom she knew intimately as a sibling, was "radicalized" to the point that Sadiqua became a target of his religious hatred. The scene she describes of an attempted exorcism speaks to the way in which religious dogma can be taught legalistically, rendering a once closely knit brother and sister as literal strangers to one another. As Sadiqua reflects on the pain of this encounter, it becomes the driving force in her pursuit of "the good." Now, she has resolved her internal tensions with the assurance that she has experienced God for herself. Her turn toward African indigenous religions, particularly as it relates to the importance of nature, serves as way for her to retain the meaning of the Five Pillars of Islam in her spiritual ritual.

Homophobia and One's Sense of Social Justice

Zipporah determined in high school that she would be an advocate for gay youth rights. Her immediate family tacitly accepted her youthful discovery. Zipporah's attraction to social justice was inspired by the story of Matthew Shepard (December 1, 1976–October 12, 1998), a student at the University of Wyoming who was beaten, tortured, and left to die from severe head injuries induced by two homophobic attackers.[39]

> *Zipporah:* I think ... well, my mom was okay with it to a degree. To the degree that she knew what was going on at the time. Like, she knew about things like Matthew Shepard. She knew like, that hate crimes were a real thing and was just like ... and she also knew that the majority of my family is like homophobic in really weird ways. Um, but I guess in her mind it was kind of like, "Oh, well you are not going to get pregnant, so I don't really care."

Her conversion to Islam led Zipporah to a mosque where she encountered homophobic teaching.

> *Zipporah:* Occasionally he would have those sermons about how homosexuality is like corrupting Islam and the black community or whatever. And I could ignore it up until a certain point, and then when I

started having issues with like chronic pain and disability I was just like, "Listen, I ain't going to sit on the carpet for like an hour to listen to some of this. It is just not ... [laughing]; this is just not my cup of tea, you know personally. Um, and I have other less savory opinions as to why he started to take that turn into the nonsensical.

As a result of exposure to international travel and her own critical research, Zipporah learned a counternarrative to the violent homophobic interpretations of Islamic texts, catapulting her to leadership status for queer Muslims.

Zipporah: That's the thing. It [the Qur'an] doesn't say, literally, anything. However, you can use what it ... the story of the prophet Lut in conjunction with layers of *fiqh*, like so ... like religious legal commentary and other forms of legal commentary to derive ... So, if you use the story of the Prophet Lut, for example, which is basically that the people of Lut got ... like God came down and annihilated the people of Lut for sodomy. That is the very surface-level interpretation of that story. You can in a theocratic context like Saudi, you can translate ... you can make the mental leap that, okay, because these people got destroyed in the Qur'an, it is somehow acceptable for us as Muslims attempting to live into that spirit of wanting to do the right thing, that that translates into punishment by death for people who are homosexual. But, if you go ... That only makes sense if you go like this [*gesturing a straight line*]; it does not make sense if you actually track the layers of *fiqh* commentary, which say ... which essentially say that okay it's not okay to be homosexual ... However, there is this other overarching principle of what is entitled to God and prophets are not necessarily entitled to man. So, there's a lot for example, that the prophet Muhammad, peace be upon him, does because he is a prophet and because he was endowed with that ability and those directives. That doesn't necessarily mean that what all of the things that all he was able to do as a prophet you are entitled to as the human, because you were not handed down those directives. You are reading the divine revelation, which chronicles the directives that he is given, but that doesn't mean, for example, that you are able to cast out people, that you are able to condemn people, that you are able to kill people, because that's not your power as a believer. So, it's very easy for people to see that "Oh, this town was destroyed for 'sodomy,' so therefore we have to destroy people for sodomy in order to prevent that corruption, that corruption" [*gesturing and chuckling as though in disbelief*] from spreading [*chuckling*].

Zipporah's social justice work focuses on promoting counternarratives. She has formed a group of like-minded young adults to stand in solidarity and address the disquieting rhetoric of Islam, which gives rise to murderous violence against LGBTQIA person within and outside of the tradition.

> *Zipporah:* Post Pulse shooting, there was a meeting of what I like to call the mainstream Muslim polity, so all the people who consider themselves leaders, mostly men, of the community wanting to talk about, you know LGBT Muslim issues 'cause you know, people raised up the fact that like Omar Mateen was someone who was struggling with their sexuality. So now, the mainstream Muslim community now has to atone for that in some way publicly, as they atone for literally everything else in the world [laughing profusely]. And, but the thing about it is, is that, like at the same time the thing that queer Muslims, including myself, started to raise on social media is that like, yeah, it's cute that organizations like CAIR say, yeah, you support the LGBT community and you don't agree with what he did, but the reality is that you still have … there are still ways in which homophobia runs like a stream through our communities, and it is not that hard to figure out why somebody who is subsequently struggling with their sexuality and is in an environment where you're literally hearing people talking about "gay people should be killed or gay people shouldn't do this, or gay people should be exiled." And you had straight Muslims in the room saying, "I didn't know it was this bad … you know, like I had no clue that these things are being said." And there was someone who works as a lawyer who was like, "No, I regularly get contacted by mosques who want to know if they can legally put in their by-laws like ways of excluding LGBT people from the mosques, like without being sued, like is there a tangible way to do that, you know?" And, it was interesting to me because I had never spent any time with people in that mainstream segment of the Muslim social justice community … had mostly avoided the majority of them because I just did not want them to know who I was, I did not want them to know about my group. I did not want the safety of my group to be compromised, and my attitude about it was like, like you can feel upset about, but you can't really do anything, you know. So, my group Third Coast Queer Muslims is kind of like a queer Muslim support group where people can get together and create safer space for themselves, especially if they do not feel comfortable going to mainstream mosques or to like mainstream Muslim events or like, even maybe you want to go and you don't want to go by yourself.

Zipporah raises the question of agency in her narrative. From an early age she self-identified as lesbian, against the indifference from within and outside of her family. Her advocacy on behalf of LGBTQIA youth is a testament to the power of difference once embraced. At all stages of her identity formation she was able to find a level of comfort with which to pursue her passions, and she embraces her difference as a badge of honor. From the selection of her own faith tradition to the preferences for her personal embodiment, to her freedom of sexual expression, Zipporah embodies the concept of liberty. Her philosophical prowess looms large in her statement about the root cause of homophobia. Zipporah suggests that "forfeiting" one's agency leads to oppression.

It was not until black women began to assert their agency that the issue of their sexuality was given voice. Audre Lorde appeared on a panel for New York University on the topic "The Personal and the Political." She named herself a "black, lesbian, feminist, mother, poet, and warrior." She mounted the podium and had these words to say:

> Those of us who stand outside the circle of this society's definition of acceptable women; those of us who have been forged in the crucibles of difference—those of us who are poor, who are lesbians, who are black, who are older—know that survival is not an academic skill. It is learning how to stand alone, unpopular and sometimes reviled, and how to make common sense with those others identified as outside the structures in order to define and seek a world in which we can all flourish. It is learning how to take our differences and make them strengths. For the master's tools will never dismantle the master's house. They may allow us temporarily to beat him at his own game, but they will never enable us to bring genuine change. And this fact is only threatening to those women who still define the master's house as their only source of support.[40]

The "culture of dissemblance," which "was seen as a way for black women to 'protect the sanctity of inner aspects of their lives,'" bred a functional façade for black women to maintain an appearance of "openness" to sexuality while simultaneously guarding their true convictions.[41]

> *Mara:* I am an adult person who is struggling to finish school because of life. I work for Blue Cross, Blue Shield, and I am single. (Identifies as lesbian and have for sixteen years.) I was married for seventeen years to what I guess would be considered my high school sweetheart. And, from that union two boys were born. So, I had my first experience with a girl at twelve. I've always known that there was something different. Ah, sixteen years ago I met a person that would help me find out what was different [giggling].

Nonetheless, Lorde urges a different paradigm where difference is considered an advantage. Being different gave Lorde the impetus to be herself. She overcame fear by first accepting herself. Lorde demonstrates the importance of being self-aware and holding one's awareness of self as sacred knowledge; such an approach is instructive for a theo-ethics that seeks liberation from a plantation mind slavery in which fear dictates that others dismiss your humanity in the effort to "please" the master/Master. It is clear from their personal reflections throughout this manuscript that Franshon, Helen, Mara, Mileece, Patricia, Sadiqua, Zachard, Benjamin, Quincy, and Tadhi found strength in accepting who they are and what they believe. In this next section, we will explore how they responded to hearing the message of Pastor Anderson while in community. Though the group represents a plurality of faith communions, their experiences found commonality in their oppressions from violent rhetoric as well as their responses to that oppression.

Group Dynamics in Focus: Listening to the Anderson Sermon

I invited each of the interviewees of my ethnography to a focus group session in which I played for them the thirty-minute video clip of Pastor Terry K. Anderson's sermon,[42] which is the preaching exemplar analyzed in Chapter 3, introducing it as a clip I had downloaded from YouTube.[43] The participants were given a meal while the video played. They were provided with a "feelings wheel" and definitions for their reference. Additionally, each participant was given a risk and benefits assessment of participating in the focus group and a list of helpful tools to address the risks. Each participant consented to the video recording of the in-group exchange. I observed the attentiveness of each participant as the video played. Some stopped eating when Pastor Anderson mentioned "same-sex marriage." Some took notes throughout the presentation. When Pastor Anderson claimed that only 2 percent of the population is gay, one participant asked, "Where did he get that statistic?"

When Pastor Anderson suggested that gay love is synonymous with bestiality, a wave of disgust moved across the room. By the time Pastor Anderson compared same-sex marriage to riding in a boat with someone who wants to drill a hole in it, two participants were looking away from the screen, and one left his seat to replenish his drink. Several participants laughed in disbelief. One person stated, "I do not have enough paper to write all of my feelings." When Pastor Anderson said he was trying to "disinfect" his sermon as much as he could, someone said, "Did he say *disinfect*?"

When Pastor Anderson mentioned his cars, the participants began to engage each other with comments, signifying an "aha" moment. When Pastor Anderson admitted to picking up the wrong key, one person said, "The wrong key, huh?" When Pastor Anderson asked, "Am I doing alright?" the participants said in unison, "No!" When he said, "If God made anything better than a woman, he kept if for himself," one self-identified lesbian minister said, "Now, I agree with that!" When Pastor Anderson noted that "this kind of preaching is not popular," a participant responded, "because it is not rational." When Pastor Anderson stated, "If you hear that Rev. Anderson was looking at some woman, you say, 'Yeah he did it, yeah, I'm praying for him; he's struggling with that; you keep him in prayer.' But if you hear that Rev. Anderson is looking at some man, you tell them, 'Now, that's a lie,'" one participant stated, "That's the first clue that he is a closeted homosexual." When the video concluded, one of the participants emphatically stated, "Thank God it's over!"

I engaged the group in a discussion after the video finished playing. Initially, I asked the group to vent their feelings. There was a consensus, though not unanimous, that the message was of no value, a source of confusion. One participant described the message as "hate speech, full of death and dying and fear." She said, "So how do you help the gay man or woman in the audience, now what's your job, leader? There is no healing, no solution." Another was incensed that Pastor Anderson would associate homosexuality with polygamy and bestiality.

One participant was enraged that the preacher boasted of having two Mercedes-Benz vehicles when some of his parishioners might be on TANF or SNAP, or might be unemployed.[44] She said, "A lot of people in congregations are low income." "A lot of people don't have a car; they take the bus to church," she continued, "so he's talking about his two cars, that's arrogance." She also interjected that Pastor Anderson projected "adult stuff" onto the kids by associating the little boy and girl holding hands with something sexual. She said, "I find it problematic because he is dumping this stuff on kids who haven't even had a concept of gender roles, sexuality. They are too young. They don't even know that concept, and he is dumping his adult stuff onto them and then that affects their outlook and their development. Then you have homosexuality equals pedophilia; that is unacceptable." Another participant said:

> I really enjoyed it, I mean, I felt, what I enjoyed about it was the aesthetics of it. So, I think that the language obviously was filled with a sense of confusion. I wouldn't term it hate. Um, and I wouldn't term it hate for two reasons. One is, he reduced himself to the equation of hate or sin, so sin seems to be the main focus. That, that unless you are in a one-to-one ratio relationship, everyone is fair game. So, I didn't really have a problem under that sense of gender equality, um, when it came to that. Um, but I did have a problem with him backing out of it.

Concerned with the impact on "hearers of the Word," another participant said:

> So as a pastor, I am always listening with a very critical ear when I hear preachers preach. And, and even when I'm preparing my own sermons I'm always very cautious of how they may or could be misconstrued or misunderstood. And so, when I'm listening to other preachers preach,

I'm always listening for the hermeneutical perspective, in other words, like, the place that they're coming from, the framework in which they're framing their theology, their theological perspective because what's being projected out impacts the inside of who we are. And, for me, having grown up Baptist, I find you know, words matter, right? And so, the language that we use in the pulpit I think we should be very cautious of, and I think we have an obligation to be well studied because we are responsible for who we speak to and what we say. Having said that, this man had so many paradoxical statements and so many un … there was no validity, there was no scripture to back up 99 percent of what he said, and then the scriptures that he did use were taken out of context. And for that, you know, he has done that congregation and the 212,000 people that have listened to that sermon a great disservice and probably more damage than he could ever even begin to imagine to some young person who is struggling with their sexuality or sexual identification.

Familiar with the Texas-based ministry of Pastor Anderson, another participant brought a depth of meaning to the communal ethos of Lilly Grove Baptist Church:

So, as I was listening to it, um, I started to thinking about the context—Houston, Texas. I don't know if anybody in here is from Houston, but Houston, Texas. Although this was preached in 2012, just last week Houston was named one of the most homophobic cities, um, in the country. The other piece to that: so, I know Terry Anderson, um, and I know Lilly Grove from the 1980s. Um, Lilly Grove had a pastor who they named, said, was gay, and they got rid of him. And he [the previous Lilly Grove pastor] became the pastor of my, of the congregation where I lived in Dallas. And, before we hired our pastor, Terry Anderson came to preach for us. So, that's how I sort of know him. So he then went to Lilly Grove, was called to Lilly Grove and he really did amazing work in terms of building a church because the church was a very small church and it's massive now, it's, you know, it's one of the largest churches, black churches in Houston. And so, that's some of the context. I am particularly interested in the pulpit antics. The sense that when the preacher stands behind the pulpit, and it's preaching time, just by looking at him, you know that you are in trouble. And then, the preacher begins to talk, begins to use his voice, use his body to take control of the people and the people endorse him, and sort of push him, propel him to continue. And what ends up happening is it sounds like you are at a lynch mob. So all of that when you talk about "what are you feeling," that's what I'm feeling; I'm feeling like I am getting ready to be lynched and I've been here before. I know about this crowd, um, who lynches gay people, and by the way, it's the same people, crowd, who was lynched. Um, so in terms of the sermon itself, um, well, it is, it is, out of all the issues pertinent to a congregation, why this one? ... is the question that I asked and then I asked "dear Terry," he protested a little too much, too much, just a little bit too much, um, and that's concerning to me. I mean if we could follow Terry a little bit closer, a little longer ...

Simultaneously, another person broke in and said:

> That's exactly what I have written on my paper, "thou protesteth too much," because I felt like I wanted to ask the question "Who are you trying to convince that *you* are not this way?" Because that is what it started to border on when he started to talk about "Oh, if you see me looking at a woman ... " Nobody should see you looking at a woman like that preacher man, I'm sorry! He never should have said that out of his mouth; that was disrespectful to his wife.

In this exchange, the participants agreed that "there *is* harm being done, we are *assuming* that there are gay people in the crowd." One person explained, "I will tell you that the director of music, minister of music of that congregation *is* gay, and I'm sitting here going 'what was *he* feeling,' I just wish the camera had panned to him because I know who that is, right?" At that juncture a participant said in response, "I hope you all know that there was more than one LGBTQIA person in that congregation." All agreed that when the camera zoomed in on the crowd, some of the congregants looked like they were shouting "crucify them!" while others looked morose, beaten, and battered by the preacher's words.

Out of the focus group came an important insight about how messages such as Pastor Anderson's might be perceived by the LGBTQIA listeners in a congregation. As a participant observer, I recorded the reactions to this sermon as each person expressed offense at the message in some respect or another. In their individual critiques, the participants discerned that Pastor Anderson's message was not God-inspired and that it harmed the LGBTQIA persons in the congregation. Their comments point to the way sermons like this leave LGBTQIA people feeling dismembered. From their myriad experiences and their responses to the video, the focus group participants noted six key points, which I summarize as the foundation for a Christian social ethics: (1) If a preached message aims to rebuke, it should also provide healing or solutions to bring balance, but not at the expense of the integrity and inherent worth of LGBTQIA persons, such as suggesting that conversion therapy, or other harmful practices, constitutes the solution. (2) The preacher's ethical mandate should not be compromised by personal biases, finances, or popularity. (3) The preacher should avoid using politics to manipulate the congregation. (4) The preacher should be studied and prepared. (5) The message should be prophetic and not simply entertaining. And (6) the preacher should follow the voice of God—the voice of reason that holds all of creation is good, that values every person, and that demands justice. These starting points require much more development and articulation of how they are inextricably interwoven than I offer here, but they fundamentally inform my black queer public theology.

The Keys to Restoration

After the focus group session with the interviewees, I met Tadhi for a follow-up conversation. His initial reactions to Pastor Anderson's sermon raised some important considerations for understanding how shifts in thinking are coded in speech acts. Tadhi recalled the moment when Pastor Anderson discussed the two keys to his two cars. Tadhi pointed out that Pastor Anderson's own capacity to shift his ideas is as simple as reflecting more deeply on the example of his car keys. In thinking about mixing up his keys, Anderson assumed that because the two keys looked alike, the one he had was programmed to start the car at the church. However, the key he had was not wired to start that particular car. No matter what maneuvers Pastor Anderson performed, no matter whether he prayed for the car to start, changed the battery in the fob, or moved toward the car, it was simply not going to happen. In effect, that same analogy works when considering the sexual orientation of LGBTQIA persons. Though some of us may look just like others in terms of basic gender norms, we are simply not wired to turn on the *same* way. We are wired differently; the keys to our desire do not work with the dominant cis-heteronormative models of gender and sexuality. It is important to note that the goal of this simplistic analogy is not to fully characterize queer desire; rather, the goal is to incite deeper reflection on how Western ontological constructs totalize the possibilities of selfhood.

Katie Cannon, in an often-overlooked volume dealing with womanist ethics for preaching and teaching, further illuminates this theo-ethical construction. Cannon emphasizes that the "Bible's testimony to the connection between morality and physical instrumentality is evident in every legitimate encounter with the living God. The biblical corpus chronicles personal encounter through prayer and the visitation of the Holy Spirit."[45] Relying on her divinity school professor Rufus Isaac Clark Sr., Cannon introduces the volume with these words:

> Read, if you will, this book as if each lecture is a definitive line drawn in the sand differentiating between jackleg preachers and professionals of the Word of God. Its overall idea forms a gargantuan divide. On one side of the chasm are fraudulent impostors who prostitute the Christian gospel as unscrupulous charlatans; on the other side are Christian ministers who embody preaching as holy intellectual inquiry.[46]

Personal encounter is lifted up as a guiding trope for any sermonic moment. That encounter encompasses the same indicia of proof as those stories in the Bible. The mysterious and the tremendous emerge from each intonation. In contrast, I have argued that mind slavery made evident through the work of racecraft has created a lore that causes some to adopt an alien narrative. How is the sacred subject formed? What are the manifestations of the sacred within the human? And more importantly, what is the responsibility of pastors to help those whom they serve live into that sacred place? The sacred subject is formed through self-understanding ritualized in concert with supportive community. The manifestation of the sacred within the human is as simple as the breath we breathe. Ritualized affirmations of the life-giving force within help us as human subjects to realize our potential for good in this world. The mindfulness necessary to achieve this place of contentment may be actualized in various religious practices. Key to this quest is the assurance that it is attainable and available to all of creation. Everyone can experience the Divine. There is no universal scriptural formula for reaching this restorative place.

Contrastingly, pastors have direct scriptural admonitions that place the onus squarely upon them to resist rhetoric that causes people to remove themselves from the "ark of safety." In Hebrew Bible scripture, pastors are warned that there is punishment for those who cause God's "flock" to retreat. For instance, the prophet Jeremiah cautions pastors to be mindful of the spoken message that "scatters" the flock.

> "Woe to the shepherds who are destroying and scattering the sheep of my pasture!" declares the Lord. Therefore, this is what the Lord, the God of Israel, says to the shepherds who tend my people: "Because you have scattered my flock and driven them away and have not bestowed care on them, I will bestow punishment on you for the evil you have done," declares the Lord. I myself will gather the remnant of my flock out of all the countries where I have driven them and will bring them back to their pasture, where they will be fruitful and increase in number. I will place shepherds over them who will tend them, and they will no longer be afraid or terrified, nor will any be missing, declares the Lord.[47]

"Scattering the flock" is a metaphor for causing people to flee the church in search of a safe space to be themselves. God prescribes punishment for those who engage in evil, ungodly messaging that causes this scattering. Moreover, God pronounces a plan to bring those who have been scattered back to the fold. This passage in Jeremiah signifies how God will usher those who have been scattered to a safe space, where they will be cared for and nurtured by God's appointed.[48]

Under King Josiah (who reigned from 640–609 BC), Judah experienced leadership with integrity. Josiah "defended the cause of the poor and the needy," but his descendants were fixated on greed, shedding innocent blood and engaging in oppressive and violent actions.[49] God's pronouncement of "woe" indicates God's pledged judgment against the injustice, inequity, and oppression exacted by pastors who mishandle the message of God to God's people.

My critique of black church public theology is meant to shine light on the divide that Cannon identifies and to explicate the fallout that occurs when preachers promote ungodly messages that "scatter the flock."[50] By the same token, I acknowledge and seriously value the work of the prophetic preachers within the black church tradition who have heeded the voice of God on behalf of LGBTQIA persons and have presented the gospel message as open to all, whether they have declared their ministries to be "open and affirming" or not.

I offered ethnographic data to demonstrate the impact of pastors and faith leaders who engage in rhetorical violence directed at LGBTQIA persons inside and outside of the black church, particularly those in Islam, and I identified six key points implicated in Christian social ethics drawn from the reactions of a focus group made up of LGBTQIA persons. In the epilogue, I will explore my theo-ethical philosophy developed in part from the witness the interviewees presented herein, prophetic preaching as I have experienced it, the theoretical framework of intersubjective relationality, and the lived experience of Audre Lorde, whose life I deem to be an exemplar of lived theology useful to this discussion.

Notes

1. Adriana Cavarero, *For More Than One Voice: Toward a Philosophy of Vocal Expression* (Stanford, CA: Stanford University Press, 2005), 22.
2. This is a popular colloquialism within black public theology.
3. Isaiah 55:8–9 (NRSV).
4. Romans 10:13–15 (NRSV).
5. This is a Latin theological phrase meaning "mission of God."
6. Mitzi J. Smith, "US Colonial Missions to African Slaves: Catechizing Black Slaves, Traumatizing the Black Psyche," in *Teaching All Nations: Interrogating the Matthean Great Commission*, ed. Mitzi J. Smith and Jayachitra Lalitha (Minneapolis, MN: Fortress, 2014), 58–60.
7. Ibid.
8. I do not intend to imply that the existential or ontological fact of LGBTQIA life is sinful. Rather, I only want to argue that for those who *do* view LGBTQIA people as "sinful" merely by their existence or their sexual practices, that alleged sinfulness has, according to common Christological understandings of Christ's death and resurrection, been subsumed in the finished work of Christ on the cross. Deeming any such "sin" intractable reduces the value of Christ's finished work and renders it insufficient.

9 Jeremiah A. Wright and Jini Kilgore Ross, *Good News!: Sermons of Hope for Today's Families* (Valley Forge, PA: Judson, 1995), 73–74.
10 Reginald L. Jones, ed., *Black Psychology*, 3rd ed. (Berkeley, CA: Cobbs and Henry, 1991), ix–xix.
11 Na'im Akbar, *Breaking the Chains of Psychological Slavery* (Tallahassee, FL: Mind Productions, 1996), v–vi.
12 Akbar, *Breaking the Chains*, viii.
13 For an illustration of how the backside of a ferociously beaten slave appeared after the wounds healed, see Orlando Patterson's *Rituals of Blood: Consequences of Slavery in Two American Centuries* (New York: Basic Civitas, 1998), between unlabeled pages in the text.
14 I acknowledge the movie *Roots* is a fictional account of very real circumstances for millions of flesh-and-blood enslaved Africans. For more scholarly accounts of the atrocities of enslavement see John Hope Franklin, *From Slavery to Freedom: A History of American Negroes* (New York: Knopf, 1988); Booker T. Washington, *Up from Slavery*, available at Documenting the American South, https://docsouth.unc.edu/fpn/washington/washing.html; Frederick Douglass, *My Bondage and My Freedom*, https://docsouth.unc.edu/neh/douglass55/douglass55.html; Frederick Douglas, *Narrative of the Life of Frederick Douglas, an American Slave*, https://docsouth.unc.edu/neh/douglass/douglass.html; Andrew Billingsley, *Yearning to Breathe Free* (Columbia, SC: University of South Carolina Press, 2007); Stephanie Camp, *Closer to Freedom: Enslaved Women and Everyday Resistance in the Plantation South* (Chapel Hill, NC: University of North Carolina Press, 2004); Thavolia Glimph, *Out of the House of Bondage: The Transformation of the Plantation Household* (Cambridge, UK: Cambridge University Press, 2008); David Brion Davis, *Inhuman Bondage: The Rise and Fall of Slavery in the New World* (Oxford: Oxford University Press, 2006); Ira Berlin, *Many Thousand Gone: The First Two Centuries of Slavery in North America* (Cambridge, MA: Belknap, 1998); Harriet Ann Jacobs, *Incidents in the Life of a Slave Girl*, https://docsouth.unc.edu/fpn/jacobs/menu.html; Sven Berkert, *Empire of Cotton: A Global History* (New York: Vintage, 2015); Edward E. Baptist, *The Half Has Never Been Told: Slavery and the Making of American Capitalism* (New York: Basic Books, 2014); David Brion Davis, *The Problem of Slavery in Western Culture* (Ithaca, NY: Cornell University Press, 1966); Eric Foner, *The Fiery Trial: Abraham Lincoln and American Slavery* (New York: W. W. Norton, 2010) (all URLs accessed July 5, 2024).
15 I use the qualifier "wholesale" here in deliberate contrast to "retail" to demonstrate that this acceptance is acquired by a cheaper mode of persuasion. Wholesale describes the large quantity of ideological goods acquired during the extended period of enslavement that have been broken up over time and retailed for more strategic consumption.
16 Smith, "US Colonial Missions," 60.
17 Fields and Fields, *Racecraft*, 18.
18 Akbar, *Breaking the Chains*, 3.
19 Ibid., 11–25.

20 Ibid., v–vi.
21 "COGIC (Church of Gays In Crisis): 'Homosexual Delivered at COGIC 107th Holy Convocation,'" posted by samson247, YouTube, November 10, 2014, https://www.youtube.com/watch?v=yIF0z3SusME</> (accessed July 5, 2024). It was later reported, as this video contends, that this scenario was in fact a hoax that the preacher arranged with the young man. I contend that this is further indication of the prevalence of shaming LGBTQIA persons and is direct evidence of the widespread intent to treat LGBTQIA persons with the "leprosy effect" inasmuch as it exposes the deep-seated mind slavery responsible for this thinking.
22 Akbar, *Breaking the Chains*, vi.
23 "The Color Purple," speech by LeVar Burton as the character Kunta Kinte.
24 Akbar, *Breaking the Chains*, viii.
25 Ariel Zambelich and Alyson Hurt, "3 hours in Orlando: Piecing Together an Attack and Its Aftermath," June 16, 2016, https://www.npr.org/2016/06/16/482322488/orlando-shooting-what-happened-update (accessed July 5, 2024).
26 "Gays Must Die Says Speaker at Orlando Mosque—WFTV 9 Orlando Report," clip from the *Rachel Maddow Show*, posted by theunitedwest, YouTube, April 6, 2016, https://youtu.be/qBlwxqqAprQ (accessed July 5, 2024).
27 "The Christian Response to the Orlando Murders Pastor Roger Jimenez VBC Sacramento CA," YouTube, https://youtu.be/xNfecFIDUMw (accessed January 5, 2017, and later removed for violating YouTube's policy on hate speech).
28 Elisabeth Schüssler Fiorenza, "Discipleship and Patriarchy," in *Women's Consciousness, Women's Conscience: A Reader in Feminist Ethics*, ed. Barbara Hilkert Andolsen, Christine E. Gudorf, and Mary Pellauer (New York: Harper and Row, 1985), 145–46.
29 "Gays Must Die."
30 Scott Siraj al-Haqq Kugle, *Homosexuality in Islam: Critical Reflection on Gay, Lesbian, and Transgender Muslims,* (London: Oneworld, 2023), 35.
31 Ibid.
32 Ibid.
33 Nuri Tinaz, "The Nation of Islam: Historical Evolution and Transformation of the Movement," *Journal of Muslim Minority Affairs* 16, no. 2 (1996): 193–209.
34 Kugle, *Homosexuality in Islam,* 21. See also Lorenza Vidino and Alexander Meleagrou-Hitchens, *Islamist Homophobia in the West: From Rhetoric to Violence* (Washington, DC: Program on Extremism, George Washington University, 2022), https://extremism.gwu.edu/sites/g/files/zaxdzs5746/files/IslamistHomophobiaintheWest090722.pdf (accessed July 5, 2024).
35 "Allahu Akbar" means "God is Great," or "God is the Greatest." "Bismillah al-Rahman, al-Rahim" means "In the name of God, the most gracious, the most merciful."
36 Kugle, *Homosexuality in Islam*, 35.

37 Ibid, 35.
38 Kugle, *Homosexuality in Islam*; and Kecia Ali, *Sexual Ethics and Islam: Feminist Reflections on Qu'ran, Hadith, and Jurisprudence* (London: Oneworld, 2017).
39 "Matthew Shepard," Biography.com, September 23, 2019, http://www.biography.com/people/matthew-shepard-092515</> (accessed July 5, 2024).
40 Lorde, *Sister Outsider*, 112.
41 "Black (W)holes and the Geometry of Black Female Sexuality," *differences: A Journal of Feminist Cultural Studies*, 6.2+3 (1994): 127–45. (Also appears in Kum-Kum Bhavani, ed., *Feminism and "Race"* [Oxford University Press, 2000].) Hammonds is quoting, in part, Darlene Clark Hines's "Rape and the Inner Lives of Black Women in the Middle West: Preliminary Thoughts on the Culture of Dissemblance," *Signs* 14, no. 4 (1989): 915–20.
42 See the transcript of the sermon in Appendix B.
43 "What Must the Church Do About Same Sex Marriage? (Matthew 13:24–30)"— Rev. Terry K. Anderson. https://youtu.be/Xs9QqJ6IEnw?si=UJY_a29IEUhqNEcM (accessed July 5, 2024).
44 TANF stands for Temporary Assistance for Needy Families, and SNAP refers to the Supplemental Nutritional Assistance Program, or food stamp program.
45 Katie Geneva Cannon, *Teaching Preaching: Isaac Rufus Clark and Black Sacred Rhetoric* (New York: Continuum, 2003), 22.
46 Ibid., 13.
47 Jeremiah 23:1–4 (NIV).
48 I read "fruitfulness" here as a metaphor for the creative nature of God such that God's creation is beckoned to become co-creators with God. Creativity, I surmise, is the hallmark of a godly life. This is not a concept necessarily wedded to reproduction, though reproduction is not excluded. In that sense, I would argue that LGBTQIA persons have successfully and creatively reproduced, both physically and figuratively, and will continue to do so until Jesus comes or the world otherwise ends, whichever comes first.
49 Jeremiah 22:16–17.
50 Jeremiah 23 (NRSV).

Epilogue

As I conclude this manuscript, my mind takes me back to my first funeral of a transgender man. His mother was a member of her church for over thirty years. She faithfully served and attended her church in northeast DC. She also faithfully and lovingly stood with her child as he navigated his identity. He completed his transition surgery and seemed to be doing fine. A month later he died. Naturally, his mother sought consolation from her pastor who immediately scorned her for asking to hold her son's final service at his home church. Not only was she summarily dismissed and told by the pastor that he would not "bury that thing," but she also received harsh words from other parishioners and family members. Her son was essentially condemned to hell. I remember feeling very strongly that it was my solemn duty and commitment to treat that mother who lost her only child with dignity and respect. Somehow that basic ethic has eluded bully pulpit preachers. It comes from a place of allegiance to standards, some patriotic and most idiotic, that I have tried to illuminate in this text. For instance, our understanding of the separation of church and state must be demythologized to recognize the multiplicity of beliefs in the US public sphere. The constructions of religious liberty recently sanctioned by the US Supreme Court effectively overturn decades of civil rights gains and moves society toward white Christian nationalism. In response, almost 400 new pieces of legislation against LGBTQIA persons, and specifically transgender persons, have been introduced in legislative bodies across the United States in the following year. Jay Michelson strikes the correct balance in saying:

> The rhetoric of victimhood notwithstanding, the conservative "religious liberty" campaign is today a well-financed strategy that has successfully limited the civil rights of others. In the last decade, groups have successfully deployed religious liberty arguments in the culture war politically, seeking legislation exempting religious acts from civil rights laws and opposing various political actions; rhetorically/culturally,

recasting antidiscrimination and reproductive health rights as oppressive of religion, creating a sense that the dominant religion in America is, in fact, being persecuted; and legally, challenging laws supporting lesbian, gay, bisexual, transgender, and queer (LGBTQ) people, defending antigay plaintiffs, and carving out religious exemptions on constitutional grounds.[1]

Dominant culture constructions of conservative religious values evolved from the logics and sociality of plantation religion, which spilled over into the white denominations from which many black denominations spawned. As a result, the conventional black church ethos regarding LGBTQIA rights aligns with ultraconservative notions of religious freedom. Those same logics that fought against women's suffrage also prevented women from preaching. And those same logics that adopted respectability politics as a means for both survival and acceptance largely view LGBTQIA folks as ontologically aberrant. The consensus born from years, decades, centuries, and indeed millennia of consistent colonial babble creates religious extremism.

The problem of religious extremism is not new. Anne Hibbens's death by hanging in 1656 was precipitated by her verbalizing her disagreement with a carpenter working on her home. The patriarchal nature of early Massachusetts ushered in a very strict social order. It promoted the Salem witch trials between 1692 and 1693, resulting in more than 200 people being accused of witchcraft, thirty tried and convicted, with nineteen (fourteen women and five men) hung from trees and others who died in jail or by other means.[2] The same religious extremism, which espoused a view that women were inherently sinful and more susceptible to damnation, would see folks put to death because of their religious convictions. Religious extremism remains a threat to religious freedom today.

In large measure the religious liberty arguments that are most extreme in our culture today, particularly around LGBTQIA issues of equality, follow the patterns of seventeenth-century extremism. Pastor Worley, Pastor Anderson, Pastor Jimenez, and Sheikh Farrokh Sekaleshfar might be some of the most extreme, but their rhetoric can be heard in the mouths of black preachers all over the nation. African Americans who invoke religious freedom are faced with a serious question regarding the width and breadth of anti-LGBTQIA rhetoric and how that rhetoric squares with their core beliefs. On the question of marriage equality, for instance, the overwhelming message from black churches was "nay." However, the gutting of the Voting Rights Act resulted in the churches calling foul. The First Amendment of the US Constitution for which many African American ancestors died is rendered weak when its five freedoms do not extend to all. The civil rights of African American LGBTQIA folks are easily trammeled as it relates to their sexual orientation. Marriage is a religious concept, and it should apply equally to LGBTQIA folks as well.

Demythologization of religious freedom serves as a precursor to a philosophical paradigm shift because it sets the parameters for examining the motivations that promote messages of doom. The fundamentalist evangelical agenda is poised to move America from a democracy to a theocracy and has already begun to do so. The black preaching and teaching examined herein is committed to this worldview and is afraid of being adjudged in violation of the "rules" of the polis—those rules that establish the circumference of moral suasion and the confines of respectability.³ This suggests that the political exchange between the church and the state does produce evil, but with a philosophical shift it can also produce good. The concept of the polis, understood as a gathered community rather than as the city-state, provides one way of understanding how this shift can take place.

The polis I envision is one without walls. In ancient Greek culture, a city-state was prominently known for being walled, and its activities took place within those walls. The story of Troy as told in *Troades* suggests that the fate of its citizens came down to the Trojan horse, which they drew into their walls, thus leaving them at the mercy of the Greeks. The walls, though considered fortification, are the structural evidence of the limits of a city-state. While walls are designed to protect the inhabitants of a city, regulate behavior within the city, and display the honor of the city, they also mark people for expulsion who do not conform to its stated polity.⁴ However, there was one city in ancient Greece, the city of Sparta, that was without walls and welcomed the stranger. It is that model that I follow in suggesting the polis as a theoretical framing of the community of folks gathered outside the gate of church communities from which they have been expelled. In essence, the prescription for survival for some is to "flee the city," for in the city the disease of stasis infects the inhabitants and embroils them in disagreement about how best to heal.⁵

Most people I surveyed grew up in a particular faith tradition, though some did not. For those who are "churched" to remain within the "walls" of the same faith tradition in which their sexual identity is frowned upon as "sinful" requires a particularized theo-ethical philosophy related to belonging. Persons outside the gate, whether driven by rhetoric away from the *temple of one's familiar* or by virtue of having grown up in an environment that does not value church participation, need a particularized theo-ethical philosophy as well. At its lowest common denominator, black church theology operates as a microcosm of the polis. It acts in many respects as a police force. It attempts to legislate morality, codifies certain behavior as sinful, and makes determinations about "sin" based on external evidence. In many respects its liberative ethos remains enslaved by Western Protestant ontology, which is, in the Levinasian sense, totalizing and lacking "ethics." However, I am not advancing a traditional view of ethics associated with the discourse on morality and virtue as is prominent in the Western Protestant tradition, though those rationalities are important; rather, I am proposing a discourse situated in the phenomenological project, which Levinas treats as an "optics" with which to view others.

Levinas determined that "ethics precedes ontology."[6] This is essential for framing a theo-ethical philosophy for engaging black queers in black churches as well as for addressing intersubjective relationality both inside and outside "the black church." I argue for a theo-ethical philosophical approach to human subjectivity and relationality that is applicable in the realm of the "religious," the "spiritual," and the "natural," as those terms have found expression within black faith and life. This way, those who have been scattered outside the gate of "normativity" within black teaching and preaching have a theoretical framework with which to engage a plurality of spaces.

Fundamentally, LGBTQIA persons are part of the bountiful blessing that is God's creation.[7] Their faith matters. God's admonition against pastors who "scatter the flock," an idea raised in Jeremiah 12:1–4, emphasizes that the privilege of guiding a flock comes with deep spiritual responsibility. Having a theology, or more particularly a Christology, grounded in an ethics of hospitality avoids the pitfalls that cause people to scatter. Philosophy understood as the guiding principle for intersubjective relationality—how we relate to each other as human beings—undergirds this idea. Engagement with ethics precedes ontological judgment—that is, the judgment of one's *beingness*. I make the claim, supported by Levinasian theory, that every human being reflects God. Levinas says it this way: "The absolutely other is the Other—*l'absolument Autre, c'est Autrui*."[8] From this perspective, I argue God might be imaged as a composite drawing of all that God continues to create. If every other is absolutely the Other, the pronouncement made in Ephesians 4:6 that "God is all in all" holds true. Indeed, Eboni Marshall Turman posits: "God's exclusively unorthodox body that defies the status quo is inclusive of, rather makes room for other(ed) bodies that are, in the first instance, characterized by worldly paradox and fragmentation, to challenge unjust norms that engender brokenness, while simultaneously pointing toward possibilities of plenitude and redemption."[9] Turman develops a theology of the incarnation that appreciates the paradoxical nature of creation in all its mystery, tension, and possibility. This aligns with biblical scholars who argue for the presence of God in the body.[10]

Mitzi J. Smith contends: "Womanist biblical scholars understand the light of God and the goodness of God to be situated in black female bodies. And we are determined to shine a light on injustice even when it is found in the black ink of the sacred text and to declare truths that can lighten and enlighten the paths of the most marginalized." Smith and Turman present a formula for womanist theological musings that I find instructive for a queer womanist theo-ethical philosophy. It is imperative that all of creation be accorded the same receptivity, particularly in the preaching moment. Starting from a perspective of all-inclusive creation memorializes the sacredness of God's creation. Only when the vision of an all-inclusive creation takes center stage and figures prominently in intersubjective dialogue can the true bounty of blessings be realized. When some "care-takers" are not welcomed to the field, the harvest yields less abundance for the reapers to gather and the bounty is diminished.

Presupposing a complex amalgamation of theoretical maneuvers, Levinas responds to the totalizing aspect of Western Protestant ontology, which advances an intersubjective relationality in which the "other" is a mere object and reflection of our gaze. As is evident in Pastor Anderson's sermon, there is the rudimentary concern with how alterity in this construct is governed within the church, and, consequently, critical thought must be given to how alterity is governed outside the gate of the church as well.

Alterity, the positioning of another person outside ourselves as other than ourselves, constitutes the basic formulation of subjectivity as a theological and ethical concern. How do we see other human beings? What are the markers for how we engage in basic human dynamics with other sentient beings? We tend to view other human beings as we view ourselves. In effect, this reduces other human beings to the same-as-we-are. The metaphysical tendency to reduce otherness to sameness presupposes that our fixation on ourselves is the only construct by which we envision all of creation, which we presume to be similarly situated. Creation must be created like "us." Male and female, then, mistakenly become reified as the sole normative gender and sexual identities, despite evidence to the contrary. For instance, the Hebrew terms *adamah* and *adam* literally mean "ground" and "human being," respectively.[11] In the Hebrew, *adam* is not a proper noun. Traditionally, however, the "*adam*" has been reduced to a singular gender, and the term has morphed into an actual proper noun—Adam. Contrastingly, in one of the two creation stories found in Genesis 2, God creates and then later surgically separates what we know from modern science to be an intersex person. This is arguably the first gender-reassignment surgery. The significance of this argument is not that there were queers in the creation, though I believe that there were; rather, the point here is that God created all that *is*. "Human being" is equally constituted as "both/and" as well as "either/or" and *all* points in between. There is no neat favoring of one or the other, as is evidenced in the diverse populations of people with fluid concepts of gender identity and sexual orientation. Diversity colors creation *ad infinitum*.

In a sermon entitled "The Wrath of God," Pastor Terry K. Anderson, whom we critically evaluated in Chapter 3, drew such close parallels to the rhetoric of Pastor Worley, introduced in Chapter 2, that it appears he was quoting Pastor Worley in his preachment:

> Here me brothers and sisters, same-sex marriage is not the goal of a homosexual agenda. Same-sex marriage is not their goal, that's a red herring, that's a red herring thrown on the track to get us off the scent; that's not their goal. Their goal is to reorder our perception of reality and

to move God absolutely out of the arena of public discourse. Because in order for you to be gay, you got to move God out of the way. In order for a man to have sexual feelings for a man, you got to rationalize that there is no God. Because anything God creates has within it a seed to reproduce itself. And everything that God made that could reproduce itself God said "and it was good." And any relationship that cannot reproduce its own kind must be evil. And if it's evil God can't bless it ... All unrighteousness, all ungodliness incurs the wrath of God.[12]

The rhetoric of the bully pulpit preachers referenced in this volume represents what many people hear on Sunday morning about Black queers from the Black preaching tradition. The nexus between the mind slavery of the plantation and the rhetoric of these preachers is undeniable, particularly as most churches in the black preaching tradition descend directly from slaveholding denominations and associations that have their heart and soul emulsified in a "moral code" that despises queers, seeks to excommunicate queers from the household of faith, and couches this hateful message in "God-talk" as though their rhetoric were God-ordained. What is more, the mimicry of white evangelicals by Black preachers fits Akbar's description of psychological slavery. Akbar declares that "in order to change the African consciousness we must change the information that is in the African mind."[13] Those chains must be broken.

Thinking of preachers as oracles who pontificate a message of hate-talk disguised as God-talk, one can see the systemic impact of their logic as they lull congregations into trances where they work their "magic" to trick people into believing that God hates LGBTQIA persons. Racecraft operates as an extension of the plantation to keep alive the essence of slaveholders' ideology that enslaved Africans were inferior chattel capable of being controlled. The social construction of gender binaries dominates the terrain by which "others" are engaged. When those of us in the LGBTQIA community do not conform to the dominant pathosis, we can face disparaging treatment, as the many examples already discussed demonstrate. Pastors need to critically reflect on their duty to speak an accurate message that does not scatter the flock. In the context of the black preaching and teaching tradition, the awareness that many are harmed by inaccurate messages and still others remove themselves from active participation in houses of worship should ring the alarm that further contemplation, meditation, and preparation is needed to be sure that what is being spoken is a direct word from the Lord. This requires more than rote memorization of the Bible. It also requires a keen appreciation for God's creation. God's creation is good and should be treated as such. All too often the preaching moment gets highjacked by charisma and the message morphs into a sideshow with little to no real connection to the heart of God. It is instructive to note that God did not specify to Jeremiah *what* message was improper, nor does Jeremiah 23 refer to a particular audience. The point of God's admonition is that there is a delicate balance that pastors are called to strike when mounting the sacred desk to bring forth the God-inspired, God-breathed word. A theo-ethical philosophy grounded in intersubjective relationality shifts the paradigmatic thinking from a strict constructionist, biblical literalism embellished by racecraft to a theo-ethical philosophy of an all-inclusive creation connected to the *imago Dei*.

Notes

1 Jay Michelson, "Redefining Religious Liberty: The Covert Campaign against Civil Rights," *Political Research Associates*, March 2013.

2 Jess Blumberg, "A Brief History of the Salem Witch Trials: One Town's Strange Journey from Paranoia to Pardon," *Smithsonian Magazine*, October 23, 2007, updated October 24, 2022, https://www.smithsonianmag.com/history/a-brief-history-of-the-salem-witch-trials-175162489/; Kristina Garcia, "Possessed: The Salem Witch Trils," *PennToday,* March 11, 2022, https://penntoday.upenn.edu/news/possessed-salem-witch-trials; and Michael Brown, "The Salem Witch Trials: Dehumanizing the Different,"*The Histories* 15, no. 1, Article 10, https://digitalcommons.lasalle.edu/the_histories/vol15/iss1/10 (all URLs accessed July 5, 2024).

3 Rosemary Radford Ruether, "The Family Agenda of the Christian Right," in *Christianity and the Making of the Modern Family* (Boston: Beacon, 2000), 156–80.

4 Valeria M. Hope and Eireann Marshall, *Death and Disease in the Ancient City* (London: Routledge, 2000), 41–43.

5 Ibid., 19.

6 Emmanuel Levinas, "Ethics as First Philosophy," in *The Levinas Reader*, ed. Sean Hand (Oxford: Basil Blackwell, 1989), 75–87.

7 Pamela Lightsey, *Our Lives Matter: A Womanist Queer Theology* (Eugene, OR: Pickwick, 2015), 51–66.

8 Emmanuel Levinas, *Totality and Infinity: An Essay on Exteriority*, trans. Alphonso Lingus (Pittsburgh, PA: Duquesne University Press, 1996), 39.

9 Eboni Marshall Turman, *Toward a Womanist Ethic of Incarnation* (New York: Palgrave-McMillan, 2013), 42.

10 Mitzi J. Smith, "'This Little Light of Mine': The Womanist Biblical Scholar as Prophetess, Iconoclast, and Activist," in *I Found God in Me: A Womanist Biblical Hermeneutics Reader*, ed. Mitzi J. Smith (Eugene, OR: Cascade, 2015), 113.

11 Another word used repeatedly in the Bible, *nephesh*, also means "living being."

12 Terry K. Anderson, "The Wrath of God," posted to YouTube, May 23, 2016, https://www.youtube.com/watch?v=jlnmKn6dKxw (accessed August 10, 2016).

13 Akbar, *Breaking the Chains*, 34.

APPENDIX A: DEATH DOCUMENTS FOR LILLIE RUTH MITCHELL

NORTH CAROLINA DEPARTMENT OF HUMAN RESOURCES
DIVISION OF HEALTH SERVICES - VITAL RECORDS BRANCH
MEDICAL EXAMINER'S CERTIFICATE OF DEATH

REGISTRATION DISTRICT NO. 008- LOCAL NO. DATE OF DEATH (Month, Day, Year): 8-20-84

NAME OF DECEASED: Lillie Ruth Mitchell Carter — SEX: Female — DATE OF DEATH: (Prob) 8-20-84

COLOR OR RACE: Black — STATE OF BIRTH: N.C. — COUNTY OF BIRTH: Bertie — DATE OF BIRTH: 03-21-51 — AGE: 33

PLACE OF DEATH — COUNTY: Bertie — CITY OR TOWN: Windsor — NAME OF HOSPITAL OR INSTITUTION: Cashie River — INSIDE CITY LIMITS: Yes

RESIDENCE — STATE: N.C. — COUNTY: Bertie — CITY OR TOWN: Windsor — STREET AND NUMBER OR RFD NO.: Route 4, Box 39 — INSIDE CITY LIMITS: No

CITIZEN OF WHAT COUNTRY: USA — MARRIED, NEVER MARRIED, WIDOWED, DIVORCED: Widowed — USUAL OCCUPATION: Homemaker — KIND OF BUSINESS OR INDUSTRY: Own Home — WAS DECEDENT EVER IN U.S. ARMED FORCES: No

SOCIAL SECURITY NUMBER: 238-90-4288

FATHER'S NAME: Tommie Mitchell — MOTHER'S MAIDEN NAME: Katherine Hoggard

INFORMANT'S NAME AND ADDRESS: Katherine H. Mitchell, Route 4, Box 39, Windsor, N.C. — RELATION TO DECEASED: Mother

PART 1. DEATH CAUSED BY:
(a) IMMEDIATE CAUSE: Asphyxia by drowning

CONDITIONS, IF ANY, WHICH GAVE RISE TO IMMEDIATE CAUSE (b): DUE TO, OR AS A CONSEQUENCE OF:
(c) DUE TO, OR AS A CONSEQUENCE OF:

PART II. OTHER SIGNIFICANT CONDITIONS: Alcohol Intoxication

AUTOPSY: Yes

ACCIDENT, SUICIDE, HOMICIDE, UNDETERMINED, NATURAL CAUSES, OR PENDING: Accident — DESCRIBE HOW INJURY OCCURRED: Fell into river — PLACE OF INJURY: River — CITY OR R.F.D.: Windsor — COUNTY: Bertie — STATE: N.C.

TIME OF INJURY: Unknown

MEDICAL EXAMINER CERTIFICATION — THE DECEDENT WAS PRONOUNCED DEAD: Approx 2400 08 22 1984 1845 — DATE SIGNED: 09-05-84

SIGNATURE: J. Ray Dawkins, M.D. — ADDRESS: Windsor, N.C. — MEDICAL EXAMINER OF: Bertie

BURIAL, CREMATION, OTHER: Burial — DATE: 08-25-84 — NAME OF CEMETERY OR CREMATORY: Hillcrest Cem. — LOCATION: Windsor, N.C.

FUNERAL HOME: Cherry's Funeral Home, Windsor, N.C. — SIGNATURE OF EMBALMER: Clatius M. Cherry, Jr. — LICENSE NO.: 1092

DATE REC'D BY LOCAL REG.: 09-06-84 — SIGNATURE OF REGISTRAR: Elizabeth Pl Joyner, MPH — Clatius M. Cherry — 1092

APPENDIX A

6346

STATE OF NORTH CAROLINA
DEPARTMENT OF HUMAN RESOURCES
DIVISION OF HEALTH SERVICES
Office of the Chief Medical Examiner
Post Office Box 2488
Chapel Hill, North Carolina 27514

CERTIFICATION FOR PAYMENT OF FEES

AUG 29 1984

"LILLIE CARTER"
Jane Doe (unknown)   8/22/84
(Decedent's Name)   (Date of Service)   Signed: Med. Exam/Reg. Path.

HOSPITAL:
1. A payment of $10.00 is made when the Medical Examiner expressly orders a body outside the hospital to be taken to the hospital for examination.
2. No payment is due when a body is taken to the hospital prior to the Medical Examiner being notified of the death.
3. No payment is due when the autopsy is performed in the hospital.

TOTAL $ _____

RADIOLOGY:
Specified fees will be paid to the radiologist or the hospital for technical services rendered on Medical Examiner cases. The radiologist can also separate fees for professional services if he interprets the films and renders an opinion in cases where the Medical Examiner or the pathologist is unable to do so.

SERVICES	(Itemization Required)	CHARGES

Total $ _____

TRANSPORTATION:
This fee is paid for transportation of bodies at the bid rate or, in case of no bid at the rate of $.50 per mile loaded. The minimum fee is $20.00. Agreement is hereby made to transport remains of the above decedent for the appropriate specified fee. This fee constitutes full and complete payment for the services provided.

FROM: BERTIE MEMORIAL HOSPITAL
TO: PCMH
FROM: PCMH
TO: CHERRY'S FUNERAL HOME

Purpose:
☐ Viewing by Medical Examiner
☑ Autopsy
☑ Other   IDENTIFICATION
   Explain

If for autopsy did you wait and return body:
Yes CHERRY'S FUNERAL HOME
         Where to
No (why not) _____

☑ Check here if you are the family designated funeral home handling final disposition of the body.

☐ Check here if additional bodies on trip. (Enter the names on top left corner of this form)

TRF 90 @ .50 = 45ᴺ

Name and Address of the Provider of Service:
CHERRY'S FUNERAL HOME
C.M. CHERRY, JR.
P.O. BOX 447, WINDSOR, N.C. 27983
710 5008 01966
(Social Security or IRS No. Required)

SIGNED: C.M. Cherry, Jr.
(Provider of Service or Authorized Agent)

APPROVED: Page Hudson, M.D.
(Chief Medical Examiner)

T08002

Date 08/23/84   Page No. 1

STATEMENT OF:

Approx. 9:30 PM 08/23/84
Kathrine Mitchell, of Rt. 4 Box 39, Windsor, N.C. came to the Sheriff's Office to report her daughter missing. Her daughter, Lillie Ruth Carter, fitted the discription of a body recovered from the Cashie River 08/22/84. According to Kathrine Mitchell, Lillie Ruth Carter had an arguement with her girl friend Josephine Wiggins from Aulander. Mrs. Carter took car keys belonging to Miss Wiggins. Patrolman Davis, Windsor Police Dept. went to the Carter residence and made Mrs. Carter return the keys belonging to Miss Wiggins. Miss Wiggins left. Patrolman Davis left the residence at 8:05 PM. According to Kathrine Mitchell, after Miss Wiggins left, Lillie Ruth Carter went to George Holley's residence. Mr. Holley lives a couple of blocks away. Lillie Ruth Carter returned home at 10:05 PM. She told her mother that she had a hundred dollars in the bank and asked her mother to take care of her child, Mark Carter, 9 yrs old. She told her mother that if she wasn't home by 11:45 PM, she wouldn't ever come home. She left the residence walking.
Dr. Harris stated the cause of death as drowning and no foul play was indicated.
I talked with Kathrine Mitchell later and she stated she don't think there was any foul play. That her daughter had killed herself.

APPENDIX B: SURVEY QUESTIONS

1. Which of the following denominations/communions have you joined over your lifetime?
    - Baptist
    - AME
    - AME Zion
    - Presbyterian
    - Episcopalian
    - Catholic
    - Church of God in Christ (COGIC)
    - Pentecostal
    - United Holy Church
    - United Church of Christ
    - Methodist
    - MCC
    - Ba'Hai
    - Judaism
    - Muslim
    - Other (please specify)
2. Where is/was your church located?
3. How long were you a member?
4. Who was the clergy person(s) at this church? Male or Female?
5. What, if anything, was ever said about sexual orientation, marriage equality or LGBTQIA persons in the preaching or teaching?
6. When did this occur? Date/Time
7. How do you self-identify in terms of sexual orientation?
8. May I contact you for participation in a focus group for this research?
9. Please state your full name.
10. What is the best means for contacting you to participate in a focus group discussion?

APPENDIX C: TRANSCRIPTION OF THE SERMON BY PASTOR ANDERSON

Pastor Terry K. Anderson
"What Must the Church Say About Same Sex Marriage?"

I want to wade further into controversy this morning by talking about an issue that is a hot button issue in our country and in our courts, and I suspect in our churches if we don't deal with it. "What Must the Church Say About Same Sex Marriage?" I do not broach this subject to be insensitive to the persons who are struggling with their sexuality because I think the mistake that the church makes in its vitriol to get heard, in its shrieking, shouting noises over the den and the dirge of other noises; I think the church makes a mistake when we make one sin bigger than any other sin. And we crow about and cry loud about same sex marriage and homosexuality and we turn our eye to adultery, to fornication, to pornography, to child abuse, to domestic violence, to sex and immorality going on in the church, we are hypocrites if we don't preach about that. But, the violent, radical gay rights agenda would have the preacher and the church to be quiet about what their real agenda is. And as God's preacher, I am called to preach the whole counsel of God. Because I think that the problem is we are trying to come up with moral and political solutions to a problem that is spiritual in nature. Moral and political solutions can't deal with a God problem. The problem is sin and sin cannot be dealt with morally because morality could be relative. Sin cannot be dealt with politically because it could be politically correct or it could be on the right or on the left; so, sin has got to be dealt with by God. God determines the standard; not the democrats, not the republicans, not the fundamental left or the liberal right; it is God who decides what the standard is. If you can remember, President George W. Bush tried to pass legislation in this marriage act that he tried to pass when he was president, to make marriage, uh, as an amendment to the constitution, that marriage was between a man and a woman. That legislation failed in Congress. And I might add, that Barack Obama who was then Senator Obama voted against that legislation. And when the President, Barack Obama, who is now in office, became President, he said marriage is between a man or a woman; but I want to leave the issue to individual states. So, the White House that is currently occupied by the current president, is straddling the fence when it comes to this business of same sex marriage. So we can't look to the President for any guidance or leadership on the issue. It must come from the word of God. My political leanings notwithstanding, I am not in any sense against or for what Mr. Obama is doing because my help does not come from the White House. He has his opinion, he has his way of legislating; he is the president and if he were to come in here right now, all of us would stand up in deference to him because he is the president of the United States. But, my help does not come from the president. My hope is not in Washington. My hope is built on nothing less than Jesus blood and his righteousness, I dare not trust the sweetest frame; but holy lean on Jesus name. On Christ, the solid rock I stand; all other ground is sinking sand. Lilly Grove, it is not enough to condemn the darkness, if we fail to be the light. I said it is not enough to condemn the darkness, if we fail to be the light. Jesus said you are the salt of the earth. If the salt loses its savor it is thenceforth good for nothing. You are the light of the world; a city that sits on a hill that cannot be hid. Men don't light a candle and put it under a bushel, but on a candlestick that it may give light to all that are in the house. So, let your light so shine before men that they may see your works, but glorify the Father who is in heaven. Now, in all honestly, how did we get here to have to even discuss same sex marriage? That was unheard of prior to this present cultural situation. How did we get here? Ironically, we got here with the heterosexual community. The invention of the birth control pill and sexual self-expression, which became the mantra in the 1960s. Sexual expression became something to be expressed publically and frequently and outside monogamous, lifelong marriage. Hue Hefner and the playboy mansion shifted the center of gravity from marital faithfulness to personal enjoyment without pain of stigma nor consequence. Free sex and the free drug movement of the 1960s have wrought devastating consequences in the 21st c. because if that is right, then this is right. If your argument is going to be rational, for one thing to be right on this side and this be wrong; you can't say this is wrong and that's right. If same sex marriage is wrong, then sex outside marriage is got to be wrong; if you're going to stand on the word of God. Aw, I don't guess you're going to buy this tape either. You, you, you might be asking what difference does it make. Live and let live. That's that man's business what he does behind closed doors; that's that woman's business what she does behind closed doors. That doesn't affect me. I am going to love my wife. I'm going to take care of my children. I'm going to have sex with my wife, it doesn't bother me what somebody else is doing in the privacy of their own home. What difference does it make? To ask that question is to have a man on a boat with a whole lot of other people on the boat and he is on his side of the boat and he has a right, because everything now is a right. He has a right to drill a hole on his side of the boat and you have no right to go to the other side of the boat and tell him you can't do that. He say, "wait a minute, stay on your side with your wife and your family. I'm on my side of the boat." But, the water is going to drown everybody. The Psalms says "if the foundations be destroyed, what then can the righteous do?" If you drill a hole in the boat all of us 'gon sink. Now brother and sisters you hear me, same sex marriage is not about marriage. That's not what it's about at all, don't be fooled. It is about destroying the Christian idea of what a family is. It's about tearing down what God has instituted. Ellen DeGeneres, Rosie O'Donnell our own mayor, it's not about same sex unions and civil unions; it's about throwing your fist in God's face saying "I know what you established, but I'm gon walk my own way." And the church is silent because they want political favors. But, you can't shake your fist in the King's face, if you're eating meat at the king's table. There's got to be a separation between a prophet and a politician; because when the world wants a word from the Lord, they don't go to the politician, they come to the church, and if our voice is hoarse…because Paul says "if the trumpet does not make a clear sound, (I wish I had a Bible reader), then the warriors will not know it's time to go into battle." Since the Holy Ghost led me to that: Jesus, in the New Testament there's a story about a field that a land owner owns and uh, in the field some tares have grown among the wheat. And, the workers got up the next morning and saw that their wheat field was full of tares. And somebody said "what happened, when we went to bed last night it was a wheat field; but now that we got up this morning there's tares among the wheat?" Somebody said, "an enemy has done this. An enemy has gotten in the field and sown some tares among the wheat." And one of the servants says, "Master you want us to pull it up?" He said "naw, naw because you might be too insensitive, you might be too coarse, you might be too judgmental, you might be too hard. Let the wheat and the tares grow together, and when I come...let the homosexual sing in the choir, let them serve on the usher board, let them come to church, you just preach the gospel and when I come...I wish I had a witness...You let the adulterer lead the music, you let the whoremonger give in the offering. Just let him hear the gospel; don't you try to tear them up 'cause you might mess something up because they don't know what you are. God is just drawing a straight line with a crooked stick. They don't know who preaching to'um. You look like a preacher; you sound like a preacher. Let the wheat and the tare grow together and when I come I will separate them. Na, naw, naw, if a same sex couple join this church, I'm not putting them out, 'cause they need to hear the gospel. Now listen, I am not going to perform a ceremony. I want you to put that on television, uh, uh camera people? I am not performing a marriage ceremony between two women or two women because it is sin. Marriage is between a man and a woman. Because anatomically, physiologically they fit together to give one another sexual pleasure. Am I doing alright? Something wrong with a man who wants another man. Something is wrong with a woman who desires sexually another woman. I oughta have some brothers help me right here. I said I oughta have some brothers help me right here. If God made anything better than a woman, he kept it for himself. Her lips are like... cheeks like pomegranates, breasts like two twin roes feeding among the lilies, her neck like the tower of David builded for an armory, lips like threads of scarlet; if God made anything better than a woman; He's hiding it. Now, y'all come on, come on get your minds back in church, come on, come on, sit down, sit down. I know y'all ready to go home right now, but sit down. You got bout 20 more minutes; sit down. Same sex marriage is not about marriage, don't be fooled. It is about destroying the Christian idea of the family as established by God in creation. He told the man have dominion, and you and your woman be fruitful and multiply and while they were doing what God said, they were naked and not ashamed. But then, sin comes in and the price tag gets switched. And what God meant for right and righteousness and pleasure becomes nasty and sinful and convoluted cause when you don't do it God's way, chaos and havoc is wreaked. There are gays in my family; but I can't not preach the truth cause I've got some gay family member. Aw no, I love them. They are my blood relatives. But I'm praying that they come out of that gay lifestyle. I'm praying that they turn that sinful lifestyle aloose. But I can't pray for them to come out of that sinful lifestyle then I get in sin and point my finger at them. No, I've got to walk worthy; if I'm going to lead them out of that sin. I can't myself be in sin and then try to talk to somebody about sin. No. no, I can't have a woman sleeping at my house and then I'm trying to tell my niece or my nephew you gotta change your lifestyle. because uh, if they were disrespectful they would say to me "Unc, you can't tell me what to do, look at what you are doing." If you're living in a glass house...I forgot what group made that, but that was a good song back in the day. In October of 2008 a first grade class in San Francisco took a field trip to City Hall to celebrate the wedding of their lesbian teacher to another woman. Earlier that same year a federal appeals court in Massachusetts said a local school district was well within its bounds to allow second graders to [1]read a book about homosexual marriage, *My Two Dads*. Now, now, now if marriage is no longer the union of one man and one woman, why not three men, why not two men and a woman, why not five women and one man, why not two brothers marry two sisters of the same family, why not polygamy, why not endogeny where a blood brother marries his blood sister, why not have sex with dogs or sheep or cows or bulls, why not bestiality? Because the Bible says it's in. Now if those that I mentioned are abnormal, then if same sex marriage is not abnormal, then I don't know what is. My favorite show used to be Grey's Anatomy until those two doctors got married and started kissing each other on prime time television. Makes me want to hurl just talking about it. But, to the world, to the culture, that's normal. They have no problem with it on The View, they have no problem with it on CBS on The Talk. They have no problem with it in prime time television with sitcoms that, that glorify and celebrate same sex unions; but the Bible says, it's a sin. You don't have to take my word for it; I don't have time to go through it all but when you read Leviticus it's an abomination. I wish I had a witness. A whole town was set on fire because angels sent from heaven had come down to talk with Lot and homosexual men were trying to tear Lot's house down to have sexual relations with angels and God blinded them and in their blindness they were still reaching for the door. And the Lord told Lot "get your whole family out of this city because this town is about to go up in smoke." Somebody ought to help me preach here. Abraham said "Lord let me go down there and talk with them." He said, "Lord if I can find 50," I wished I had a Bible reader, "would you spare the city?" The Lord said, "I'll do it for you Abraham for 50." Abraham said, "well maybe 40?" The Lord said, "if you can find 40 who executes judgment and walks uprightly, I will save the city." Then, Abraham said well maybe 30, how about 20, 10...Abraham couldn't find one man who walked right before God.

---

[1] Lillygrovembc, "What Must the Church Do About Same Sex Marriage?," YouTube, April 15, 2012, accessed July 18, 2016, https://www.youtube.com/watch?v=SfpVPydcNrQ.

INDEX

1 Corinthians 6:9–10 42
1 Corinthians 13:11 66
The 700 Club 42, 43

accommodation 79–81
Adam and Eve 11, 21, 41, 85, 87–8
adamah/adam 135
Africentrism 14, 63–4, 66, 104
agapé (God's love and love for God) 59
Ahmed, Sarah 27–8
Akan people of Africa 53–4
Akbar, Na'im 9, 104, 105–7, 109
    see also "mind slavery"
al-mus-tad'afun fi al-ard 109
Amos, prophet 83–5
Anderson, Terry K. 11, 14, 26, 82–6, 125
    Black Lives Matter 82–3
    "do no harm" principles 91–2
    group dynamics 121–5
    and the prophet Amos 83–5
    and Solomon, son of David 85–6
anti-LGBTQIA *see* slurs
Apostle Paul 66, 99–100

Bahati, David 108
Baldwin, James 79–80
bestiality 86–7
Bible 40–2, 55, 87–8, 107, 126, 100, 101, 103–4
    Adam and Eve 11, 21, 41, 85, 87–8
    Community influence 2
    see also individual Biblical passages ...
Black Church theology as accommodation 79–81
Black Lives Matter 80–1
    and Audre Lorde 81
    Frantz Fanon 81–2
    Terry K. Anderson 82–3

Black Psychology (Jones) 104
"Black Sexuality: A Pawn of White Culture" (Douglas) 39–40
Black Skin, White Masks (Fanon) 27
blackface stereotypes 18–19, 54
    "The Blackface Stereotype" by Townes 18
    perpetuating evil 18
blood sacrifices 87–8
Bonhoeffer, Dietrich 91–2
Boone, Wellington 35–6, 42–3
Breaking the Chains of Psychological Slavery (Akbar) 104, 105–7, 109–10
Brotherhood Organization of a New Destiny (BOND) 51–2, 81
Brown, Brian 45
Buber, Martin 89
"bully pulpit" 9, 13, 31–71
    anatomy of racecraft 82–3
    black preachers and the way of love 61–2
    covenants 56–7
    deconstruction 32–3
    encountering freedom 58–9
    ethical considerations, identity 53–5
    faith formation 66
    finding strength amidst struggle 45–50
    free from judgment 57–8
    gendered rhetorical violence 51–3
    intentional false prophecy messaging 40–1
    interconnection between racism/racecraft 38–40
    invisible ontology 35–7
    managing devaluation 64–5
    moral and spiritual freedom 55–6
    philosophical implications 59–61
    racist ontology of black preachers 37–8

slurs and misogyny 50–3
spiritual formation 63–4
ties that bind 33–5
Burton, LeVar 104–5
Bush, George W. 40
Butler, Keith 35–6, 43

Camper, Peter 74
Cannon, Katie 27, 125, 127
Carter, Lillie Ruth Mitchell 3–5, 63–4
catechesis 99–101
Cavarero, Adriana 99
chattel slavery 22, 105–6, 136
cultural hegemony 22–3
childhood connections of the author 3
Church of God in Christ (COGIC) worship 106–7
church and state 101–3
civil rights movement 1, 32, 42, 64–5, 83, 131–2
Clark Sr., Rufus Isaac 125
CNN broadcasting 33–4, 39
COGIC *see* Church of God in Christ worship
colonialism 22, 27
see also slavery
community, sense of 110–13
"compassionate conservatism" 40
concentration camps 89–92
Cone, James H. 91
Cooper, Anderson 33–4, 39
Copeland, M. Shawn 56–7, 58–9
countermemory
navigating outsider status in the Church 20
perpetuating evil 18
whiteface stereotypes 18–20
covenants 56–7
Critical Ethnography: Methods, Ethics, and Performance (Madison) 9
cultural hegemony 22–3
see also hegemony
"culture of dissemblance" 120

death squads 108
DeGruy, Joy 65
Deuteronomy 22:5 41–2
DeVaughan, Quentin 50–1
DeVaughn, William 86–7

Diawara, Manthia 18–19
"do no harm" principles 91–4
Dodson, James 42
doublemindedness 74
Douglas, Kelly Brown 6–8, 39–40, 88–9
"dreamers" 74–5
Du Bois, W. E. B. 73, 74, 94

Eden *see* Adam and Eve
"enfleshing freedom" 58–9
Enuma Elish 87–8
"Eros", *eros* (intimate love) 13–14, 58–9
erotic, the 60–1, 62
estrangement 7–8
ethics 2, 25, 53–5, 89–90, 125
Moral Majority 24
"Ethics as First Philosophy" (Levinas) 89–90
evangelicalism 13, 54–5
Black Church theology as accommodation 79
countermemory and whiteface stereotypes 19
and George W. Bush 40
perpetuating evil 18
right-wing fundamentalism 24–5
slave catechisms 100–1
see also "bully pulpit"
evil 18

face of the other *see* whiteface stereotypes
faith formation, "bully pulpit" 66
Falwell, Jerry 24–5
family 42, 56, 113–17
Fanon, Frantz 27, 81–2
fault lines 103–4
Fields, Karen 35, 36–7
see also racecraft
Fields, Karen E. & Barbara J. 82
Focus on the Family 42
Foucault, Michel 18, 22
freedom 13–14, 55–9, 101, 119–20
Fruit of Islam (FOI) 111
Full Gospel Baptist Church Fellowship International 50–1
fundamentalism 23–5
see also evangelicalism

Galatians 4:19 2
Garrett, Michael 48
"Gatekeepers" network 45
gay bashing *see* slurs
gender
    male–female relationality 59–60
    misogyny 50–3
    rhetorical violence 51–3
    womanism and the LGBTQIA body 6–7
Genesis 13:13 41–2
"ghost of the plantation" 106–7
"God's Purpose in Marriage" sermon (Boone) 42–3
God's rule 88–9
    see also imago Dei
Golden Rule 54
"good life", living 25–7
"good news" Gospels 100, 101, 103–4
    see also Mark Gospels; Matthew Gospels
"Good News for Homosexuals" (Wright) 103
Graham, T. J. 44–5
Gramsci, Antonio 18
"Great Commission" 8, 37–8, 40, 100
Greater Mt. Cavalry Holy Church of America 47–8
Greco-Roman cultures 22

Hagar story in the Bible 55
Hebrews from Egypt 87–8
hegemony 10, 22–3
Heidegger, Martin 89–90
heteronormativity 53, 58, 125
Hill, Renee 63, 66
The History of White People (Painter) 74
Holocaust 89–92
Holy Spirit 8, 79, 125
homophobia *see* slurs
Homosexuality in Islam: Critical Reflection of Gay, Lesbian, and Transgender Muslims (Kugle) 109
Hope Christian Church, Maryland 46–7
Husserl 27
Hutcherson, Ken 45

"I and thou" (Buber) 89
identity 17–18, 53–5, 101–3
    Africentrism 14, 63–4, 66, 104
imago Dei 10, 89–91, 94
implicit bias 91
intentional false prophecy messaging 40–1
Interfaith Council 48
intersubjective relationality 89–91
invisible ontology 35–7
    see also racecraft
Irigaray, Luce 9, 58–60, 62
Islamic faith traditions 14, 107–9, 110–21

Jackson, Harry 46–7
James 3 92
Jesus of Nazareth 2, 17, 21, 56–8, 63–6, 88–9
"Jewish Question" 89–92
    see also Holocaust
Jimenez, Roger 107–8
Joe stereotypes 54
Johnson, Rader 37–8
    interconnection between racism/racecraft 38, 39
Jones, Reginald L. 104
Josiah, King 126–7
judgment 57–8
justice 32–3

"Kill the Gays" bill 108
King Jr., Martin Luther 1
kneeling for prayer 36–7
Kosofsky, Eve 44
Kugle, Scott Siraj at-Haqq 109
    Homosexuality in Islam 109

Lavater, Johann Kaspar 74
"Letter from a Birmingham Jail" (Amos) 83
Levinas, Emmanuel 9, 13–14, 89, 94
    and otherness 89–91
Leviticus 18:22 41–2
liberty *see* freedom
Lightsey, Pamela 84–5
Lilly Grove Missionary Baptist Church, Houston, Texas 11, 123–4
    see also Anderson, Terry K.

A Litany of Survival (Lorde) 74–6
logos 99
Long, Charles H. 22, 28
   cultural hegemony 22–3
Lorde, Audre 13–14, 17–18
   Black Church theology as accommodation 79–81
   Black Lives Matter 81
   black preachers and the way of love 62
   "enfleshing freedom" 58, 59
   living the "good life" 26–7
   minstrelsy, minstrel shows 74–6
   philosophical implications, bully pulpit 60–1
   sense of social justice 120–1
   Sister Outsider 35
love 59–62
   agapé (God's love and love for God) 59
   "Eros", *eros* (intimate love) 13–14, 58–9
Lovin, Robin 25

Mack, Jon 48
McMickle, Marvin 32–3, 41
Maddow, Rachel 108
Madison, Soyini 9
male–female relationality 59–60
Mammy stereotypes 54
Mark Gospels 101
marriage, marriage equality 41, 42, 59
   parroting 42–3, 44–5
   see also Adam and Eve
Mateen, Omar 107
Matthew Gospels 40, 100, 101
"Mayday for Marriage" rally 45
Meeks, James 45
"mind slavery" 9, 22, 86–7, 106–7, 109, 120–1, 126, 136
minstrelsy, minstrel shows 54, 74–9
misogyny 50–3
missionizing 108–9
Mohammed, Warith Deen 106–7
morality *see* ethics
morphóö, Christian maturity 63–4
Morton, Paul 50–1
mosques 117–18
   see also Islamic faith traditions

Mt. Cavalry Holy Church 92–3
Muhammad, Elijah *see* Nation of Islam
Muslim faith *see* Islamic faith traditions
mutuality among women 63

Nation of Islam (NOI) 110–17
National Organization for Marriage 45
navigating outsider status in the Church 20–2
Nazi concentration camps 89–92
Need: A Chorale for Black Woman Voices (Baldwin) 79–80
The Negro Church (Du Bois) 74
Negro inferiority *see* racism
"New World" 22
Niebuhr, Reinhold 91

Obergefell v. Hodges 42
Oduyoye, Mercy Amba 57
Office of Faith-based and Community Initiatives 40
On Physiognomy (Lavater) 74
"otherness" 10–12, 14, 100
   see also racism; whiteface stereotypes
Our Lives Matter: A Womanist Queer Theology (Lightsey) 84–5
Owens, Alfred 47–8

Painter, Nell 74
parroting 42–5
patriarchy 10, 54–5
Patterson, Jesse 36
Peele, William & Glen 5–6, 8
perpetuating evil 18
personal identity *see* identity
Peterson, Jesse Lee 51–2, 81
philia (friendship) 59
philosophical implications, "bully pulpit" 59–61
Post Traumatic Slave Disorder 64–5
pro forma heteronormativity 53
Protestantism 59, 89
psyche 100
Pulse Nightclub massacre 107–8

qualitative method informing public theology 9–12
Qu'ran 109
  see also Islamic faith traditions

racecraft 35, 37–40, 82–3, 91
Racecraft: The Soul of Inequality in American Life (Fields & Fields) 82
racism, racialization 37–41, 44–5, 54, 74, 100
  civil rights movement 1, 32, 42, 64–5, 83, 131–2
  minstrelsy, minstrel shows 54, 74–9
  see also whiteface stereotypes
Ray, Stephen 91–2, 94
right-wing fundamentalism 23–5, 45
  see also evangelicalism
Riley, Cole Arthur 21, 35
Robertson, Pat 42, 43
Rock, Chris 19
Romans 1 41–2, 88
Roots: The Next Generation (1979) 104–5

salvation 7, 88–9, 91
Sambo stereotypes 54
Sanders, Cheryl 54
scapegoating 87–8
"scattering the flock" 126
Sekaleshfar, Farrokh 107
self-love 66
  see also identity; love
sense of community 110–13
sense of family 113–17
sense of social justice 117–21
sexual difference 13–14, 17–18, 61–2, 91
sexuality and the Sacred 5–6, 58–9
Shepard, Matthew 117
sin 91–2, 101
Sister Outsider (Lorde) 35
sisterhood 63
slavery 28, 99–101, 104–7, 109
  chattel slavery 22, 105–6, 136
    cultural hegemony 22–3
  "mind slavery" 9, 22, 86–7, 106, 107, 109, 120–1, 126, 136

slurs 6–7, 11–12, 31–2, 50–1, 82, 107–17
  sense of community 110–13
  sense of family 113–17
  sense of social justice 117–21
  see also racism
Smallwood, Mattie Matilda Cherry 1–2
Smith, E. Dewey 92–3
Smith, Mitzi J. 100
social justice, sense of 117–21
"solidarity with the oppressed" 109
Souls of Black Folk (Du Bois) 74
Southern Baptist Convention (SBC) 39, 40
spirituality 55–6, 58–9, 63–4
stereotypes 18–20, 54, 74–9
  blackface stereotypes 18–19, 54
    "The Blackface Stereotype" by Townes 18
  perpetuating evil 18
  see also racism, racialization; slurs; whiteface stereotypes
Stranger at the Gate: To Be Gay and Christian in America (White) 24
strength amidst struggle 45–50
Strength for the Journey (Falwell) 24–5
suicide 3–5

techné 60–1
Terrell, JoAnne Marie 87–8
Thurman, Howard 93–4
Townes, Emilie M. 12–13, 18, 19, 22, 54–5
Trans-Atlantic slave trade 28
  see also slavery

Uganda 108–9
ungrievable lives 3–4
United Church of Christ, Chicago 103–4
United Methodist Church 40

Verity Baptist Church, Sacramento, California 107–8

The Way of Love (Irigaray) 59–60, 62
West, Traci 23–4, 64

"What Must the Church Do about Same Sex Marriage" (Anderson) 82
Where Have All the Prophets Gone? (McMickle) 32–3
White, Mel 24, 26–7
whiteface stereotypes 38, 73–98
   anatomy of racecraft, "bully pulpit" 82–3
   Anderson, Terry K. 82–6
      and bestiality 86–7
      and the prophet Amos 83–5
      and Solomon, son of David 85–6
   Black Church theology as accommodation 79–81
   Black Lives Matter 80–1
      and Audre Lorde 81
      and Frantz Fanon 81–2
   blood sacrifices 87–8
   countermemory and stereotypes 18–20
   "do no harm" principles 91–4
   doublemindedness 74
   face of the other 13–14, 73, 89–91
   God's rule 88–9
   minstrelsy as trope 74–9
   perpetuating evil 18
whiteness 9
   as orientation 12–13, 27–8
Wiley, Christine & Dennis 48
Williams, Anthony 48
Williams, Delores 55–6

womanism and the LGBTQIA body 6–7
Womanist Ethics and Cultural Production of Evil (Townes) 18
women hating *see* misogyny
Wood, Frances E. 20
Word of Faith International Christian Center 35–6
Worley, Charles 31–5
   CNN coverage 33–4, 39
   interconnection between racism/racecraft 38–9
   invisible ontology 35–6
   parroting 44
"wounded healers" and wounded people 14, 99–130
   breaking the chains 109–10
   breaking the chains, Na'im Akbar 104, 105–7, 109–10
   challenge of personal identity 101–3
   group dynamics 121–5
   keys to restoration 125–7
   Muslim faith traditions 107–9
   sense of community 110–13
   sense of family 113–17
   sense of social justice 117–21
   slavery catechisms 99–101
   theological fault lines 103–4
The Wretched of the Earth (Fanon) 81–2
Wright, Jeremiah A. 103–4